D0524184

CAFE
OKLAHOMA

Casual Recipes For The Casual Sooner Lifestyle

**PRESENTED BY THE
JUNIOR SERVICE LEAGUE
OF MIDWEST CITY, OKLAHOMA**

Bon Appetit, y'all!

APRIL 19, 1995, 9:02 A.M.

It's a moment burned into all of our memories — the moment the massive blast in downtown Oklahoma City destroyed the Alfred P. Murrah Federal Building, taking with it the lives of 168 innocent Oklahomans.

Here in Oklahoma, we grieved for the dead and injured, but we also felt pride in the living. Throughout the ordeal, so many Oklahomans responded with courage, compassion and selflessness. For us, it was a reaffirmation — we've always believed in the essential goodheartedness of Oklahomans, and it was clear that we were right.

This is the third printing of a book dedicated to the wonderful food of Oklahoma, and as always we've seasoned it with Oklahoma stories and history, and served it all up with a generous helping of pride. The events surrounding April 19 are another chapter in our history, and add depth to our pride. We are pleased to share all of it with you.

At the same time, we dedicate this book to everyone who was lost, everyone who was found, and everyone throughout Oklahoma and America who gave of themselves so selflessly. They give new depth to the phrase, "America's Heartland".

Additional copies may be obtained at the cost of $16.95, plus $2.50 postage and handling, each book. Oklahoma residents add appropriate city and state sales tax, each book. Send to:

> Junior Service League of MWC
> P. O. Box 10703
> Midwest City, OK 73140

ISBN: 0-9641096-0-3
Library of Congress Number: 94-75929

Copyright © 1994 Junior Service League, Midwest City, Oklahoma

First Printing	5,000 Books	September, 1994
Second Printing	5,000 Books	March, 1995
Third Printing	10,000 Books	September, 1995

Printed in the USA by

WIMMER
The Wimmer Companies, Inc.
Memphis • Dallas

TABLE OF CONTENTS

Since the inception of this project, many members have touched the development of "**Cafe Oklahoma**" in their own special way. Although too numerous to mention everyone, the following individuals have contributed countless hours in helping this vision become a reality. Our thanks and gratitude go to them as well as to their families for their patience and support.

Chairman

Diane Joy-Sisemore

Co-Chairman

Teresa Sanders

Sharon Breeden	Dara McGlamery
Debbie Clark	Cindy Mikeman
Pam Dimski	Theresa Todd
Pam Hall	Margenia Wicker
Lezlie Hudiburg	Eileen Wilson
Cheryl Johnson	

Computer Input: Suzi Byrne

Cover Concept: Bob Haydon

Copy, Illustration & Production: Steve Young, Young at Art

OKLAHOMA:
THE CAFE AT THE CROSSROADS

Dear Friends:

The members of the Junior Service League of Midwest City, Oklahoma are proud to present you with a labor of love we call "Cafe Oklahoma." There's a great deal of all of us in these pages, because interspersed among the hundreds of tantalizing dishes – and we can vouch for how tantalizing they are! – are our own personal recollections, and the historical glimpses that make Oklahoma what it is to us – home.

From Oklahoma's picturesque beginning as Indian Territory, through the dark days of the Depression, to the heady times of the Oil Booms, a way of life has developed here that is distinctly Oklahoma. It's composed of equal parts of friendliness and hospitality, together with pride in the past and faith in the future. At the same time, there's an easygoing tolerance and a willingness to get along with your neighbor, whatever his background might be.

And in Oklahoma your neighbor can come from a lot of different backgrounds, because this is indeed America's crossroads. Less than a century ago, many different kinds of people, from many different places, converged all at once in America's heart and made a State out of it, all in an astonishingly short time. No other State grew to maturity so fast – that's why they say Oklahoma was "born grown." It's an amazing story, and we're pleased to share it with you.

Most of all, we're pleased to share this wonderful collection of recipes, handed down by generations of pioneers of many colors and cultures and origins. We've tried to represent all of them here, because it takes all of them to make Oklahoma, well, Oklahoma.

Welcome to Oklahoma, then – and . .

Bon Appetit, y'all!

5

This book contains the favorite recipes of our members, their friends and families. We do not claim that all of these recipes are original, only that they are our favorites. Unfortunately, due to duplication or similarity, we could not include all recipes that were submitted.

Throughout this book, we have attempted to be as specific as possible on measurements, ingredients and pan sizes. At times, measurements are left to the particular tastes of the cook. Below are a few explanations and suggestions that may make your cooking experience easier.

1. Sugar is granulated. Any other sugar will be specified.

2. Flour is all–purpose flour. Any other flour will be specified.

3. Confectioner's sugar and powdered sugar are the same.

4. Margarine, oleo and butter are interchangeable in most recipes. When butter is mandatory or recommended, it will be specified.

5. Oil refers to a vegetable oil, and is not interchangeable with solid shortenings, butter or margarine.

6. Condensed milk is a sweetened canned milk and is not interchangeable with evaporated milk.

SPECIAL NOTES:
****If you are among the individuals who are concerned about bacterial problems associated with uncooked eggs, certain recipes contained in this book should be avoided or modified. Individuals at special risk may be infants, pregnant women, the elderly, and anyone with impaired immune system.

****Some recipes contained in this book call for home canning methods of food preparation. Although canning directions may be supplied, please contact your local County Extension Office for the most up–to–date methods for safe home canning.

THE VERY FIRST WEDDING IN OKLAHOMA

Oklahoma very nearly became *two* states.

For years, there had been strong sentiment for admitting the Indian Territory as the Indian State of Sequoia. Neighboring Oklahoma Territory, meanwhile, would become the State of Oklahoma.

Constitutions were written for both, but in the end the two Territories were joined into one and admitted to the Union as Oklahoma.

It remained for them to seal that emotional issue in some way, and they arrived at a quaint solution.

They had a wedding on Statehood Day.

The bride, representing the Indian Territory, was a beautiful dark-haired, dark-eyed lady of Cherokee descent, Anita Trainer Bennett. From Oklahoma Territory came tall, fair-haired C. G. "Gristmill" Jones. The ceremony took place in the Territorial capital, on the steps of the library, before an immense crowd of people – the whites in their Sunday best, the Indians in feathered headdress and blanket, the women with their babies in brightly beaded cradleboards.

It was a brilliant November day, and the ceremony was lavish – the bride in a lavender satin floor-length gown with a picture hat and gloves, the bridegroom in striped pants and black formal coat. All the peoples were represented – giving the bride away was a future Choctaw chief, with judges, politicians and the about-to-be-inaugurated first governor in attendance.

There's a suggestion of the sensitivity of the event in the vows that were read.

". . . To you, Mr. Jones, as the representative of Oklahoma, I present the hand and fortune of Miss Indian Territory . . Despite the unhappy circumstances of her youth, which have cast a shadow of sorrow over a face by nature only intended to give back warm smiles of God's pure sunshine, this beautiful maiden comes to him as the last descendant of the proudest race that ever trod foot on American soil . . . Although an orphan, Miss Indian Territory brings her spouse a dower that, in fertile fields, productive mines and sterling and upright citizenship, equals the fortune of her wooer. Mr. Oklahoma, into whose identity Indian Territory is about to be merged forever, must be entrusted to care for this princely estate . . ."

The crowd cheered as the bride, whose identity had been a closely-kept secret, stepped forward, lifted her veil and waved a greeting. She shielded her eyes from the bright sun with a mauve chrysanthemum – even that was symbolic, as it was to be the official flower of the newly-born State.

A choir of Cherokee girls sang "The Star Spangled Banner," and the crowd cheered.

The two Territories had become one State.

Thank you for your financial support of the Junior Service League of Midwest City. Your purchase of Cafe Oklahoma will help to support projects such as:
Drug Detection Canine
A project that provides the Midwest City Police Department with a golden retriever trained in detecting drugs. In a 20-month period, "Country" was initialized 302 times, resulting in 249 arrests and removing drugs valued at $11,778,763 from the streets of the community.

NEW YEAR'S GOOD LUCK BRUNCH

APPETIZERS
CHILI CHEESE PUFFS
ORANGE JUICE FREEZE
BURGUNDY SUNSET

BREAKFAST ITEMS
BRUNCH SPINACH QUICHE
SOUR DOUGH FLAPJACKS WITH WARM CHERRY SAUCE
MOM'S SAUSAGE GRAVY AND COUNTRY FRESH BISCUITS

SIDE DISHES
HOPPEL POPPEL
SCALLOPED PINEAPPLE
"OKIE" GOOD LUCK PEAS

MAIN DISHES
SOUR CREAM TENDERLOIN
CHICKEN IN LEMON SAUCE

BREADS
ORANGE BOWKNOTS
APRICOT ALMOND BREAD
BLUEBERRY BUTTERMILK BISCUITS

SWEETS
SOUR CREAM APPLE PIE
BLUEBERRY STREUSEL
CHERRY PECAN BREAD

W9-AKV-649

OKLA–HOE–DOWN

APPETIZERS

SOONER SALSA & CHIPS
PICKLED OKRA
CANDIED DILL PICKLES

SALADS

CORNBREAD SALAD
OKLAHOMA SLAW

SIDE DISHES

FRIED OKRA
PAN FRIED TATERS
WILD BILL'S BAKED BEANS

MAIN DISHES

DOWN HOME BRISKET
OLD OKLAHOMA CATFISH FRY & HUSHPUPPIES
BARBECUE BEEF RIBS

BREADS

TERRITORIAL LIGHT BREAD
SWEET CORNBREAD

SWEETS

OKLAHOMA CRUDE CAKE
DOUBLE LAYER PEACH COBBLER

STROLL THRU THE SOUTH

APPETIZERS

SHRIMP AND ARTICHOKE HEART DIP
CRABMEAT CHEESE DIP
BLACK–EYED PEA PINWHEELS

SALADS

BROCCOLI BACON SALAD
OKRA SALAD

SIDE DISHES

HOMINY–SQUASH CASSEROLE
SWEET POTATO PRALINE CASSEROLE
CHEESE GRITS

MAIN DISHES

SHRIMP CREOLE
CAJUN BLACK BEANS AND RICE

BREADS

BUTTERMILK BISCUITS
QUICK HERB ROLLS

SWEETS

PECAN PIE TOFFEE BARS
CURRIED FRUIT
PRALINE PUMPKIN PIE

BLACK GOLD BUFFET

APPETIZERS
CRABMEAT BALL
BACON STUFFED CHERRY TOMATOES
OKLAHOMA CAVIAR

SALADS
MEDITERRANEAN PASTA
CAESAR SALAD

SIDE DISHES
BROCCOLI CHEESE SOUP
CARROTS GLAZED WITH MAPLE BUTTER
ASPARAGUS CASSEROLE

MAIN DISHES
CORNISH HENS WITH ALMOND RICE STUFFING
HAM WITH AMARETTO SAUCE
BEEF TENDERLOIN DELUXE

BREADS
ROSIE'S BUNS

SWEETS
CARROT CAKE AND CREAM CHEESE FROSTING
WHITE CHOCOLATE CHEESECAKE
ALMOND LEMON TART

RUSTLER'S ROUNDUP

APPETIZERS
RANCH SNACK MIX

SALADS
BARBECUE PIG IN THE GREENS

SIDE DISHES
WILD BILL'S BAKED BEANS
POTATO SALAD

MAIN DISHES
GREEN CHILE CHILI
COWBOY BEDROLL
BOOT-SCOOTIN' STEAK
BAR–B–QUICK SAUCE

BREADS
CATTLE RUSTLER CORNBREAD
COWHAND SODA BISCUITS
BUTTERMILK BISCUITS WITH CHOCOLATE GRAVY

SWEETS
WHITE CHOCOLATE DREAMS
ULTIMATE CHOCOLATE CAKE

SOUTHWEST SOIREE

APPETIZERS
ROSY CHAMPAGNE PUNCH
SUSAN'S MUSHROOM SANDWICHES
WRANGLER ROLL–UPS

SALADS
CABBAGE ONION SALAD
RAW VEGETABLE SALAD
SPINACH SALAD WITH DRESSING

SIDE DISHES
LAYERED BROCCOLI CASSEROLE
SCALLOPED CORN CASSEROLE

MAIN DISHES
HONEY BAKED HAM WITH CINNAMON APPLE RINGS
TENDERLOIN OF BEEF IN WINE SAUCE
CHICKEN CORDON BLEU

BREADS
DILLY BREAD
SESAME–SWISS CHEESE BREAD

SWEETS
CHILLED CHOCOLATE TORTONI
ROCA CHEESECAKE

SUNDAY AFTER MEETING

APPETIZERS

STUFFED FRENCH LOAF

SALADS

SOUR CREAM CORN SALAD
BLACK–EYED PEA SALAD
SPINACH SALAD AND DRESSING

SIDE DISHES

POTATOES, HONEY
FRESH CORN FRITTERS
LUSCIOUS LIMAS

MAIN DISHES

OLD FASHIONED CHICKEN–N–DUMPLINGS
SOUTHERN FRIED CHICKEN
BEEF POT ROAST IN BEER

BREADS

GRANDMA'S OATMEAL BREAD
GRAMMY'S BISCUITS

SWEETS

CINNAMON CHOCOLATE SHEET CAKE
BANANA NUT ICE CREAM

TEX–MEX FIESTA

APPETIZERS

FIESTA CHEESE BALL
CHILI RELLENOS DIP
STUFFED JALAPEÑOS

SALADS

AVOCADO SALAD
MACHO SALAD

SIDE DISHES

MEXICAN TACO SOUP

MAIN DISHES

CHICKEN ENCHILADAS
BEST OF THE WEST BURRITOS

BREADS

MEXICAN CORNBREAD
BEAN BREAD

SWEETS

PANCHETTA'S COOKIES
VANILLA ICE CREAM & PRALINE SAUCE

ROUTE 66 TAILGATE PARTY

APPETIZERS
NUTS, BOLTS & JOLTS
BLOODY MARY'S

SALADS
COLD RICE & BEAN SALAD

SIDE DISHES
HONEY BAKED BEANS

MAIN DISHES
BLUE RIBBON BRISKET

BREADS
BEER BREAD
GOLDEN CHEESE LOAVES

SWEETS
PECAN PIE TOFFEE BARS
LANDRUN BROWNIES

AFTER THE HUNT

APPETIZERS
PUMPKIN DIP & GINGERSNAPS
HOT BUTTERED RUM MIX

SALADS
GREEN BEAN AND RED ONION SALAD
WITH DILLED DRESSING

SIDE DISHES
CHEESE PACKED POTATOES
COPPER CARROTS

MAIN DISHES
VINITA VENISON CASSEROLE
QUAIL IN CREAM

BREADS
HONEY CORN MUFFINS

SWEETS
CHEESE BARS
APPLE CAKE WITH HOT BUTTER SAUCE

WINTER WARM–UP

APPETIZERS

HOT BACON MIX
HOT CINNAMON CIDER

MAIN DISHES

JOE'S GREEN CHILI STEW
WHITE CHILI
STEW WITH A KICK

BREADS

CHUNK OF CHEESE BREAD
BUTTERMILK CORNBREAD

SWEETS

DEEP DISH APPLE PIE
CHOCOLATE POUND CAKE

HOLIDAY CAROLING CELEBRATION

APPETIZERS

HOLIDAY CHEESE BALL
OVEN CARAMEL CORN
HOT CINNAMON CIDER

SALADS

CRANBERRY SALAD
NAPPA SALAD

SIDE DISHES

ITALIAN GREEN BEANS WITH POTATOES & ONIONS
POTATO CORN CHOWDER

MAIN DISHES

MEAT LOAF DIJONNAISE
ITALIAN ROAST PORK WITH WINE SAUCE

BREADS

CHEDDAR BACON OLIVE BREAD

SWEETS

PEANUT BRITTLE
CANDY CANE COOKIES
AUNT BILL'S BROWN CANDY
PRALINES
EGGNOG PIE
SANTA'S WHISKERS

CAFE
OKLAHOMA

OKLAHOMA SPECIALTIES

MAYBE ROME WASN'T BUILT IN A DAY, BUT . . .

At sunup April 22, 1889, Oklahoma City consisted of a train depot, a couple of wooden buildings, and a water tank.

At sundown, it was a tent city with 10,000 residents.

It was the first of the great Land Runs, and America had never seen anything like it.

The word went out that there was free land, available in claims of 160 acres, on a first-come, first-served basis, and if you were hardy enough to be an 89er, it was yours for the taking. All you had to do was line up at the border – along with the other 50,000 prospective homesteaders – and wait for the U.S. Cavalry to give the signal. . .

And line up they did, weeks in advance. In prairie schooners, buckboards, buggies, bicycles, on horseback, even on foot. Others rode one of 15 railroad trains. Lined up along the northern border of the Oklahoma District, they waited – most of them.

As always, there was an unscrupulous few who entered the District early, in secret, and staked claims earlier than the rules allowed. Some of them hid in ravines and waited, but others were outright brazen – the story goes that one homesteader arrived at a choice parcel only to find it occupied by a character who had already planted a vegetable garden. He explained the days-old sprouts by saying, "The soil's so rich, I planted those onions an hour ago, and up they came!" Since they claimed land sooner than was legal, that's what they were called – Sooners. Being a Sooner guaranteed you good land, but it had its downside, too – from being disqualified, to being lynched, to just being shot on sight.

At noon, the bugles blew and the pistols fired, and the thousands thundered across the prairie into what they hoped would be a new beginning and a better life. One cowpuncher recalled the sound more than anything, saying it was much like the sound of 10,000 cattle on a stampede.

Those who had a prior acquaintance with the land were in great demand, and many of them, like legendary Indian scout Pawnee Bill Lillie, did quite well for themselves serving as guides to groups of newcomers.

Some staked out claims for farmland, others staked "town plots" for property in one of the new cities – Guthrie, Perry, Norman, and Oklahoma City. They used anything they could find to stake a claim – sticks, blankets, even pantaloons and petticoats nailed to posts and fluttering in the springtime breeze.

Unlike cities in other states, these cities had no growing up process. In Oklahoma City, surveyors were among the first to arrive, using knotted lariats to lay out the street grids the afternoon of the Run. In the confusion of that first day, two competing survey parties almost came to blows over whether the streets should be aligned with true north or with the existing railroad.

Somehow, that dispute got settled, and so did the city. A temporary government was set up the first month, a City Directory published shortly thereafter, and the first elections followed soon behind. Although there were no taxes, schools, or formal laws during that first year, the social amenities that would form the foundation of the city – The Ladies Whist Club, the Opera House, the Five O'Clock Tea Club and the Ladies Chautauquah Circle – had already begun to appear. . .

The evening of the Run, as darkness fell, the sound of a distant voice rang out on the still air.

"Oh, Joe, here's your mule!"

Another voice took it up, and another, and still another, until it seemed that everybody within earshot was announcing that Joe's mule had been found.

Having taken care of that, the brand new city settled down to its first night's sleep.

CANDIED DILL PICKLES

You'll love the unusual combination of flavors!

½ gallon whole Kosher or
   dill pickles
1 teaspoon celery salt
1 stick cinnamon

3 cups sugar
1 cup cider vinegar
2 teaspoons mustard seeds
½ teaspoon ground allspice

Yield: ½ gallon of pickles

Remove pickles from jar and discard juice. Cut pickles into 1-inch chunks and replace in jar. Boil remaining ingredients for 1 minute, stirring constantly. Pour over pickles. Replace the lid and store in the refrigerator.

Note: See special note on page 6 regarding home canning.

PICKLED OKRA

5 pounds medium okra,
   trimmed
6 cloves garlic
3 cups white vinegar

3 cups water
1½ cups sugar
salt (non-iodized)

Yield: 6 pints

Remove the stem of the okra and trim the top of the pod. Pack the okra and garlic into sterilized pint jars. Combine the vinegar, water and sugar in a saucepan and bring to a boil. Pour over the okra and add ½ teaspoon salt to each pint. Seal the jars and process for 10 minutes in a boiling water bath.

Note: See special note on page 6 regarding home canning.

RUSH SPRINGS WATERMELON RIND PRESERVES

A 54–year Oklahoma Tradition!

4 pounds watermelon rind
8 cups water
9 cups sugar
4 lemons, sliced

4 4–inch cinnamon sticks, broken into pieces
4 teaspoons whole cloves
green or red food coloring, optional

Yield: 6 pints

Select melons with thick rinds. Remove the green peel from the rind and discard. Dice remaining white watermelon rind, (makes approximately 11 cups). Soak in mild salt water overnight (½ cup salt to 1 gallon water); drain. In large Dutch oven, cover diced rind with clear water and bring to a boil. Allow to cook approximately 30 minutes or until tender; drain well. Make a syrup of water, sugar, and lemon slices. Tie cinnamon and cloves in cheesecloth bag and add to syrup; allow syrup to boil 5 minutes. Add rinds and continue to cook until rinds are transparent. If desired, a few minutes before preserves are done, add enough green or red food coloring to tint the preserves. Remove spice bag; pour preserves into sterilized jars, filling to within ½-inch of top. Put on cap and screw band on tightly. Process in boiling water bath 10 minutes. (See special note on page 6 regarding home canning.)

Note: Rush Springs, Oklahoma has hosted their annual Watermelon Festival on the second Saturday in August, since 1940. A weekend full of watermelon exhibits, stage shows, carnivals, arts and crafts shows and, of course, a watermelon seed spitting contest, await the thousands of people that attend each year. Over 50,000 pounds of watermelon are obtained from area growers for the festival. Each year, area growers enter their largest and best melons in the various contests offered. Prize watermelons are then auctioned to the highest bidder. Since 1965, the largest Rush Springs melon entered in the annual contest was in 1988 and weighed in at 134½ pounds!!

SOONER SALSA

A quick and easy salsa!

1 16–ounce can stewed
tomatoes
4 medium tomatoes,
chopped

3 small jalapeño peppers,
chopped & seeded
⅓ cup chopped onion
½ teaspoon salt
½ teaspoon cayenne pepper

Yield: 4 cups

Combine tomatoes, peppers and onions in food processor and process until desired consistency. Add salt and cayenne pepper, process again to mix. Store in refrigerator.

Note: With jalapeños – keep as many or as few seeds as you wish; the more seeds, the hotter the salsa.

OKLAHOMA CAVIAR

1 14–ounce can black–eyed
peas, drained
1 15½–ounce can white
hominy, drained
2 medium tomatoes, seeded
& chopped

4 green onions, very thinly
sliced
2 garlic cloves, minced
1 medium green pepper,
finely chopped
1 cup regular (or hot)
picante sauce

Yield: 7 cups

Combine all ingredients, tossing to mix well. Chill at least 2 hours or up to 24 hours, stirring occasionally. Serve as a dip with tortilla chips or as a side salad.

TORTILLA WAGONWHEELS

2 8–ounce packages cream cheese, softened

3 tablespoons sour cream

1 4–ounce can mild chopped green chilies, drained

1 cup finely diced bell pepper

4 slices bacon, cooked and crumbled (can substitute real bacon bits)

3 tablespoons chopped pimiento

4 green onions, finely chopped

seasoning salt and garlic to taste

6 – 8 large flour tortillas

Yield: 7–8 dozen

Mix cream cheese and sour cream until smooth. Add remaining ingredients, except tortillas, and combine well. Spread mixture ⅛-inch thick on each flat tortilla. Tightly roll each tortilla, jelly roll style. Chill. Cut in ½-inch slices and serve.

BLACK MESA BREAKFAST

1 pound bulk sausage

2 slices bread, cut into ½–inch cubes

1 cup (4–ounces) shredded sharp Cheddar cheese

6 eggs

2 cups milk

½ teaspoon salt

½ teaspoon dry mustard

Yield: 6–8 servings

Crumble sausage in a medium skillet; cook over medium heat until browned, stirring occasionally. Drain well. Spread bread cubes in a buttered 12 x 8 x 2-inch baking dish; top with sausage, then cheese. In a mixing bowl combine eggs, milk, and seasonings; beat well, and pour over cheese. Cover and refrigerate overnight. Bake in oven preheated to 350° for 30 to 40 minutes or until set.

GOOD MORNIN' OKLAHOMA BRUNCH

Buttermilk Cornbread:

1 cup yellow cornmeal
⅓ cup all-purpose flour
1 teaspoon baking powder
½ teaspoon salt

¼ teaspoon baking soda
1 egg, beaten
1 cup buttermilk

Egg Topping:

3 tablespoons butter or
    margarine
3 tablespoons all-purpose
    flour
2 cups milk
¼ teaspoon salt

⅛ teaspoon pepper
6 hard-cooked eggs, peeled
    and chopped
½ cup mayonnaise or salad
    dressing

Garnish:

chopped green onion
crumbled cooked bacon

shredded Cheddar cheese

Yield: 9 servings

Preheat oven to 400°. For cornbread, combine dry ingredients; add egg and buttermilk, mixing well. Pour batter into a greased 8-inch square pan. Bake for 20 minutes or until lightly browned. While cornbread is baking, prepare topping by melting butter in a heavy saucepan over low heat; add flour, stirring until smooth. Gradually stir in milk; cook until thickened and bubbly. Add salt, pepper, eggs and mayonnaise, mixing well. To serve, slice cornbread squares in half horizontally, spoon egg mixture over cornbread, garnish with onion, bacon and cheese.

PRAIRIE PANCAKES

A Sunday morning favorite!

6 tablespoons vegetable oil	**¼ cup wheat germ**
1 large egg	**½ cup sugar**
1¼ cups milk	**1 tablespoon baking powder**
1¼ cups flour	**¼ teaspoon salt**

Yield: 15 pancakes

Mix liquid ingredients together in large bowl, blending thoroughly. Combine all dry ingredients in separate bowl. Add flour mixture to liquid mixture slowly, combining well after each addition. Pour ¼ cupful of batter onto hot greased griddle. Cook until top surface is bubbly and edges are lightly browned. Turn and cook other side until slightly browned. Remove from griddle and serve warm with maple syrup.

Note: My grandmother, Opal McGlocklin, was born in Henderson, Oklahoma on January 21, 1911. I was born on January 21, 1956. Being her first granddaughter as well as sharing her birthday, it seems we always had special times that I will always remember. One of the funniest things we always laughed about years later, was the morning grandmother fixed pancakes for me for breakfast. Grandmother realized she didn't have any store bought syrup, so that morning I curiously watched her make sugar syrup. The syrup she made was much runnier than store bought syrup, and as she poured it on my pancakes I remember whining because I thought she was pouring "water" on my pancakes. She explained to me that when she was a little girl her mother always made that kind of syrup for her. After a little coaxing, I finally tasted the syrup she made and was amazed it tasted so good! — DeAnn Bower

INDIAN FRY BREAD

Dough:

2 cups flour
1 heaping tablespoon baking
    powder

1 teaspoon salt
1 cup milk
2 cups vegetable oil

Seasoned Flour:

1 cup flour
1 tablespoon ground black
    pepper
1 tablespoon salt
1 teaspoon parsley

1 teaspoon ground garlic
½ teaspoon oregano
½ teaspoon poultry
    seasoning
¼ teaspoon cayenne pepper

Yield: 8 servings

For dough, mix dry ingredients in 4–quart mixing bowl and form a well in the center. Slowly add milk, a little at a time, while stirring with index finger to work mixture together. Mix well until dough forms ball. Divide dough into 8 balls and allow to rest for 10 minutes. Combine all ingredients for seasoned flour and use only seasoned flour on hands, table and for all frying purposes. Flatten balls and work dough with hands or rolling pin until each is ¼ to ½-inch thick and approximately 6–inches in diameter. Poke a hole in the center to "Let the Spirits Out". In an 8–10-inch skillet, heat 2 cups oil until temperature reaches 350°. (You can test oil readiness by placing a dime–sized piece of flattened dough in oil. When dough touches oil, it should float on top and bubble around the dough piece.) When oil is ready, gently place flattened dough in oil and allow to float freely on the hot oil and turn when lightly golden brown, approximately 30 seconds per side. Take out of hot oil and drain on paper towel. Serve hot with butter or syrup or serve with taco meat and toppings.

MOM'S SAUSAGE GRAVY AND COUNTRY FRESH BISCUITS

A stick–to–your–ribs Oklahoma breakfast!

Biscuits:

6 cups flour
½ cup instant nonfat dry
   milk powder
¼ cup double–acting baking
   powder (yes, ¼ cup)

¼ cup sugar
2 teaspoons salt
2 teaspoons cream of tartar
2 cups shortening
1½–2 cups water

Gravy:

1 pound sage–flavored bulk
   pork sausage
6 tablespoons flour
1 quart milk
½ teaspoon poultry
   seasoning

½ teaspoon ground nutmeg
¼ teaspoon salt
dash Worcestershire sauce
dash Tabasco sauce

Yield: 8–10 servings

Preheat oven to 400°. Prepare biscuits by mixing dry ingredients together in large bowl. With pastry blender, cut shortening into flour mixture to resemble coarse crumbs. Stir in 1½ cups water until moistened. If mixture is too dry, add ¼ to ½ cup additional water. Turn dough onto floured surface. With floured hands, knead 8 to 10 times until smooth. With floured rolling pin, roll dough to ¾–inch thickness. With a floured 2½–inch round cookie cutter, cut out biscuits and place 1–inch apart on cookie sheet. Press trimmings together, re-roll and cut. Bake 20 to 25 minutes until golden. While biscuits are cooking, prepare gravy by browning crumbled sausage in 12–inch skillet. Drain, discarding all but 2 tablespoons of drippings and set cooked sausage aside. To drippings, stir in flour and cook over medium–low heat about 6 minutes or until mixture bubbles and turns golden. Add milk, stirring constantly. Return sausage to pan with remaining seasonings and continue to cook and stir until thickened. To serve, split warmed biscuits and top with hot gravy.

Note: My mother always took the "trimmings" of the biscuits, dipped them in melted butter and then rolled them in a sugar and cinnamon mixture. It was our treat on Saturday mornings that made us all stand in line for our "doughy" breakfast. We loved it, but now that I have children of my own I am just now realizing why the yield has

Continued on next page

never quite agreed. When it states 2 dozen, my recipe will only yield 2 biscuits. Hardly seems worth the trouble of turning on the oven ... plus the worst is I still have to share, first with my brother and sisters and now with my children. I long for the day I can yield all 24 "doughy" biscuits by myself. — Teresa Sanders

P.S. Who knows if they're good with gravy? We never had enough biscuits!

GRAMMY'S BISCUITS

4 cups flour
2 tablespoons baking
   powder
1 teaspoon baking soda

2 teaspoons salt
½ cup shortening
2 cups buttermilk

Yield: 2 dozen

Preheat oven to 450°. Combine all dry ingredients in large bowl; cut in shortening. Add buttermilk and combine until dough forms. Roll dough on floured surface to ½-inch thickness. Cut with biscuit cutter or glass dipped in flour. Place on lightly greased baking sheet and put in oven immediately. Bake 10 to 15 minutes or until light brown.

TERRITORIAL LIGHT BREAD

½ cup sugar
½ cup shortening
2 teaspoons salt
1 cup hot milk

2 beaten eggs
2 packages dry yeast
1 cup warm water
6 – 6½ cups flour, divided

Glaze:
2 eggs
2 tablespoons water

sesame seeds or poppy
  seeds

Yield: 2 loaves

Preheat oven to 350°. Place sugar, shortening and salt in large mixing bowl; add hot milk to mixture and stir to soften. After mixture has cooled, beat in eggs. In separate bowl, soften yeast in warm water (not more than 110°), and stir into shortening mixture. Add 4 cups of flour, beating until smooth. Add enough remaining flour (2 cups) to make soft dough. Turn dough on floured board and knead 10 minutes or until smooth. Place in greased bowl and allow to rise 1 to 1½ hours, or until doubled in size. Punch dough down and allow to rise an additional 10 minutes. Place dough in 9 x 5 x 3-inch loaf pans and allow to rise again until doubled in size. Beat together egg and water to make glaze and brush on top of loaves. Sprinkle loaves with sesame or poppy seeds if desired. Bake for 25 to 35 minutes or until golden brown.

Note: Christmas Eve at my grandparent's farm home was always such a special time. Every year when we would arrive, grandmother would have sheaves of grain tied with colored ribbons, placed in the corners of the room with silent prayers for a good harvest in the next season. Under the Christmas tablecloth, a thin layer of hay was placed in memory of Jesus in the manger. Before sitting down to the table for dinner, all family members would break bread with each other and wish all a year of peace, good health and love. — Eileen Wilson

SWEET CORNBREAD

1½ cups flour
3 tablespoons baking
  powder
⅛ teaspoon salt
1½ cups yellow cornmeal

½ cup sugar
½ cup vegetable oil
2 eggs, beaten
1 cup milk

Yield: 9 servings

Preheat oven to 400°. Mix together flour, baking powder, salt and cornmeal; set aside. In separate bowl, combine sugar, oil and eggs. Add this mixture to dry mixture alternately with milk, mixing well after each addition. Pour into greased and floured 9-inch cake pan and bake 30 minutes.

CATTLE RUSTLER CORNBREAD

½ pound ground beef
1 cup plus 1 tablespoon
  cornmeal, divided
¾ teaspoon salt
½ teaspoon baking soda
1 cup milk
1 17–ounce can cream style
  corn

2 eggs, well–beaten
¼ cup vegetable oil
2 cups shredded colby
  cheese
1 large onion, chopped
2–4 jalapeño peppers,
  seeded & chopped,
  optional

Yield: 6 servings

Preheat oven to 350°. In 10–inch cast iron skillet, brown and crumble ground beef; drain, remove from pan and set aside. While skillet still has some beef drippings in it, lightly dust bottom of pan with 1 tablespoon cornmeal. Combine 1 cup cornmeal, salt and baking soda; add milk, creamed corn, eggs and vegetable oil and mix well. Pour ½ of batter into skillet. Sprinkle with shredded cheese, chopped onion, beef and jalapeño peppers, if desired; top with remaining batter. Bake for 50–60 minutes. Cool and cut before serving.

INDIAN TACOS

Filling:

1 pound ground beef	1 15–ounce can pinto beans
½ cup chopped onions	salt and pepper to taste

Fry Bread Dough:

2 cups flour	1 teaspoon salt
1 heaping tablespoon baking powder	1 – 1½ cups evaporated milk
	2 cups vegetable oil

Toppings:

sour cream	black olives
shredded cheese	green chilies
lettuce	tomatoes

Yield: 6–8 servings

For taco filling, brown ground beef and onion in skillet and drain well. Add undrained can of pinto beans and allow to simmer, stirring occasionally, for 20 minutes. Salt and pepper to taste. Keep the filling warm while frying bread. For fry bread, combine flour, baking powder and salt in large mixing bowl. Stir in 1 cup canned milk; combine until mixture forms ball. Additional milk or flour may be added to gain right consistency. Divide dough into 8 small balls; cover and set aside for 10 minutes. Flatten balls and work dough with hands or rolling pin until it is ⅛–inch thick and approximately 6–8 inches in diameter. Poke hole in center of each dough round to allow for puffing. Heat oil in skillet until very hot, approximately 375°. Carefully place dough in hot grease. Grease should bubble around floating dough. Fry each side approximately 30 seconds or until golden brown. To "assemble" Indian Taco, place fry bread on plate, top with large spoonful of taco filling and layer on toppings of choice.

Note: There are a number of different recipes for Indian Fry Bread and Indian Tacos. Hopefully this is an easy combination of all those submitted. Also, Fry Bread is an art! It'll be worth the wait and your family will love it while you practice! Fry Bread is also wonderful served hot with butter and honey.

BLUE RIBBON BRISKET

1 5–pound beef brisket
1 teaspoon onion salt
1 teaspoon celery salt
1 teaspoon garlic salt
3½ ounces liquid smoke

salt and pepper to taste
3 tablespoons
　Worcestershire sauce
1 cup barbecue sauce
　(optional)

Yield: 8–10 servings

Trim all fat from brisket; place in pan deep enough so foil placed over top of pan will not touch top of meat. Sprinkle with onion, celery and garlic salts, and pour liquid smoke over brisket. Cover pan with foil and allow to marinate overnight. Preheat oven to 275°. Before roasting, sprinkle with salt, pepper and Worcestershire sauce. Cover tightly with heavy duty foil and bake 5 hours. Thirty minutes before end of baking time, remove foil and pour barbecue sauce over meat, if desired. When cooking time is done, allow meat to cool before slicing.

HICKORY RIBS

4 – 6 pounds spare ribs
1 8–ounce can tomato sauce
½ cup sherry
½ cup honey
2 tablespoons wine vinegar

2 tablespoons minced onion
1 clove garlic, minced
¼ teaspoon Worcestershire
　sauce

Yields 2–4 servings

Preheat oven to 350°. Place ribs in roasting pan and bake for 30 minutes. To prepare sauce, combine all remaining ingredients and simmer for 6 minutes; set aside. Using hickory charcoal, prepare barbecue grill. When coals are completely ashed, push them to one side of the grill. Place ribs on the other side of the grill, away from the coals. Grill in this manner for approximately 40 minutes. Then, move the ribs directly over the coals and grill for an additional 20–30 minutes, brushing frequently with sauce. Remove from grill and serve.

BARBECUE BEEF RIBS

Absolutely fabulous!

4 pounds beef ribs
½ cup chopped onion
½ cup molasses
½ cup ketchup
2 teaspoons shredded
    orange peel
⅓ cup orange juice
2 tablespoons cooking oil
1 tablespoon vinegar
1 tablespoon bottled steak
    sauce

½ teaspoon mustard
½ teaspoon Worcestershire
    sauce
¼ teaspoon garlic powder
¼ teaspoon salt
¼ teaspoon black pepper
¼ teaspoon Tabasco sauce
⅛ teaspoon ground cloves
¼ cup bourbon

Yield: 6 servings

Place beef ribs in Dutch oven and add enough water to cover ribs completely. Cover and bring to a boil; reduce heat and simmer for 45 minutes, or until ribs are tender. Drain thoroughly. While ribs are cooking, prepare barbecue sauce by combining all remaining ingredients in 4-quart saucepan. Bring to a boil; reduce heat and allow to simmer, uncovered, for 15 minutes. Set aside. Grill cooked ribs over slow coals for 40 minutes, turning approximately 3 times and basting with sauce. Serve ribs with remaining sauce.

TWO–STEP TENDERLOIN WITH A KICK

2 tablespoons Dijon mustard
1 tablespoon olive oil
1 4–pound beef tenderloin, trimmed
1 tablespoon freshly ground black pepper
1 tablespoon dried leaf oregano, crushed

1 tablespoon dried leaf thyme, crushed
1 tablespoon finely snipped chives
2 cloves garlic, minced
1 teaspoon salt

Mustard Sauce:
½ cup mayonnaise
½ cup sour cream
¼ cup Dijon mustard
1 tablespoon white wine vinegar

1 tablespoon snipped chives
1 teaspoon Worcestershire sauce

Yield: 12 servings

Preheat oven to 425°. Combine mustard and olive oil; brush on all sides of tenderloin. Combine pepper, oregano, thyme, chives, garlic and salt. Pat seasoning mixture on all sides of roast. Place tenderloin on a rack in a large shallow roasting pan; let stand at room temperature for 30 minutes. Insert meat thermometer; place in oven about 45 minutes or until thermometer registers 140° for rare meat. Remove from oven; let stand for 45 minutes, then wrap and chill. Meanwhile, make Mustard Sauce by combining mayonnaise, sour cream, mustard, vinegar, chives and Worcestershire sauce in a small mixing bowl. Cover and chill. Before serving meat, allow tenderloin to stand at room temperature for 2 hours. Slice roast and serve with Mustard Sauce.

CHICKEN FRIED STEAK AND GRAVY

2 pounds round steak
   cutlets, tenderized
vegetable oil
1 egg

½ cup milk
1–2 cups flour
1 teaspoon pepper
1½ teaspoons salt

Gravy:
3 tablespoons flour

1–1½ cups milk

Yield: 4 servings

Trim fat from meat. In heavy skillet, heat oil until very hot. Blend egg and milk together in bowl; set aside. In shallow pan, combine flour and remaining ingredients. Dip meat into egg mixture, then coat well with flour. For extra crispy steak, repeat this process. Place steak cutlets into hot oil and cook 3-4 minutes on each side. To keep the coating on well, the oil has to be very hot to begin, then heat may be lowered. After meat is done, make gravy from drippings, if desired. Remove meat and reduce heat to low. Leave 3 tablespoons of oil in pan and add 3 tablespoons flour. Brown flour and add 1-1½ cups of milk slowly while stirring. Continue to stir until gravy thickens to desired consistency.

COWHAND CHILI & RICE

1 pound lean ground beef
½ cup chopped onion
1 clove garlic, minced
2 teaspoons chili powder
¼ teaspoon red pepper
½ teaspoon oregano
1 16–ounce can ranch style
   beans

1 16–ounce can stewed
   tomatoes
½ cup water
6–8 cups cooked rice
2 cups grated Cheddar
   cheese

Yield: 4 servings

In a large skillet, brown meat, onion and garlic; drain. Add chili powder, red pepper, oregano, beans, tomatoes and water, stirring well. Reduce heat and simmer 1 hour. Serve over rice and top with grated cheese.

RED DIRT CHILI

6 pounds roast
1 32–ounce can tomatoes
1 24–ounce can tomato
   sauce
4–6 cloves garlic, minced
3 teaspoons cumin
2 teaspoons paprika

2 tablespoons chili powder
1 tablespoon cayenne
   pepper
1 tablespoon cocoa
1 12–ounce can of beer
1 tablespoon sugar
salt to taste

Yield: 20 servings

Trim fat from roast and cut into small cubes. In very large, heavy cooking pot, brown meat and onions until juices are cooked out. Add tomatoes and sauce, breaking or chopping tomatoes as needed. Add remaining ingredients. If chili is too thick, additional beer or water may be added. Cook uncovered over low heat, stirring often for 4 hours or until meat is tender.

CHICKEN ON THE BRICKS

2 tablespoons lime juice
2 tablespoons vinegar
⅛ teaspoon Tabasco sauce
½ teaspoon garlic salt
¼ cup cooking oil
1 tablespoon Worcestershire
   sauce

1 teaspoon sugar
½ teaspoon paprika
1 teaspoon salt
1 cut up fryer or
6–8 boneless, skinless
   chicken breasts

Yield: 6 servings

Thoroughly mix all ingredients, except chicken. Pour marinade over chicken, cover and refrigerate at least 3 hours. Grill chicken 10 to 12 minutes per side or until done, depending upon flame.

OLD FASHIONED CHICKEN–N–DUMPLINGS

Almost like Grandma used to make!

3–4 pound chicken	**1 teaspoon salt**
water	**2 teaspoons baking powder**
salt	**½ cup margarine**
3 cups flour	**1 cup milk**

Yield: 8 servings

Cut chicken into serving pieces, debone if desired, and place into a large pot. Cover chicken with salted water; cover with lid and bring to a boil. Reduce flame and allow to simmer until chicken is tender. While chicken is cooking, combine dry ingredients in large bowl and cut in margarine with pastry blender. Add milk and mix until dough forms. Turn dough out onto lightly floured board and knead lightly. Roll out to ⅛-inch thickness and cut into 3 to 4-inch strips, 1-inch wide. When chicken is tender, drop strips into pot with chicken, stir and cover; continue to simmer 20 minutes or until dumplings are thoroughly cooked.

Note: As a child, my family always went to grandma's for Sunday dinner after church. Since my grandmother had 5 children and they all lived in the same area, there was always a large group of cousins with which to play. My favorite Sunday meal was chicken and dumplings made from scratch. Since grandma never measured any of her ingredients, she was never able to write down the recipe for me. Grandma has since passed away, but the memories of chicken and dumplings, family, and food still linger.

— *Wyvonna Folks*

OVEN BARBECUED CHICKEN

3 tablespoons vegetable oil
3–4 pounds chicken, cut in
 pieces
⅓ cup chopped onion
3 tablespoons butter or
 margarine
¾ cup ketchup
⅓ cup vinegar

3 tablespoons brown sugar
½ cup water
2 teaspoons prepared
 mustard
1 tablespoon Worcestershire
 sauce
¼ teaspoon salt
⅛ teaspoon pepper

Yield: 6–8 servings

Preheat oven to 350°. Heat oil in a large skillet. Fry chicken pieces until browned on all sides; drain and arrange chicken in a 13 x 9 x 2-inch baking dish. In a saucepan, sauté onion in butter until tender; stir in remaining ingredients. Simmer mixture, uncovered, for 15 minutes. Pour over chicken. Bake for approximately 1 hour, basting occasionally.

CHUCKWAGON BEAN BAKE

Guaranteed to be a hit!

1 pound bacon, diced
1 pound ground beef
1 medium onion, diced
2 15–ounce cans pork and
 beans
1 15–ounce can large butter
 beans, drained

1 16–ounce can kidney
 beans, drained
¼ cup brown sugar
½ teaspoon liquid smoke
3 tablespoons vinegar
¼ cup ketchup
3 tablespoons molasses

Yield: 6 servings

Preheat oven to 350°. Brown bacon, beef and onion together in large skillet; drain well. Place mixture in oven roasting pan along with remaining ingredients and combine well. Bake 3 hours, stirring occasionally. If mixture becomes dry while cooking, water may be added.

Note: This has a very unusual, but delicious flavor.

SOUTHERN FRIED CHICKEN

1 3–pound chicken
2 tablespoons salt
2 tablespoons pepper
2 large eggs
1 cup evaporated milk
2 cups flour

2 teaspoons paprika
½ teaspoon dried thyme,
  crushed
1 teaspoon garlic powder
1 quart vegetable oil

Yield: 4 servings

Cut chicken into serving pieces. If desired, take skin off chicken and discard. Place chicken in shallow baking dish, salt and pepper as desired. In a separate bowl, beat eggs and milk until well–blended. Pour milk and egg mixture over chicken and let stand at least 5 minutes. In heavy brown paper bag, combine remaining ingredients, except oil, and shake to mix well. Drain chicken and add to paper bag, 1–2 pieces at a time. Shake bag until chicken pieces are well–coated with flour. In well-seasoned 10 to 12-inch iron skillet, heat oil until drop of water sizzles. Fry chicken in batches, making sure not to crowd. Cover skillet and allow chicken to cook 15 minutes. Remove cover, turn chicken pieces and cook, uncovered, approximately 15 minutes to allow chicken to crisp. Remove pieces from skillet and drain on paper towels.

Note: I will always remember my grandma, Anna Karban, for her fried chicken. We would go almost every weekend to Enid, Oklahoma to visit my grandparents. They lived on a farm and raised chickens, cattle and wheat. Grandma loved to cook and always had fried chicken, and mashed potatoes and gravy for lunch. My grandma is gone now, but I always think of her when I eat fried chicken, even though it never tastes as good as hers did!

— *Karel Nichols*

PANHANDLE BEANS

2 cups dried pinto beans
6 cups water
1 2-ounce piece of salt pork, rind removed
4 dried, hot red chilies, stemmed, seeded and pulverized in a blender

1 medium onion peeled and sliced
1 teaspoon salt
1 recipe of salsa cruda to garnish (see following recipe)

Yield 4–6 servings

Wash the beans in a colander under cold running water. In a heavy 3–4 quart saucepan, bring the water to a boil over high heat. Drop the beans in and cook briskly, uncovered for 2 minutes. Turn off the heat and let the beans soak for 1 hour. Add the salt pork, chilies and onion slices, and return to a boil over high heat. Reduce the heat to its lowest setting, simmer for 5½ hours, stirring occasionally. Stir in the salt and simmer an additional 30 minutes. (Add more boiling water by the ¼ cup if necessary. The beans should have absorbed most of the liquid when fully cooked.) Ladle the beans into individual bowls and serve with Salsa Cruda on top.

SALSA CRUDA

1 16-ounce can tomatoes, drained and finely chopped
1 4-ounce can chopped green chilies

½ cup finely chopped onion
1 tablespoon white vinegar
1 teaspoon sugar

Yield: 6 servings

Combine tomatoes, chilies, onions, vinegar and sugar in a bowl and stir until well–mixed. Taste for seasoning. Let the salsa rest at room temperature for 30 minutes before serving. Salsa Cruda may top Panhandle Beans, tacos or enchiladas.

JOE'S GREEN CHILI STEW

3 pounds of pork chops or
   pork roast
3 tablespoons vegetable oil
1 clove garlic, diced
3–4 cups water
1 4–ounce can chopped
   green chilies
1 10¾–ounce can diced
   tomatoes with green
   chilies

3 tablespoons chicken
   bouillon crystals
2 medium onions, chopped
5 medium potatoes, peeled
   and cubed
1 6–ounce bag frozen,
   breaded okra
salt and pepper to taste

Yield: 4-6 servings

Trim fat from pork and cut into bite–sized cubes. Brown pork with 3 tablespoons of oil in Dutch oven. Dice garlic and add to pork as it browns. After pork browns, add 3 cups water, green chilies, tomatoes and chicken bouillon and bring to a boil. Add onions, potatoes and breaded okra. Simmer 2 hours, stirring occasionally to keep okra from sticking to bottom of pan. Salt and pepper to taste.

Breaded okra will thicken the stew, so, if necessary, add water for desired consistency.

POLITICALLY CORRECT HAM LOAF

From the Boren family — an Oklahoma political tradition!

1 pound beef
¾ pound smoked ham (not fresh)
½ pound veal
1 egg
1 teaspoon dry mustard
1 teaspoon salt

1 teaspoon pepper
1 teaspoon paprika
½ clove garlic, finely minced
1½ cups plus ⅓ cup tomato juice cocktail, divided
1¼ cups dry bread crumbs, finely crushed, divided

Yield: 6–8 servings

Preheat oven to 350°. Have meat market coarsely grind together beef, ham and veal. In separate bowl, slightly beat egg and mix in all seasonings. Add 1½ cups of tomato juice cocktail and thoroughly combine. Add 1 cup bread crumbs to meat and lightly mix. Gently add egg mixture to ground meats and combine thoroughly. Place entire mixture into 7½ x 11 x 2-inch baking pan and very gently pat into place, making sure not to pack down the meat. Sprinkle the top with remaining bread crumbs and pour ⅓ cup of tomato juice cocktail around (not on top) of loaf. Bake uncovered for one hour.

Note: This recipe was submitted by Christine M. Boren, mother of Oklahoma's former U.S. Senator, David Boren. Senator Boren and his father, Lyle, played an important part of Oklahoma's political history for many years.

SUSAN'S MEATLESS CHILI

A Miss America favorite!

2½ cups dry kidney beans
6–8 cups water, divided
1 teaspoon salt
1 cup bulghur (cracked wheat)
1 12-ounce can tomato juice cocktail
¼ cup olive oil
1 cup diced carrots
1½ cups diced Spanish onions
1 cup diced celery
1 cup diced red or green pepper
5 large cloves garlic, crushed
1 teaspoon basil
1 teaspoon cumin
1½ teaspoons chili powder
½ teaspoon black pepper
½ teaspoon Tabasco sauce, optional
2 tablespoons tamari (or soy sauce)
3 cups stewed or fresh chopped tomatoes
juice of half a lemon
3 tablespoons tomato paste
3 tablespoons dry red wine
2 tablespoons chopped fresh cilantro

Yield: 6–8 servings

Place kidney beans in Dutch oven with six cups of water and allow to soak 4 hours. Add additional 2 cups of water, plus 1 teaspoon salt and cook about 1 hour until tender, watching to make sure the beans keep their shape. Keep an eye on the water level; add more if necessary. Place the bulghur in the tomato juice cocktail and allow to soak 30 minutes; set aside. In olive oil, sauté the carrots, onions, celery and green pepper; add garlic and cook until tender. Combine all spices, including tamari and Tabasco sauce and add to vegetables. Combine tomatoes, lemon juice, tomato paste and red wine and add to cooked kidney beans. Add cooked vegetables and spices to bean mixture and allow to simmer for 1 to 3 hours – the longer the better, stirring as needed. Fifteen minutes before serving, add the bulghur mixture. Just before serving, garnish with cilantro.

Note: This recipe is a favorite of Susan Powell, Miss America 1981. Susan, from Elk City, Oklahoma is proud of her Oklahoma heritage and shares with us, "I always love to tell people that my mother's grandparents were in the Oklahoma land run, and were original settlers in western Oklahoma (Elk City). Her mother, my grandmother, was born in a half-dugout in 1897 in what is now rural Elk City and lived in or around that area until her death in 1990. She was a real pioneer woman!! As long as she lived, she had a cow to milk and we had fresh milk, sweet cream and homemade butter year round. Times have certainly changed...."

"OKIE" GOOD LUCK PEAS

It's traditional in Oklahoma to eat black–eyed peas on New Year's Day to insure good luck for the coming year.

1 wood–burning fireplace with a crane for hanging pots

1 4–quart cast iron pot suitable for hanging

½ pound dry black–eyed peas

1 shank portion of a smoked ham, approximately 4 pounds

1 large or 2 small cloves of garlic

½ medium yellow onion

1 medium stalk celery

¼ teaspoon hot pepper sauce

Yield: 6–8 servings

Build a fire in the fireplace using well–seasoned oak or hickory wood. Allow to burn until you have a hot, slow–burning fire. You want a good bed of coals that will last at least three hours. Wash the peas thoroughly, put them in a pot, cover with water and bring to a boil. Remove from the stove and let stand for 1 hour. Remove skin and most of the fat from the ham (for dieters). Cut most of the ham from the bone and cut into 1–inch squares or chunks. Crush the garlic, and dice the onion into about ¼–inch pieces. Slice the celery into ¼-inch slices. Pour the peas and liquid into the cast iron pot, add garlic, onion, celery, ham bone and hot pepper sauce. Save the ham squares, or chunks, for addition to the pot later. Cover the mixture with approximately 1½ inches of water. Stir the mixture gently so as not to bruise or mash the peas excessively. Hang the pot on the crane in the fireplace so as to get enough heat to allow the liquid to simmer. Cover the pot with a lid or aluminum foil to keep the liquid from evaporating too rapidly. Stir the mixture very gently every 30 minutes, for two hours. It should begin to smell pretty darn good about this time. After 2 hours, remove the ham bone, trim the rest of the meat and return meat to the pot. Add the ham chunks. Leave uncovered and cook for another hour. This last hour allows the mixture to absorb that good smoked flavor that only makes something good, a little bit better. In event you do not have a fireplace, similar, but not near as good results can be obtained by cooking on a kitchen range.

Note: This recipe was submitted by Bill and Allison Kaiser, long–time residents of Midwest City. To retain its true Oklahoma flavor, this recipe was edited only slightly, trying to keep Mr. Kaiser's original comments in for added spice. Mr. Kaiser also adds, "This pot of peas, served with butter and a mess of cornbread, will feed 6–8 hearty appetites and assure a year of 'Oklahoma Good Luck.'"

OLD OKLAHOMA CATFISH FRY

An Oklahoma pioneer favorite!

3 gallons vegetable oil	6 tablespoons salt
20 pounds catfish fillets	3 tablespoons pepper
3 pounds yellow cornmeal	

Yield: 40 servings

Fill wash pot or butane fish cooker with cooking oil. Build fire under wash pot and heat until oil is bubbling. Roll each fish fillet in mixture of cornmeal, salt and pepper. Drop each fillet into hot oil and cook until fillet floats on surface of oil, brown and crisp. Mix leftover cornmeal mixture with water to moisten. To make hush puppies, shape cornmeal mixture into walnut–size balls and drop into hot oil until brown and crisp.

David Steen submits the following commentary with this recipe.

FISH FRY IN A CAST IRON WASH POT

The large cast iron wash pot used to boil the white clothes in the laundry can still be seen in antique shops and as flower planters in farm yards. On wash days the pot was filled with about twenty gallons of water. A fire was made under the pot, which would set the pot of water to a boil. If you were seven or eight years old, you got the job of "poking the clothes" with a sawed–off broom stick. It would take a lot of bleach to get things that white now.

The wash pot had another purpose. Transported to the edge of a lake or river it became a fish cooker when filled with MRS. TUCKERS' LARD and heated to the bubbling stage.

While these preparations were being made, the fishermen were out catching stringers of fish to bring back to the cook pot while the fish were still jumping. These were really fresh fish! Immediately, they would clean the fish, roll them in seasoned corn meal and drop them into the boiling oil. In just a couple of minutes the cooked fish would pop to the surface all brown and crispy.

A long–handled spoon was used to lift the fish from the cauldron. Each person carried his own tin plate or a cedar shingle to hold the fish while they picked the sweet, moist meat from the bones.

The only thing you need to go with the fish is hush puppies. These corn bread delights got their name when hungry puppies would gather

Continued on next page

around the cooking pot and the cook would throw one to the dog and say "hush puppy". Add enough water to cornmeal to make a ball and drop into the hot grease with the fish. When they turn golden brown they are ready to eat.

CORNBREAD SALAD

Great for a summer picnic!

1 8½–ounce box corn muffin mix
½ cup sugar
9 slices bacon, cooked & crumbled

1 small white onion, chopped
1 bell pepper, chopped
2 small tomatoes, seeded & chopped
1 cup real mayonnaise

Yield: 8 servings

Make 9 x 9-inch pan of cornbread according to package directions, adding sugar to batter. Cool cornbread, crumble into bowl and add remaining ingredients. Mix well and refrigerate overnight.

Note: This is a great recipe to double for a large group and tastes best if made 1 – 2 days ahead of time. Very unusual, but very good.

BARBECUE PIG IN THE GREENS

Barbecue salad at its best!

Salad:

9 cups salad greens
½ cup celery
¾ cup chopped green
   pepper
½ cup sliced carrots
1 cup (4 ounces) shredded
   Cheddar cheese

1 cup (4 ounces) shredded
   Monterey Jack cheese
1 cup cherry tomato
   quarters
3½ cups shredded cooked
   pork

Dressing:

1 cup mayonnaise
½ cup sour cream
½ cup buttermilk
1 cup barbecue sauce
2 tablespoons minced onion

2 teaspoons salt
4 tablespoons lemon juice
1 teaspoon black pepper
1 tablespoon sugar

Yield: 6–8 servings

Prepare salad by combining all ingredients except pork; toss well. Just prior to serving salad, top with pork and salad dressing. Prepare dressing by combining all ingredients with a wire whisk and chill until ready to serve. Pour dressing on individual salads to serve.

Note: Great use for leftover smoked pork or beef.

OLD STAND–BY POTATO SALAD

6 medium size baking
   potatoes, diced
2 teaspoons salt
3 celery stalks, diced
3 large sweet pickles, diced
6 fresh green onions, diced

6 black or stuffed green
   olives, sliced
salt and pepper to taste
6 hard–boiled eggs
1 cup real mayonnaise

Yield: 12 servings

Peel and chop each potato into approximately 16 pieces. Place cut potatoes in bowl of cold water for 15 minutes to allow potatoes to absorb any possible water loss. Drain potatoes and place in Dutch oven or other large pot. Add salt and enough water to cover the potatoes by 3 inches. Bring salted water to a boil and allow potatoes to cook just until potatoes are firm but have no raw taste. When potatoes are done, drain and allow to cool. While potatoes are cooling, mix celery, pickles, onions and olives in small bowl with small amount of pickle juice to marinate. When potatoes are cool, add salt and pepper to taste and pickle mixture to potatoes. Mix by gently lifting salad so the potatoes will not wear off their edges. Reserving 3 egg yolks, chop remaining eggs and stir mayonnaise into potato mixture until each potato piece is lightly covered. Press reserved yolks through sieve and use to sprinkle over potato salad. Can garnish with extra sliced olives.

Note: This recipe, along with a few others, was submitted to us by David Steen of Norman, Oklahoma. Mr. Steen is the 70–year old father of Service League member, Kathy McLaughlin, and considered by all that know him as an "Original" Oklahoman. With each of his recipes, a very colorful story was attached. Following is a portion of his commentary on Potato Salad, unedited, truly showing his Oklahoman spirit and sense of humor. "Potato salad is a standard – most everybody likes dish. It is easy to make in quantity for wakes or weddings. The damn stuff is dangerous tho – I remember watching a fly light on a bowl of potato salad. It happened to set down on the piece of egg yellow so when the fly left, the cluster of white fly eggs on the yellow was quite visible. This is of no importance, except being a Biologist, I thought that it was interesting and a good warning to keep potato salad cold, covered and co–insured."

PAWNEE BILL POTATO SALAD

1½ cups mayonnaise
1 tablespoon prepared
   mustard
½ teaspoon garlic salt
2 tablespoons vinegar
dash of salt and pepper
4 large potatoes, peeled

½ cup chopped onions
1 cup real bacon bits
4 large eggs, hard–boiled,
   chopped
1 8–ounce jar sweet pickles,
   diced

Yield: 4–6 servings

The evening prior to serving the salad, prepare dressing by combining mayonnaise, mustard, garlic salt, vinegar, salt and pepper; cover and refrigerate. To prepare salad, boil potatoes until done; allow to cool. Cut into chunks and mash all or part of the potatoes. Combine with onions, bacon bits, chopped egg and pickles. Just before serving, pour dressing over salad and toss to coat evenly.

PAWHUSKA POTATO SALAD

5 medium red potatoes
1¼ teaspoons salt
¼ teaspoon pepper
5 green onions, thinly sliced

6 hard–boiled eggs, peeled &
   diced
1 medium bell pepper, diced
paprika, optional

Dressing:
1½ cups mayonnaise
1 teaspoon sugar
2 tablespoons dill pickle
   juice

1 tablespoon vinegar
1 tablespoon sweet relish
¼ teaspoon celery salt

Yield: 8 servings

Prepare red potatoes by boiling with skins on until tender. Allow to cool slightly, remove skins and dice (about 6 cups). Combine diced potatoes with salt and pepper in large bowl. Combine all dressing ingredients in separate bowl and stir well. Pour dressing over still warm potatoes and mix thoroughly. Let stand in refrigerator for at least 2 hours (overnight is preferred). Add green onions, peppers and eggs. Mix thoroughly. Garnish with paprika. Serve chilled.

BLACK-EYED PEA SALAD

Salad:
3 10–ounce packages frozen black–eyed peas

1 medium red bell pepper, chopped

⅓ cup fresh chopped parsley, divided

1 small red onion, thinly sliced, divided

Vinaigrette Dressing:
1 cup red wine vinegar

1 cup sugar

¼ cup vegetable oil

1¾ teaspoons salt

¾ teaspoon coarsely ground black pepper

⅛ teaspoon minced garlic

Yield: 12–14 servings

Cook frozen black–eyed peas according to package directions and drain. In large bowl, combine black–eyed peas with remaining salad ingredients, holding out 1 tablespoon parsley and some red onion slices for garnish. For vinaigrette dressing, whisk vinegar and sugar until sugar is dissolved. Gradually whisk in oil and remaining ingredients until thoroughly combined. Pour dressing over salad and allow to marinate 2 hours in refrigerator before serving. Salad can be placed on large platter lined with lettuce leaves and garnished with remaining parsley and red onion slices.

PAN FRIED TATERS

¼ cup chopped onion

3 tablespoons bacon grease

5–6 medium brown potatoes, finely diced

salt and pepper to taste

Yield: 4–6 servings

Sauté onion in bacon grease in 10 to12-inch frying pan. Add potatoes, cover and cook over medium heat, stirring occasionally until brown, about 30 minutes.

DALE'S FOURTH OF JULY BEANS

1 gallon can pork & beans	½ cup honey
1 medium white onion, diced	½ cup ketchup
1 large bell pepper, diced	3 tablespoons
6 fresh jalapeño peppers, sliced	Worcestershire sauce

Yield: 20 servings

Preheat oven to 350°. Mix all ingredients in a large baking dish or roasting pan. Bake 2 hours, stirring occasionally.

Note: Pam and Dale Matherly have had an annual 4th of July party for years. The names and faces of the guests may change a bit from year to year, but there's one thing that you can depend on — Dale's wonderful baked beans! Dale adds a special note to this recipe, "If your cholesterol really needs a boost, add about ½ pound of fat trimmings off of whatever you have in the smoker and 3 sliced hot links."

WILD BILL'S BAKED BEANS

1 52–ounce can pork and beans	2 apples, peeled, cored and chunked (optional)
1 medium onion, chopped	1½ cups packed brown sugar
1 medium green pepper, chopped	1 cup ketchup
5 slices bacon, cut in pieces	2 tablespoons prepared mustard

Yield: 10–12 servings

Preheat oven to 350°. Combine all ingredients into large 9 x 13-inch casserole dish, mixing until brown sugar is dissolved and all ingredients are mixed. Bake uncovered for 2 hours.

OKRA SALAD

1 16–ounce package frozen,
  sliced and breaded okra
1 bunch green onions,
  chopped
2 medium tomatoes,
  chopped

5 slices bacon, cooked crisp
  and crumbled
¼ cup vegetable oil
¼ cup sugar
⅛ cup vinegar

Yield: 6 servings

Fry okra according to package directions, drain and allow to cool completely. In a large bowl, combine okra with onions, tomatoes and crumbled bacon; mix gently. Add mixture of oil, sugar and vinegar; toss to coat. Chill until ready to serve.

FRIED OKRA

1–2 pounds fresh okra
2 eggs, beaten
1 cup flour

1 cup cornmeal
vegetable oil

Yield: 4–6 servings

Wash, dry and remove stems from okra. Slice okra into ¼ to ½-inch pieces and dip in beaten eggs. Combine flour and cornmeal in bowl. Remove okra from eggs and toss in cornmeal-flour mixture until pieces are thoroughly coated. In 12–inch black skillet, heat ½ to 1-inch vegetable shortening until very hot. Add okra to hot oil and fry on all sides until brown and tender. Remove from pan and drain.

Every down–home Oklahoma cook has their own recipe and secrets to frying okra, but three hints seem to show up often. First, a black cast iron skillet is a must. Secondly, the cooking oil must be very hot, so the okra will brown quickly. The final hint is to stir the okra as little as possible while it is cooking. This will help to keep the coating on the okra pieces.

OKRA FRITTERS

¼ cup cornmeal
¼ cup flour
½ cup finely chopped onion
½ cup evaporated milk
1 large egg slightly beaten
3 tablespoons chopped fresh
 parsley

2 tablespoons grated
 Parmesan cheese
½ teaspoon salt
¼ teaspoon red pepper
1 pound fresh okra, sliced
vegetable oil

Yield: 4–6 servings

Combine first 9 ingredients; stir in okra. Pour oil to depth of 2 inches in Dutch oven and heat to temperature of approximately 350°. Drop mixture by teaspoonful into oil. Cook until golden brown, turning once. Drain on paper towels. Sprinkle with salt, if desired, and serve immediately.

OKLAHOMA SLAW

1 large head cabbage,
 shredded
1 large onion, chopped
1 cup sugar
1 cup vinegar

¾ cup vegetable oil
1 tablespoon ground
 mustard
1 teaspoon celery seeds
1 tablespoon salt

Yield: 6–8 servings

In large bowl, toss cabbage and onion; sprinkle with sugar, but do not stir. In medium saucepan heat remaining ingredients, bringing to a boil. Pour hot mixture over cabbage and onion mixture, but do not stir. Cover and refrigerate 4 days before serving.

CHEESE GRITS

Great for a brunch!

6 cups water
1¾ cups grits
½ teaspoon salt
½ cup margarine

¾ pound box of Velveeta,
  shredded
3 eggs, well–beaten
4–6 dashes Tabasco sauce
paprika, optional

Yield: 12 servings

Preheat oven to 275°. In a large sauce pan, bring water to a boil; add grits and cook according to package instructions until done. Remove from heat and add salt, margarine and grated cheese. Stir until margarine and cheese are melted; allow to cool slightly. Stir in beaten eggs and Tabasco sauce and pour entire mixture into deep baking dish that has been sprayed with non–stick vegetable spray. Sprinkle with paprika, if desired. Allow to bake 1 hour or until grits in the center of the dish are set.

WAGON WHEEL COOKIES

4 eggs
2 cups sugar
2 teaspoons vanilla
4 squares baking chocolate,
  melted
½ cup melted shortening

2 cups flour
2 teaspoons baking powder
1 teaspoon salt
½ cup chopped pecans
powdered sugar

Yield: 4 dozen

Preheat oven to 350°. Beat eggs, sugar and vanilla until smooth. Blend in chocolate and shortening. Sift together dry ingredients and add to creamed mixture until thoroughly combined. Stir in chopped pecans. Roll dough into 1–inch balls and then roll each in powdered sugar. Place 2 inches apart on ungreased cookie sheet and bake 10–15 minutes.

OATMEAL SOUR CREAM COOKIES

¾ cup softened margarine
2 cups firmly packed brown
   sugar
2 eggs, beaten
¾ cup sour cream
1 teaspoon baking soda
2 cups flour

2 cups oats
pinch of salt
½ teaspoon cinnamon
1 teaspoon vanilla
1 cup raisins
1 cup chopped nuts

Yield: 6 dozen

Preheat oven to 350°. In large mixing bowl, cream together margarine, brown sugar, eggs, sour cream and baking soda. Beat well. Stir in remaining ingredients. Drop by teaspoonful onto lightly greased cookie sheet. Bake 15 minutes.

Note: I was born on January 10, 1936, in Harrah, Oklahoma, the youngest child of Raymond and Opal McGlocklin. My older brothers and I attended a small Oklahoma grade school and always looked forward to after school snacks. Mother would bake something every day for us. One of our favorite things was cookies, and as you know, with four kids, it was always difficult to agree on what kind of cookies mom should bake. Since mother realized we all had our preferences, she would make half the cookies with raisins and half without raisins. I guess I always appreciated that she would go to the trouble of making some without raisins, because I was one of those kids who wouldn't touch them! — Dolores Knox

DEEP DISH APPLE PIE

Pastry:
1 cup flour
½ teaspoon salt

⅓ cup plus 1 tablespoon
   shortening
2 – 3 tablespoons cold water

Filling:
1½ cups sugar
½ cup flour
1 teaspoon nutmeg
1 teaspoon cinnamon

¼ teaspoon salt
12 cups thinly sliced, pared
   apples
2 tablespoons margarine

Yield: 8 servings

Preheat oven to 425°. Prepare pastry by combing flour and salt in large bowl; cut in shortening. Sprinkle with cold water, 1 tablespoon at a time, mixing until all flour is moistened and dough almost clings to side of bowl. Set aside. Make filling by stirring together sugar, flour, nutmeg, cinnamon and salt. Mix gently with apples. Turn mixture into ungreased 9 x 9 x 2-inch baking pan; dot with margarine. Roll pastry on lightly floured board. Roll into 10-inch square; fold pastry in half. Place pastry over apples, unfold and fold edges just inside pan. Cut 4 to 5 small slits on top of pastry. Bake 1 hour or until juice begins to bubble through slits in crust. Best served warm with ice cream.

STRATFORD PEACH FRIED PIES

From the Peach Capital of Oklahoma!

Pastry:
2 cups flour
1 teaspoon salt
1 cup real butter or
    shortening

⅓ cup cold water

Filling:
3 tablespoons cornstarch
¾ cup sugar
¾ cup water

pinch of salt
2 cups peeled and diced
    fresh peaches

Yield: 1½ dozen

Prepare pastry by thoroughly combining flour and salt; cut in butter until mixture resembles coarse meal. Add cold water and continue to mix with hands until soft dough forms. Roll dough ⅛-inch thick on floured board. With large 2–inch cookie cutter, cut dough into rounds. Make peach filling by mixing cornstarch, sugar, salt and water in small saucepan until thoroughly dissolved. Cook over low heat, stirring constantly until thick and clear. Add diced peaches and stir until coated with sauce, mashing slightly. In each round, place 1½ tablespoons mashed peaches. Moisten edges with water, fold rounds to make semicircle and press edges together with fork. Fry in deep, hot, grease until golden brown, turning only once.

Note: On the twin virtues of quality and quantity, Stratford, Oklahoma claims itself to be the Peach Capital of Oklahoma. Stratford, located in the Lake Country of South Central Oklahoma, opens its doors each year for their annual Peach Festival — three days of activities, contests, exhibits, a rodeo and the crowning of the Peach Festival Queen and Princess. Each year, peach growers in the Stratford area contribute peaches to be auctioned. In the past, a bushel of prize peaches has brought as much as $2,600.

DOUBLE LAYER PEACH COBBLER

8 cups sliced fresh peaches
2¼ cups sugar
3 – 4 tablespoons flour
½ teaspoon ground
  cinnamon

½ teaspoon ground nutmeg
1 teaspoon vanilla extract
⅓ cup margarine
2 8-inch unbaked pastry
  shells

Yield: 8 servings

Preheat oven to 425°. In Dutch oven combine peaches with sugar, flour, cinnamon and nutmeg; toss to coat well. Bring mixture to a boil; reduce heat and allow to cook 10–15 minutes. Remove from heat; add vanilla extract and margarine, stirring until margarine melts. Roll half of pastry to ⅛-inch in thickness on floured surface; cut out an 8–inch square. Lightly butter an 8-inch square baking dish and fill with half of peach mixture; lay pastry square on top of peaches. Bake 15 minutes. Remove from oven and spoon remaining peaches over pastry. Roll remaining pastry to ⅛-inch and cut into 1-inch strips. Arrange strips in lattice design over peaches. Return to oven and bake an additional 15–20 minutes or until golden brown.

OKLAHOMA CRUDE CAKE

2 cups sugar
1 cup shortening
4 eggs
1½ cups flour
¼ teaspoon salt
⅓ cup cocoa

3 teaspoons vanilla
1 cup chopped pecans
  (optional)
1 7–ounce jar marshmallow
  creme

Icing:
⅓ cup cocoa
1 16-ounce box of powdered
  sugar
2 sticks of margarine,
  softened

⅓ cup evaporated milk
1 teaspoon vanilla
1 cup pecans, chopped

Yield: 12 servings

Preheat oven to 350°. For cake, cream together sugar and shortening; add eggs and continue to beat. In separate bowl, sift together flour, salt and cocoa and gradually add to creamed mixture. Add vanilla and nuts, if desired. Pour batter into 9 x 13-inch cake pan and bake 25 to 30 minutes. Remove cake from oven. While cake is still hot, spread marshmallow cream on top; allow to cool. For icing, mix together cocoa and sugar; add margarine and remaining ingredients. Spread icing on top of marshmallow layer. Store in tightly covered cake pan.

CINNAMON CHOCOLATE SHEET CAKE

2 cups sugar
2 cups flour
½ cup shortening
½ cup margarine
1 cup water
¼ cup cocoa

½ cup buttermilk
2 eggs, beaten
1 teaspoon baking soda
1 teaspoon vanilla
1 teaspoon cinnamon

Frosting:
½ cup margarine
4 tablespoons cocoa
⅓ cup milk

1 1–pound box powdered
  sugar
1 teaspoon vanilla
1 cup chopped pecans

Yield: 18 servings

Preheat oven to 400°. In large mixing bowl, sift together sugar and flour and set aside. In 4–quart sauce pan on top of stove, heat shortening, margarine, water and cocoa until mixture comes to a boil. Pour hot mixture over flour mixture and combine. Add buttermilk, beaten eggs, baking soda, vanilla and cinnamon to batter and thoroughly blend. Pour mixture into a well–greased 15 x 10-inch cake pan. Allow cake to bake for 20 minutes. While cake is baking, prepare frosting by bringing margarine, cocoa and milk to a boil; add powdered sugar, vanilla and nuts and thoroughly combine. Spread warm frosting on cake while still warm.

OKLAHOMA DEPRESSION CANDY

6 cups sugar
2 cups water

peels from 12 oranges (thick
  peels preferred)

Dissolve sugar in water in 2–quart saucepan. Boil sugar water until a drop of syrup forms a ball when dropped in cold water. Cut orange peel into pieces approximately 1–inch square. Drop orange peel into syrup and stir until coated, a few pieces at a time. Lift peel out of syrup with fork and place on wax paper until cool.

Note: This recipe started during the Depression when candy was hard to come by and provided the entire family with a sweet to chew on for just a few pennies.

AUNT BILL'S BROWN CANDY

An Oklahoma holiday tradition!

6 cups white sugar, divided
2 cups evaporated milk
¼ pound butter
¼ teaspoon soda

1 teaspoon vanilla
2 pounds pecans, broken
into pieces

Yield: 10 dozen pieces

Pour 2 cups sugar in iron skillet and place over low heat. Stir with wooden spoon until sugar turns the color of light brown sugar and begins to melt. Be sure to keep sugar moving (takes about ½ hour) and do not let sugar smoke or burn. When sugar starts to melt in skillet, place remaining 4 cups of sugar and canned milk in heavy saucepan over low heat; cook slowly. When sugar in skillet is completely melted, begin slowly pouring into the sugar and milk mixture. The real secret of combining these two mixtures is to pour a very fine stream of melted sugar from the skillet. Aunt Bill said to pour no larger stream than a knitting needle and stir across bottom of the pan all the time. Continue cooking until combined mixtures reach the firm ball stage. Remove from heat and add soda, stirring vigorously as it foams. Add butter and continue to stir. Remove from heat for 20 minutes. Add vanilla to mixture and beat until thick and heavy with dull appearance. Add broken pecans and mix. Pour into 2 buttered 9 x 13-inch cake pans and allow to cool. Cut into 1-inch pieces to serve. Allow 2½ hours and 2 people to make.

Note: Each Christmas season, my sister, Cheryl and I would plan an entire day to spend at our grandmother's house to make Aunt Bill's. Grandmother would always use the same black iron skillet – she insisted that no other pan would work. Being the younger, I always tried to outlast my sister in stirring the candy, but never could. Of course, it was grandmother that outlasted us both! — Diane Joy–Sisemore

CAFE
OKLAHOMA

APPETIZERS & BEVERAGES

SOME DAYS IT JUST RAINED OIL

If anything symbolized the Oklahoma Oil Boom, it was the Wild Mary Sudik.

Oil had first been discovered in the Choctaw Nation in the 1850's, and by the turn of the century there were derricks here and there around the Oklahoma landscape. But many producing wells were like the Nellie Johnstone No. 1 in northern Oklahoma Territory – even though proven producers, they were capped until the railroads came, when it would be economically feasible to get their oil to market.

In 1905, it became economically feasible.

Underneath Ida Glenn's farm in northeast Oklahoma that year they discovered an enormous pool of oil. Ever after called the Glenn Pool, it mushroomed into a forest of no fewer than 500 producing oil wells, and it made nearby Tulsa legendary as a wildcatter's heaven and The Oil Capital of the World.

Much of the strike was in the old Osage Nation, and since the tribe had managed to retain their mineral rights, overnight they found themselves to be among the richest people on Earth.

There were big strikes all over the state. And then the great Oklahoma City field exploded in 1928.

The great pool was directly under the city – Petunia No. 1 was drilled from a flower bed south of the State Capitol, 6,000 feet down to a pool *directly under the building itself.* It was said that the field was so rich, a driller's chances of striking it rich were better than nine out of ten.

And the Wild Mary Sudik?

Even though it happened in 1930, they still talk about that day. They say the well came in like an earthquake, with a thundering black geyser that shot oil hundreds of feet skyward, blowing heavy iron drillpipe with it like matchwood. It went on out of control for eleven straight days, 10,000 barrels of oil a day raining down in a fine black mist as far as 20 miles away. You didn't dare hang the washing out on the clothesline, for fear of getting it soaked in crude oil. And for days, nobody in Oklahoma City dared strike a match, for fear of igniting the very air, laden as it was with natural gas.

You just couldn't escape it. Unlike booming Oklahoma City, beautiful Tulsa had a strict prohibition against drilling in the city limits, so the skyline never developed the rows of derricks that Oklahoma City so prided itself on. In 1934, though, permission was given for one well to be drilled at the International Petroleum Exposition, simply to demonstrate drilling equipment.

It goes without saying that – purely by accident – they struck oil. . .

Big Oil imprinted Oklahoma's landscape with a unique forest of oil derricks that remained a proud trademark for decades. And though the wildcatters are gone, they left behind plenty of producing wells and a legacy that remains to this day.

Thank you for your financial support of the Junior Service League of Midwest City. Your purchase of Cafe Oklahoma will help to support projects such as:

The Child Abuse Response & Evaluation Center

The CARE Center provides an innovative approach to the investigation and treatment of child sexual and physical abuse. The CARE Center strives to minimize each child's trauma, to provide timely treatment and services, and to ensure the proper investigation of abuse cases.

OKLAHOMA COOLER

Perfect for hot Oklahoma summers!

½ cup lemon juice
¼ cup lime juice
2 cups cold water

4 teaspoons honey or sugar
2 cups ginger ale
4 thin lime slices

Yield: 4 servings

In a 2-quart pitcher, combine and mix well the lemon and lime juices, water and honey and set aside. Divide the lemon–lime juice mixture into 4, 12-ounce glasses filled with ice cubes. Fill the remainder of the glass with ginger ale. Stir briskly and garnish each glass with a lime slice.

CHIP'S FRUIT SMOOTHIE

A quick, early morning eye–opener!

½ banana
4–5 strawberries, fresh or
  frozen
4–5 ice cubes

1 packet artificial sweetener
  or 1½ teaspoons sugar
1–2 cups apple juice

Yield: 1 12–ounce drink

Place fruits, ice cubes and sweetener into blender. Fill remainder of blender pitcher with apple juice. Cover and blend 30 seconds, stopping once. Pour into glass and serve at once.

Most any fruit can be used for this frothy, frozen, healthy drink.

YOGURT FRUIT SHAKE

¾ cup milk
6 ounces plain yogurt
⅓ cup strawberry or apricot
  preserves

1 small banana cut into
  chunks

Yield: 2 1–cup servings

Place all ingredients into blender. Cover and process on high speed until thick and foamy. Serve immediately.

Note: Great for a quick on–the–go breakfast!

ORANGE JUICE FREEZE

1 6–ounce can frozen orange
    juice
1 tablespoon honey
½ teaspoon vanilla

½ cup water
½ cup milk
4 ice cubes

Yield: 2 servings

Combine all ingredients in blender. Cover and process approximately 30 seconds or until desired consistency.

FRUIT PUNCH

6 cups water
4 cups sugar
1 48–ounce can pineapple
    juice
2 12–ounce cans frozen
    orange juice concentrate,
    thawed

1 12–ounce can frozen
    lemonade concentrate,
    thawed
6 bananas, pureed
6 quarts ginger ale

Yield: 2 gallons

Mix water and sugar together in saucepan and heat until sugar is dissolved. Remove from heat and cool. When mixture is cool, add fruit juices and bananas. Place mixture in containers to freeze. Take out 2 hours prior to serving. When ready to serve, add ginger ale.

ROSY CHAMPAGNE PUNCH

8 cups ripe strawberries
1 cup fine granulated sugar
2 bottles (750 ml) dry white
    wine, chilled

4 bottles (750 ml)
    champagne, chilled
2 cups strawberry juice or
    similar berry juice, chilled

Yield: 35–40 servings

Wash and hull strawberries. If very large, cut in half. Place strawberries in a large punch bowl, sprinkle with sugar and toss gently. Pour the wine over berries and allow to set in cool area 2 to 3 hours. Just before serving add chilled champagne and berry juice.

BLOODY MARYS

Settle back and relax!

3 cups tomato juice
1 cup vodka
2 tablespoons fresh lemon
  juice
1 tablespoon fresh lime juice
1 teaspoon Worcestershire
  sauce

½ teaspoon Tabasco sauce
freshly ground pepper
4 lime wedges, for garnish
4 small celery ribs with
  leaves, for garnish

Yield: 4 servings

Combine all liquid ingredients and mix thoroughly. Pour into 4 ice–filled glasses. Dust with a small pinch of pepper. Garnish each glass with lime wedge and celery rib.

HOT BUTTERED RUM MIX

1 pound butter, softened
1 pound packed light brown
  sugar
1 pound powdered sugar
2 teaspoons cinnamon

2 teaspoons nutmeg
1 quart vanilla ice cream,
  softened
1 jigger of rum per serving

Garnish:
whipped cream   cinnamon stick (optional)

Yield: 40–50 8–ounce cups

In large bowl, cream together butter, sugars and spices until light and fluffy. Blend in ice cream. Place in container and keep in freezer. To serve, place 3 tablespoons of mix and 1 jigger of rum into large mug. Fill with boiling water and top with whipped cream. Serve with cinnamon stick.

HOT CINNAMON CIDER

Warm, soothing and wonderful!

1 teaspoon whole cloves
1 teaspoon whole allspice
1 3-inch cinnamon stick
½ peeled lemon, sliced

½ cup sugar
2 quarts cider
½ quart cranberry juice

Yield: 2½ quarts

Bundle spices in cheesecloth. In 4-quart saucepan place spices with remaining ingredients, stir and allow to thoroughly heat. Serve warm.

BURGUNDY SUNSET

6 cinnamon sticks
1 tablespoon whole cloves
10 cups water

4 6-ounce cans frozen apple
   juice concentrate
8 cups burgundy wine

Yield: 40 servings

In large Dutch oven, place cinnamon, cloves and water. Bring to boil, then reduce heat; cover and simmer 10 minutes. Add apple juice concentrate and return to boil. Add wine and allow to heat thoroughly. Serve warm.

TANTALIZING TEA

6 cups boiling water
3 family size tea bags
1 cup sugar

1 6-ounce can lemonade
2½ cups pineapple juice
4 6-ounce cans water

Yield: 10-12 servings

In a large saucepan add tea bags to boiling water. Allow to steep for approximately 5 minutes. Turn off heat and add sugar to hot tea so that the sugar can dissolve. Add remaining ingredients and stir thoroughly. Serve cold with mint leaves.

SHRIMP DIP

1½ cups cooked, peeled & chopped shrimp
1 8–ounce package cream cheese, softened
1 16–ounce carton sour cream

1 .7 ounce package dry Italian dressing mix
⅛ teaspoon liquid smoke
⅛ teaspoon Worcestershire sauce
¼ teaspoon garlic powder
1 cup chopped green onion

Yield: 10 servings

Combine all ingredients thoroughly; cover and chill overnight. Serve with crackers.

AVOCADO CRAB DIP

1 large ripe avocado, mashed
1 tablespoon fresh lemon juice
2 tablespoons grated onion
1 teaspoon Worcestershire sauce

1 8–ounce package cream cheese, softened
½ cup sour cream
½ teaspoon salt
1 7½–ounce can crab meat, drained & flaked

Yield: 1 cup

With electric mixer, combine mashed avocado with lemon juice, onion and Worcestershire sauce. Thoroughly mix in cream cheese, sour cream and salt. Remove from mixer, and by hand, gently stir in crab meat. Serve with your favorite crackers.

GRINGO GUACAMOLE

8 medium, ripe avocados, peeled & chopped
½ teaspoon oregano
½ teaspoon cumin
dash of chili powder
juice of 1 lemon

3 medium tomatoes, diced
1 tablespoon salt
¼ onion, grated
½ cup grated Monterey Jack cheese

Yield: 8 servings

Combine prepared avocados with next 4 ingredients and mash. Add diced tomatoes, salt and onion to mixture; stir to blend. Cover with plastic wrap (place wrap directly on guacamole, allowing for no air). Refrigerate until ready for use. Sprinkle with grated cheese and serve with corn chips.

CHILI RELLENOS DIP

3 large tomatoes, diced
1 4–ounce can chopped
   green chilies, drained
2–3 chopped green onions

1 4–ounce can chopped
   black olives, drained
2 tablespoons vegetable oil
1½ teaspoons garlic salt

Yield: 6 servings

Mix all ingredients together; cover and chill several hours until flavors are blended. Serve with corn tortilla chips.

CURRY DIP

1 cup real mayonnaise
1 3–ounce package cream
   cheese, softened
1 teaspoon tarragon vinegar

½ teaspoon prepared
   horseradish
½ teaspoon garlic salt
1 teaspoon curry powder

Yield: 1½ cups

Thoroughly combine all ingredients and allow to chill overnight. If needed, milk may be added prior to serving to make dip smoother. Serve with a variety of raw dipping vegetables.

VEGETABLE DILL DIP

⅔ cup mayonnaise
⅔ cup sour cream
1 tablespoon dried parsley
   flakes
1 tablespoon dried chopped
   onions

1 teaspoon Accent
1 teaspoon seasoning salt
1 teaspoon dill weed
dash of Tabasco sauce

Yield: 1⅓ cups

Combine all ingredients in bowl and mix well. Cover and refrigerate at least 2 hours to allow flavors to blend. Serve with assortment of raw vegetables.

Note: For a different taste, fill hollowed-out round bread with dip. Use the excess bread for dipping.

OKLAHOMA CAVIAR

(See recipe in Oklahoma Specialties Section)

STAR BURST DIP

¼ cup finely chopped
  cucumbers
½ cup finely chopped green
  pepper
1 7–ounce jar chopped
  pimientos, drained

1 cup sour cream
1 cup mayonnaise
1 2–ounce package dry
  ranch dressing

Yield: 2½ cups

Thoroughly mix all ingredients. Serve as a dip with vegetables or crackers.

CRABMEAT CHEESE DIP

2 6½-ounce cans crabmeat
  or 1 pound frozen
  crabmeat, thawed
6 tablespoons margarine,
  melted
6 tablespoons flour
1½ cups chicken broth
1½ cups evaporated milk

1 medium onion, chopped
1 tablespoon Accent
3 tablespoons chopped
  pimiento
⅓ pound Gruyère (Swiss)
  cheese, grated
¼ pound fresh Parmesan
  cheese, grated

Yield: 8 cups

Drain and flake crabmeat; set aside. In a medium saucepan over low heat, combine margarine and flour, blending until smooth. Combine chicken broth with evaporated milk and gradually add to flour mixture. Continue to heat, stirring constantly until smooth and thickened. Add chopped onion, Accent, pimiento, cheeses and crabmeat to saucepan and continue to heat until cheese melts. Transfer to a chafing dish set on low heat. Serve warm with chips.

SHRIMP & ARTICHOKE HEART DIP

1 3–ounce package cream
   cheese, softened
½ cup mayonnaise
½ cup picante sauce
1 cup shredded (not grated)
   Parmesan cheese

1 6–ounce can tiny shrimp,
   drained
1 14–ounce can artichoke
   hearts, drained & diced

Yield: 10–12 servings

Preheat oven to 350°. In medium bowl, blend together cream cheese, mayonnaise, picante sauce and shredded Parmesan. Gently stir in shrimp and artichoke hearts and transfer to 8 x 8-inch ovenproof dish. Bake for 30 minutes. Serve warm with your favorite crackers.

HOT BACON MIX

½ pound slab bacon, cubed
1 sweet bell pepper,
   chopped
1 small onion, chopped

¾ pound Cheddar cheese,
   grated
shredded wheat crackers

Yield: 8–10 servings

Preheat broiler to low heat. In food processor, or meat grinder, process bacon, bell pepper and onion until mixture has a spreading consistency. Mix with grated cheese. Spread a small amount of mixture on shredded wheat cracker and place under broiler for about 5 minutes until bacon cooks and cheese bubbles.

Watch to avoid burning. Shredded wheat type of crackers are a must for this dish.

Note: This recipe was submitted by Melba Lovelace. Melba's column, "Melba's Swap Shop" has appeared in The Daily Oklahoman for many, many, years. Through her column, Melba gives household hints, exchanges reader information and recipes and has cultivated thousands of friends throughout her loyal readers.

THUNDERBIRD BEAN DIP

1 16-ounce can bean dip
1 cup prepared brick chili
1 pound hot sausage,
    browned
1 teaspoon garlic salt
2 tablespoons chopped
    onion

1 4-ounce can chopped
    green chilies, drained
2 ounces picante sauce
1 cup shredded jalapeño
    cheese

Yield: 6–8 servings

Combine all ingredients in medium saucepan. Cover and cook over medium heat until entire mixture is thoroughly warmed. Transfer to serving dish and serve with corn chips.

MACHO NACHO DIP

1 pound ground beef
1½ teaspoons chili powder
½ teaspoon cumin
1 16-ounce can refried
    beans
1 4-ounce can chopped
    green chilies, drained

1½ cup shredded Monterey
    Jack cheese
1½ cup shredded sharp
    Cheddar cheese
1 cup taco sauce

Garnish:
1 cup sour cream
1 8-ounce carton guacamole
1 cup chopped green onions

1 4½-ounce can chopped
    black olives, drained

Yield: 12 servings

Preheat oven to 350°. Brown ground beef seasoned with chili powder and cumin and drain. Spread refried beans in 10–inch greased round or quiche pan. Evenly layer on the seasoned beef, green chilies and both cheeses. Pour on taco sauce and bake for 25 to 30 minutes. Garnish immediately with sour cream, guacamole, onions and olives. Serve warm with corn tortilla chips.

CHUTNEY DIP

A nice change for a brunch!

Cheese Ball:

1 8–ounce package cream
cheese, softened

8 ounces Cheddar cheese,
grated

1 teaspoon curry powder

½ cup golden raisins

½ cup chopped pecans

Topping:

1 8–ounce jar mild chutney

4–6 green onions, chopped

Yield: 8–10 servings

Combine cheeses, mixing well. Add remaining ingredients, form into a ball and refrigerate 1–2 hours. Combine chutney and onions, pour over ball when ready to serve. Serve with wheat wafers.

Note: You must try this to enjoy the unique flavors.

DOUBLE CHEESE DIP

½ cup margarine, softened

2 3–ounce packages cream
cheese

1 cup flour

1 small Gouda cheese round

1 4–ounce can chili peppers,
drained (optional)

Yield: 6–8 servings

Preheat oven to 425°. Combine margarine, cream cheese, and flour to make a dough. Form into a ball and chill for 1 hour. Pat or roll out dough until it reaches a size sufficient to cover Gouda cheese round. Place cheese round in the middle of the dough. Spread chili peppers over cheese (if desired). Bring edges of pastry up to cover cheese and peppers; seal edges. Excess pastry may be used to decorate top. Place in baking dish that is close–fitting (the appetizer will take the shape of the container). Bake for 25 minutes. Serve hot with crackers.

FRIED CHEESE

6 ounces Cheddar cheese
2 eggs, beaten

¾ cup all purpose flour
1½ cups bread crumbs

Yield: 4–6 servings

Cut cheese into 1–inch cubes. Dip into beaten eggs and dredge in flour. Dip again in the egg and roll in bread crumbs, pressing firmly. Place on wax paper that has been sprayed with non–stick vegetable spray and chill for 30 minutes. Deep fry in hot oil (375°) until golden brown. Drain on paper towels.

Note: Great with Honey–Mustard Dressing.

HOLIDAY CHEESE BALL

2 8–ounce packages cream
   cheese, softened
1 8½–ounce can crushed
   pineapple, drained
2 tablespoons finely
   chopped onion

½ cup finely chopped green
   pepper
½ teaspoon salt
1 cup finely chopped pecans

Yield: 15 servings

Combine cream cheese, pineapple, onion, green pepper and salt. Form into 1 large or 2 small balls. Roll in pecans, refrigerate on wax paper and allow to chill overnight for flavors to blend. Serve with crackers.

FIESTA CHEESE BALL

2 8–ounce packages cream
   cheese, softened
2 cups shredded sharp
   Cheddar cheese
1 tablespoon chopped
   pimiento
1 tablespoon finely chopped
   green pepper

1 tablespoon finely chopped
   onion
2 teaspoons Worcestershire
   sauce
1 teaspoon lemon juice
dash cayenne pepper
dash salt
finely chopped pecans

Yield: 10–12 servings

Combine all ingredients, except pecans, until well blended. Roll mixture into ball and roll in chopped pecans to cover. Refrigerate until ready to serve. Serve with crackers.

CRABMEAT BALL

1 8–ounce package cream
   cheese, softened
8 green onions, thinly sliced
   (including greens)
1½ tablespoons
   Worcestershire sauce
1 cup chili sauce
1 tablespoon horseradish

½ teaspoon Tabasco sauce
1 6–ounce package frozen
   crabmeat, thawed &
   drained
½ cup chopped parsley
fresh lemon juice to taste
1 cup chopped pecans

Yield: 8 servings

Mix thoroughly all ingredients, except pecans, and allow mixture to firm slightly in refrigerator, approximately 30 minutes. Remove from refrigerator, form into a ball and coat in chopped pecans. Refrigerate until ready to serve. Serve with your favorite crackers.

VEGGIE WEDGIES

1 package crescent rolls
1 1.0–ounce package ranch
   dressing mix
1 8–ounce package cream
   cheese, softened
1 cup mayonnaise
½ cup chopped broccoli
½ cup chopped green
   pepper

½ cup sliced or chopped
   cucumber
1 carrot, shredded
1 bunch green onions,
   chopped
1½ cups grated Cheddar
   cheese

Yield: 6–8 servings

Preheat oven to 400°. Press crescent rolls into pizza pan, slightly overlapping edges, and prick with a fork. Bake 10 minutes, remove from oven and allow to cool. (This step can be done in advance). Mix dry dressing mix into cream cheese; add mayonnaise and blend into frosting consistency. Spread mixture over crust. Sprinkle chopped vegetables evenly over cream cheese mixture and top with grated cheese. Cut into wedges to serve.

BACON STUFFED CHERRY TOMATOES

25 cherry tomatoes
1½ pound bacon
½ cup finely chopped green
  onions

½ cup mayonnaise
fresh parsley to garnish –
  optional

Yield: 12 servings

Wash and remove stems from tomatoes. Place tomato stem side down on cutting board and slice thin slice off of the top. With small spoon, scrape out pulp and discard. Invert tomatoes on paper towel and allow to drain thoroughly. Cook bacon until crisp; drain, cool and crumble into medium bowl. Mix bacon with green onions and mayonnaise. Fill tomatoes with bacon mixture. Allow tomatoes to refrigerate at least two hours before serving. Garnish with parsley.

BLACK–EYED PEA PINWHEELS

1 15–ounce can black–eyed
  peas, drained
¼ cup margarine
¼ teaspoon seasoned salt
2 ounces chopped green
  chilies, drained
dash of garlic powder

2 3–ounce packages cream
  cheese, softened
1 10–ounce package 6 x 4-
  inch ham slices
10 green onions, cut into 6-
  inch lengths

Yield: 6 dozen

Combine black–eyed peas, margarine, seasoned salt, chilies and garlic powder in a saucepan; bring to a boil. Reduce heat and simmer uncovered for 15 minutes stirring occasionally. Position knife blade in food processor bowl, add black–eyed pea mixture and cream cheese. Process 3 to 5 seconds. Stop processor and scrape sides of bowl with a rubber spatula. Process an additional 5 seconds or until mixture is well–blended. Spread about 3 tablespoons of pea mixture on each slice of ham; place a strip of green onion lengthwise in middle of ham slice. Roll up ham lengthwise; chill. To serve, cut each roll into ½–inch slices and arrange cut side up on a serving platter.

AVOCADO BACON BOATS

Great for pool parties!

3 large avocados
1 tablespoon lemon juice
6 slices bacon, cooked and
  crumbled
½ cup sour cream

2 tomatoes, diced
2 tablespoons sliced green
  onions
¼ teaspoon salt

Yield: 6 servings

Half each avocado and gently scoop out avocado meat, reserving skins intact. Dice avocados and sprinkle with lemon juice. Gently toss avocado with remaining ingredients and spoon back into avocado shells to serve.

NACHO CHEESECAKE

⅔ cup finely crushed tortilla
  chips
2 tablespoons margarine,
  melted
1 cup cottage cheese
3 8-ounce packages cream
  cheese, softened
4 eggs
10 ounces shredded sharp
  Cheddar cheese

1 4-ounce can chopped
  green chilies, drained
1 8-ounce container sour
  cream
1 8-ounce container
  Jalapeño-Cheddar dip
1 cup chopped tomatoes
½ cup chopped green onions
½ cup pitted ripe olive slices

Yield: 10-12 servings

Preheat oven to 325°. Combine the tortilla chips and margarine and press onto the bottom of a 9-inch springform pan. Bake for 15 minutes. While crust is cooking, place the cottage cheese in a blender or food processor. Cover and process on high speed until smooth. In large mixing bowl, combine the cottage cheese and cream cheese, mixing at medium speed until well blended. Add the eggs, one at a time, mixing well after each addition. Blend in the shredded Cheddar cheese and chilies. Pour the mixture over the baked crust. Return the pan to the oven and bake for 1 hour. Combine the sour cream and dip; mix thoroughly. Spread mixture over the hot cheesecake; return to the oven and continue baking for 10 minutes. Remove from the oven and allow to cool slightly. Loosen the cake from the rim of the pan; cool completely before removing the rim. Refrigerate the cheesecake until ready to serve. Top with tomatoes, green onions and olives before serving. Serve with tortilla chips.

TORTILLA WAGONWHEELS

(See recipe in Oklahoma Specialties Section)

STUFFED JALAPEÑOS

1 16–ounce can jalapeño
  peppers
1 8–ounce package cream
  cheese, softened

1 tablespoon sour cream
¼ cup chopped pecans
garlic salt, to taste

Yield: 10–12 servings

Drain peppers; slit down one side, remove seeds under running water and pat dry. Combine cream cheese with sour cream and garlic salt to taste; blend in pecans. Stuff each pepper with cheese mixture, press closed and chill until firm. Slice peppers into bite–sized pieces and serve.

Note: These peppers can be stuffed with wide variety of fillings: shrimp, salmon or crab blended with sour cream or any softened seasoned cheese.

CHILI CHEESE PUFF

10 eggs
1 pint cottage cheese
1 pound Monterey Jack
  cheese, grated
1 4–ounce can chopped
  green chilies, drained

½ cup flour
1 teaspoon baking powder
½ teaspoon salt
½ cup butter, melted

Yield: 10–12 servings

Preheat oven to 350°. Beat eggs till lemon colored, add cheeses and chilies. Stir in dry ingredients, add butter and mix. Pour into buttered 13 x 9 x 2-inch baking dish, and bake for 35 minutes. Cut in 2-inch squares to serve.

Note: Layers of cooked sausage can be added to this recipe.

CHILI SQUARES

Also great for a breakfast treat!

1 4–ounce can whole green
   chilies, drained
2 cups grated Cheddar
   cheese

2 eggs
2 cups milk
½ cup flour
½ teaspoon salt

Yield: 8–10 servings

Preheat oven to 350°. Remove the seeds and strings from green chilies and layer in the bottom of a buttered 9 x 9-inch baking dish. Top evenly with Cheddar cheese. Beat together eggs, milk, flour and salt and pour over chilies and cheese. Bake for 1 hour or until knife blade inserted in center comes out clean. Cut into 2-inch squares to serve.

Note: Best when served hot.

CHEESE–OLIVE PUFFS

2 cups grated Cheddar
   cheese
1 cup flour
½ teaspoon paprika

½ cup margarine, softened
3–4 dozen small pimiento-
   stuffed olives

Yield: 3–4 dozen

Preheat oven to 400°. Mix first four ingredients, blending well into a smooth dough. Drain olives well, allowing to dry on a paper towel. For each puff, shape a generous teaspoonful of dough around an olive, making sure olive is fully enclosed. Bake on ungreased cookie sheet for 15 minutes, until dough is cooked but not browned.

Note: Prior to baking, puffs may be frozen on cookie sheet and stored in plastic freezer bag. Thaw before baking.

HOT & SPICY MEAT BALLS

1 pound ground beef
¾ cup cracker crumbs
½ cup chopped onion
2 teaspoons prepared
   horseradish

4 drops Tabasco sauce
¾ teaspoon salt
½ teaspoon pepper
2 eggs

Sauce:
¾ cup ketchup
½ cup water
¼ cup vinegar
2 tablespoons brown sugar

2 tablespoons minced onion
4 teaspoons Worcestershire
   sauce
3 drops Tabasco sauce

Yield: 10–15 servings

Preheat oven to 350°. Combine ground beef and next 7 ingredients and mix thoroughly, using hands if necessary. Form into 1 to 1½-inch balls and brown, either by baking, broiling or frying. Place meatballs in 9 x 9-inch casserole dish and set aside. Prepare sauce by combining all ingredients in medium bowl, mixing well. Pour over meatballs and bake 20 minutes. Serve warm with wooden picks.

SHRIMP EGG ROLLS

½ onion, chopped
2 tablespoons vegetable oil
4 cups shredded cabbage
1 cup chopped carrots

soy sauce to taste
2 6–ounce packages shrimp,
   thawed
1 package egg roll wrappers

Yield: 25 servings

Sauté onions in vegetable oil in a large skillet. Add cabbage and carrots; continue cooking until cabbage is clear in color (5-10 minutes). Add soy sauce. Add shrimp to cabbage mixture, stir and heat thoroughly. Place scant ¼ cup cabbage/shrimp mixture on egg roll wrapper. Roll on the diagonal, folding sides toward the center while rolling and ending with "v" shape. Seal with water. Fry in hot oil 2–3 minutes or until golden. Drain and serve warm.

ZUCCHINI SQUARES

1 cup biscuit baking mix
½ cup grated Parmesan
  cheese
2 teaspoons dried parsley
½ teaspoon salt
½ teaspoon oregano

¼ teaspoon garlic powder
½ cup vegetable oil
4 eggs, slightly beaten
dash of pepper
3 cups chopped, unpeeled,
  zucchini

Yield: 2 dozen

Preheat oven to 350°. Mix all ingredients together and spread evenly into a greased 9 x 13-inch pan. Bake 25 minutes or until golden brown. Cut into 2–inch squares and serve warm.

SPINACH BALLS

Easy! Can do ahead and freeze!

3 10-ounce boxes frozen
  spinach
1 large bag herb–seasoned
  stuffing
1 pound mozzarella cheese,
  grated

9 eggs, beaten
2 onions, diced
1 cup margarine, melted
2 teaspoons garlic powder
1 teaspoon black pepper

Yield: 5 dozen balls

Preheat oven to 375°. Combine all ingredients well and form into 1-inch balls. Bake on cookie sheet that has been sprayed with non–stick vegetable spray for 15–20 minutes. Serve hot.

Note: After balls are formed, they can be frozen on a cookie sheet and stored in zip top bags. Bake frozen in preheated oven for 20 minutes.

SPINACH EMPANADAS

Filling:

4–5 slices bacon, cooked, drained and crumbled
1 tablespoon bacon drippings
¼ cup finely chopped onion
3 cloves garlic, minced

1 10–ounce package frozen chopped spinach, thawed and drained
1 8–ounce container cottage cheese
¼ teaspoon black pepper
⅛ teaspoon ground nutmeg
salsa

Pastry:

2 8–ounce packages cream cheese, softened
¾ cup margarine, softened

2½ cups flour
½ teaspoon salt
1 egg, beaten

Yield: 5 dozen

Preheat oven to 450°. Prepare filling by cooking bacon in 12-inch skillet until crisp; drain bacon, reserving drippings. In drippings, sauté onion and garlic 3–4 minutes until tender; remove from pan. In large mixing bowl, combine spinach, cottage cheese, pepper and nutmeg with crumbled bacon, onion and garlic. Combine all thoroughly and allow to cool while making pastry. For pastry, combine softened cream cheese with margarine, flour and salt until soft dough forms. Roll pastry on lightly floured surface until it is ⅛-inch thick. Using a 3-inch biscuit cutter (or glass) cut out as many pastry circles as possible. Place 1 teaspoon of cooled filling on one half of each pastry circle. Moisten the edges of the circle with egg and fold the other half of the circle over the filling. Place filled pastries on ungreased baking sheet. Gently seal the edges of the Empanadas with tines of a fork. Brush Empanadas with beaten egg. Using the tines of a fork, prick a small vent in each pastry. Bake 10–12 minutes until golden. Serve with salsa.

Note: This recipe was a 4–H Award winner for 14–year old, Caralee Buchanan. Caralee also recommends using low fat cream cheese, margarine and cottage cheese in this recipe if you're watching calories.

SUSAN'S MUSHROOM SANDWICHES

20 slices thin–sliced white
 bread
2 tablespoons grated onion
¼ cup real butter
¾ pound fresh mushrooms,
 finely chopped
2 tablespoons flour

½ teaspoon Tabasco sauce
1 teaspoon salt
⅛ teaspoon pepper
½ cup half–and–half cream
extra butter and vegetable
 oil for frying

Yield: 6 servings

Cut each slice of bread with a biscuit cutter into four 1¾-inch rounds. Sauté onion in butter; add mushrooms and continue to sauté until all moisture is cooked out of mushrooms. Add flour and stir until thickened. Add Tabasco sauce, salt, pepper and half–and–half; cook until thick. Spread 1 teaspoon of mushroom mixture on 20 of the bread rounds. Top with remaining bread rounds to make sandwiches. Fry sandwiches in equal portions of hot butter and oil until brown and crisp, about 1 minute for each side. Drain on paper towel. Keep warm, uncovered in a 300° oven.

WRANGLER ROLL–UPS

1 can crescent rolls
1 8–ounce package cream
 cheese, softened
2–3 green onions, chopped
 with tops

1 2.5–ounce jar chopped
 mushrooms
1–2 tablespoons garlic salt
1 egg yolk, beaten
poppy seeds

Yield: 4-6 servings

Preheat oven to 350°. Flatten crescent rolls into a rectangle, pinching together perforated edges to form solid sheet of dough. Evenly spread cream cheese over dough and top with green onions and mushrooms. Sprinkle evenly with garlic salt. Roll dough jelly-roll style using longer side. Cut dough into ½-inch slices and place on greased cookie sheet. Using pastry brush, brush slices with egg yolk and sprinkle with poppy seeds. Bake 15 minutes.

Note: For a variation, add 6–ounce can of chicken on top of cream cheese.

SPANISH ROLLS

Great for afternoon snacks.

1 pound ground round
2 ounces olive oil
salt and pepper to taste
1 clove garlic, chopped
6 green onions, finely
  chopped

1 4½-ounce can ripe black
  olive slices, drained
1 4-ounce can tomato sauce
2 tablespoons taco sauce
1 pound American cheese,
  grated
20-30 sour dough rolls

Yields: 20-25 servings

Preheat oven to 350°. In large skillet, brown ground round in olive oil with salt and pepper; drain well. Add garlic and remaining ingredients, except rolls, and allow to cook 5 – 10 minutes and remove from heat. Slice top of roll, folding back top to scoop out centers. Fill each roll with meat mixture, close top of roll and wrap loosely in foil and heat 20 – 30 minutes.

Note: Perfect to make ahead, freeze, and heat as needed.

SNAPPY JACK BREAD

1 cup melted margarine
1 cup real mayonnaise
2 4-ounce cans chopped
  green chilies, drained

3-4 loaves French bread,
  halved lengthwise
8-ounces Monterey Jack
  cheese, grated

Yield: 14-16 servings

Combine margarine, mayonnaise and green chilies. Spread evenly on top of bread. Sprinkle all with cheese. Place under broiler and heat thoroughly (watch closely). Slice to serve.

STUFFED FRENCH LOAF

1 16–ounce loaf French
    bread
8 ounces spicy bulk pork
    sausage
⅓ cup chopped onion
1 clove garlic, minced
1 egg
3 teaspoons Dijon–style
    mustard, divided

2 tablespoons chopped
    parsley
¾ cup grated extra sharp
    Cheddar cheese
½ cup grated Parmesan
    cheese
¼ cup olive oil
1 teaspoon pepper

Yield: 14–16 servings

Preheat oven to 350°. Slice the bread in half lengthwise and slightly hollow out each half, leaving ½-inch of bread. Place the bread crumbs in a food processor and process 15 seconds; set aside. Cook the sausage, onion and garlic in a skillet over medium heat until meat is brown; drain well. In a large bowl, combine bread crumbs, meat mixture, egg, 1 teaspoon mustard and parsley and set aside. Using a food processor, process the cheeses, olive oil, 2 teaspoons mustard and pepper until mixture forms a paste (approximately 1 minute). Spread cheese mixture evenly over the inside of each bread half. Spoon meat mixture into the cavity of each bread half. Place bread halves together and wrap foil around loaf. Bake 30 to 35 minutes, slice and serve.

Note: Serve as an appetizer or with your favorite soup.

CHEESE CRISPS

2 cups flour
¼ teaspoon salt
½ teaspoon cayenne pepper
1 cup margarine, softened

10 ounces extra sharp
    Cheddar cheese, grated
2 cups crispy rice cereal

Yield: 8 dozen

Preheat oven to 350°. In a large mixing bowl, combine flour with salt and cayenne pepper; cut in margarine. Add grated cheese and cereal and blend with hands. Using about 1 tablespoon of mixture for each, press dough into firm 1½-inch patties about ¼–inch thick. Place on cookie sheets that have been prepared with a non–stick vegetable spray. Bake 15 minutes; cool and store in air tight container.

OVEN CARAMEL CORN

3¾ quarts popped corn
1 cup packed brown sugar
½ cup margarine

¼ cup light corn syrup
½ teaspoon salt
½ teaspoon baking soda

Yield: 15 cups

Preheat oven to 200°. Divide popped corn between 2 ungreased 9 x 13-inch pans. In saucepan, heat brown sugar, margarine, corn syrup and salt, stirring occasionally until bubbly around edges. Continue cooking over medium heat for 5 minutes. Remove from heat and stir in soda until foamy. Pour on pop corn until well coated. Bake 1 hour, stirring every 15 minutes.

RANCH SNACK MIX

1 1.0–ounce package dry
   ranch–style dressing mix
1 teaspoon lemon pepper
   seasoning
1 teaspoon garlic salt
1 teaspoon dill weed
1 cup vegetable oil
Use ½ box of each:
1 10–ounce box mini round
   buttery crackers

1 8–ounce box thin wheat
   crackers
1 8.5–ounce box pretzel
   chips
1 7–ounce box cheese
   crackers
1 12–ounce box square
   wheat or rice cereal

Yield: 15–20 servings

Combine dressing mix with next 4 ingredients in jar and shake well. In a large paper sack, pour all crackers and shake to mix. Pour dressing over cracker mixture and shake very well to evenly coat. Let soak in paper bag 2–3 hours, shaking occasionally until oil is absorbed.

NUTS, BOLTS AND JOLTS

½ cup margarine
½ cup bacon drippings
2 tablespoons
    Worcestershire sauce
1 teaspoon garlic salt
1 teaspoon celery salt
1 teaspoon seasoned salt
1 teaspoon red pepper

10 cups square wheat, rice
    or corn cereal
5 cups round oat cereal
1 10–ounce package
    pretzels, broken
1 7–ounce can peanuts or
    mixed nuts
2 cups pecan halves

Yield: 20 cups

Preheat oven to 250°. Melt margarine and bacon drippings in sauce-pan. Add seasonings and simmer. Mix cereal, pretzels and nuts in large cake pan. Pour margarine mixture over cereal mixture and mix gently. Heat 1 hour, stirring gently every 20 minutes. Store in sealed container.

PUMPKIN DIP

A "must try" recipe for fall!

4 cups powdered sugar
2 8–ounce packages cream
    cheese, softened
1 30–ounce can solid pack
    pumpkin

2 teaspoons ground
    cinnamon
1 teaspoon ground ginger
gingersnap cookies

Yield: 7 cups

In a large mixing bowl, combine powdered sugar and cream cheese, beating with mixer until well–blended. Beat in remaining ingredients (except cookies). Store in air tight container in refrigerator. Serve as a dip with gingersnap cookies.

Note: Beautiful served in pumpkin that has been hollowed out with fall leaves at the base.

CANDIED DILL PICKLES

(See recipe in Oklahoma Specialties Section)

ICE BOX PICKLES

8 cups sliced cucumbers
1 cup thinly sliced celery
1 medium green pepper,
  thinly sliced
1 large onion, finely
  chopped

1 3¼–ounce jar chopped
  pimiento, drained
1½ tablespoons salt
2 cups sugar
1 cup white vinegar
1 teaspoon celery seed
1 teaspoon mustard seed

Yield: 8 pints

In a large, non–aluminum bowl mix all vegetables with salt and set aside for one hour. During this time, combine sugar with vinegar, celery seed and mustard seed in medium saucepan. Heat mixture to boiling, stirring until sugar is dissolved. Remove from heat and allow to cool. Pour liquid over vegetables, cover and refrigerate until thoroughly chilled. Pour mixture into glass jars and store in refrigerator.

PICKLED GREEN TOMATOES

8 cups green tomatoes (golf
  ball size)
1 Bermuda onion, sliced

3–4 cups white vinegar
½ teaspoon "Steen's Fire"
  (found on following page)

Yield: 1 quart

Thoroughly wash tomatoes and cut into quarters. Alternate tomatoes and onion slices in quart–size jar with tight fitting lid. Fill jar with white vinegar until the tomatoes are totally covered. Add "Steen's Fire" and seal jar. Allow tomatoes to refrigerate at least 72 hours before serving.

Note: See recipe on next page for Steen's Fire.

PICKLED OKRA

(See recipe in Oklahoma Specialties Section)

RUSH SPRINGS WATERMELON RIND PRESERVES

(See recipe in Oklahoma Specialties Section)

SOONER SALSA

(See recipe in Oklahoma Specialties Section)

WILDFIRE

1 pound fresh jalapeño peppers
2 large carrots, cut into quarters
1 onion, cut in quarters

2–3 cloves of garlic
⅓ – ½ cup safflower oil
⅓ cup cider vinegar
1 teaspoon salt

Yield: 2 cups

Chop first four ingredients in food processor. Combine with oil, vinegar and salt in bowl. Mix well. Store in refrigerator in well–sealed container. Serve with corn chips or warm tortillas.

STEEN'S FIRE

1 pound jalapeño peppers
1 large bell pepper
1 large Bermuda onion

2 teaspoons Tabasco sauce
½ cup vinegar

Yield: ½ pint

Clean and remove stems from jalapeño peppers. Clean and section bell peppers and onion. Alternately feed onion, bell pepper and jalapeño peppers into food grinder, allowing to fall into a large bowl. Use vinegar to wash out grinder and collect into ground vegetable mixture. Add Tabasco sauce and stir well. Cover with plastic wrap and refrigerate 12 hours, stirring occasionally, to allow flavors to blend. For longer storage, place mixture in glass jar with tight fitting lid and refrigerate.

Note: Dave Steen adds, "Don't make this unless you are in a creative mood and have at least a pint of whipping cream available to overcome the tasting process required."

PEPPER RELISH

4 cups bell pepper pieces
3 cups onion, coarsely
   chopped
3 cups vinegar, divided

2 cups water
3 cups sugar
1 tablespoon salt

Yield: 4 pints

Process bell pepper and onion through grinder using medium blade. Heat ground vegetables in Dutch oven with 1 cup of the vinegar and water. Bring mixture to a boil and allow to boil 5 minutes; cool slightly and drain well. Add sugar, remaining vinegar and salt to vegetables and heat again. Allow mixture to cook 15 minutes. Pour relish into jars and store in refrigerator.

HOT PEPPER JAM

6½ cups sugar
1½ cups white vinegar
¾ cup chopped red bell
   pepper
½ cup chopped hot red or
   green peppers

1 6-ounce bottle liquid fruit
   pectin
red food coloring
1 8-ounce package cream
   cheese

Yield: 7 cups

Mix sugar and vinegar together in large saucepan and bring to a boil. Add peppers and boil an additional 10 minutes. Remove from heat and add liquid pectin. Add red food coloring until desired color is reached. Let stand and cool, stirring occasionally until jam begins to thicken. Pour into sterilized jars, store in refrigerator. To serve, pour 1 cup jam over softened cream cheese and eat with thin wheat crackers.

JEZEBEL SAUCE

1 18-ounce jar pineapple
  preserves
2 18-ounce jars apple jelly
1 ¼-ounce can dry mustard

2½ ounces horseradish
1 8-ounce package of cream
  cheese

Yield: 10-15 servings

Mix all ingredients together, adding horseradish to desired taste. Serve by pouring 1 cup sauce over cream cheese and serve with crackers.

Note: More horseradish may be added for a zestier taste.

HEAVENLY JAM

1 quart fresh strawberries,
  washed and hulled
1 12-ounce can crushed
  pineapple, drained

2 tablespoons lemon juice
1 1¾-ounce package of fruit
  pectin
5 cups sugar

Yield: 4 (8-ounce) jars

Crush strawberries, slightly; put into large kettle. Add remaining ingredients except sugar. Bring mixture to a boil; add sugar. Place over high heat and bring to a full rolling boil; allow to boil 1 minute. Remove from heat. Stir for 5 minutes while skimming froth; allow to cool slightly. Ladle into hot sterilized jars; seal with hot paraffin.

Note: Contact your local County Extension Office for most current home canning and processing methods.

CAFE
OKLAHOMA

BREADS

A TRADITION OF OUTLAWRY

If there's a touch of larceny in the Sooner soul, we come by it, well, honestly.

Since this part of the country was set aside early as a place where the Indian tribes came to be resettled – our founding fathers' thinking was a little hazy on exactly how that was to be organized – it was by definition outside the jurisdiction of white lawmen.

In other words, it was a tough place.

Which is why Oklahoma's past is peopled with the likes of the Dalton Gang, Belle Starr, and Bonnie Parker and Clyde Barrow.

The Panhandle was so full of them, they called it "Robbers Roost." Meanwhile, at the opposite end of the Territory, was "Robbers Cave," where Belle Starr's gang hid out.

Belle Starr. While there's no real record of her having actually killed anybody, she sure had the reputation. It started early – by age 16, she was riding with the Jesse James Gang, which is where she met and romanced Cole Younger (which is another story entirely). She was no doubt the best-dressed horsethief America ever produced – she loved velvet gowns with ostrich-plumed hats, and always wore a pair of matched Colt .45's to complete the ensemble. The *National Police Gazette* styled her "The Petticoat Terror;" she herself said simply, "I regard myself as a woman who has seen much of life."

Later, in the 1880's, the Dalton Gang operated out of Oklahoma Territory, robbing trains in neighboring Indian Territory well into the '90's. It was a way of life that was fast vanishing, though, because the law was making inroads into the outlaws' haven. As far as the Daltons were concerned, they just bit off more than they could chew – most of the gang got gunned down in Kansas when they tried to rob two banks at once.

Still later, the 1930's produced its own crop of Oklahoma outlaws. At about the same time Bonnie and Clyde were going on raids into Kansas and Missouri and returning to hide out in Oklahoma – nothing new there: the Plains Indians had founded the practice years before – there was Charles Arthur Floyd.

Everybody knew him as "Pretty Boy" – he loved fast cars, flashy clothes, and flashier women. He was from the northeastern hills in the old Cherokee Nation, and he always took care of his own. In 1931, when the Oklahoma governor put a $7,000 reward on his head, he responded with a postcard, saying, "I have robbed no one but moneyed men." His poor neighbors in the Cookson Hills would agree, because he shared much of the proceeds of his bank robberies with them (consequently, no one tried to collect the reward).

Somehow, an Oklahoman can usually find just a little bit of a soft spot for a desperado, especially one as generous as Pretty Boy Floyd. That's part of the reason 20,000 people came to Pretty Boy's funeral to pay their respects.

He was one of their own.

The Law caught up with him, of course; it caught up with all of them who hid out here – Bonnie, Clyde, Machine Gun Kelly, the Daltons, the Youngers. But all those legends still echo across Oklahoma.

You can still visit Belle Starr's grave, with its elaborate headstone. Alongside the carving of her pistols, it has a carving of her favorite horse. A beautiful horse it was, naturally: she only stole the best.

Thank you for your financial support of the Junior Service League of Midwest City. Your purchase of Cafe Oklahoma will help to support projects such as:

Mid-Del Group Homes

These group homes allow mentally handicapped young adults to live in a supervised independent setting.

 **Breads**

OVERNIGHT CRUNCH COFFEE CAKE

⅔ cup margarine or butter
½ cup brown sugar
1 cup sugar
2 eggs
2 cups sifted flour
1 teaspoon baking soda

1 teaspoon baking powder
1 teaspoon cinnamon
1 teaspoon salt
1 cup buttermilk or sour
   milk

Topping:
½ cup brown sugar
½ teaspoon cinnamon

½ cup walnuts, chopped, or
   pecans
¼ teaspoon nutmeg

Yield: 12 servings

Cream margarine and sugars until fluffy; add eggs, one at a time, beating well. Sift together dry ingredients and add alternately with buttermilk. Spread in greased and floured 13 x 9 x 2–inch pan. Combine topping ingredients and sprinkle over batter. Refrigerate overnight or for 8 hours. Bake in 350° oven for 45 minutes or until done. Cut into squares and serve warm.

Note: I remember spending the night with my Granny, Frances Knox, so many times when I was a little girl. Granny was born in Tecumseh, Oklahoma on July 15, 1906. She would always tell me stories about how things were when she was a little girl, and she was raised by her Father. One of the stories she told me was how her Daddy would fix her coffee to drink while he had his coffee in the mornings. Of course, I thought that sounded so grown up and asked her if I could have some coffee. With a smile on her face, she fixed me a cup of coffee (actually a lot of cream and sugar and a little coffee), just as her father had done for her. I thought I was all grown up as we sat and drank our coffee together. Granny is 87 years old now and we still "have coffee together."—De Ann Bower

SOUR DOUGH FLAPJACKS WITH WARM CHERRY SAUCE

Sauce:

1½ cups sugar
3 tablespoons cornstarch

2 20-ounce cans sour or tart
  pitted cherries
½ cup margarine

Flapjacks:

2 packages dry yeast
½ cup warm water
2 eggs, beaten

3 cups milk
4 cups biscuit baking mix

Yield: 6-8 servings

For cherry sauce, mix sugar and cornstarch with juice from cans of cherries in medium–sized heavy saucepan. Cook over low heat and stir constantly until mixture begins to thicken. Add cherries and margarine and continue to stir until margarine is melted. Keep warm while preparing pancakes. To make flapjacks, soften dry yeast in warm water in a small cup and set aside. In large bowl, place beaten eggs and add milk and biscuit baking mix, stirring until blended; add dissolved yeast. Cover bowl with thin towel and set in warm place to rise for 1½ hours. Do not stir mixture during this time. Heat griddle. Lift large spoonful, one at a time from the bottom of the bowl and place on griddle. Allow to brown and turn. Serve with syrup, honey or warm cherry sauce.

Note: You can keep pancakes warm until ready to serve by placing them on a plate or baking dish in a 200° oven. Layer paper towels between them to absorb steam and to keep them from getting soggy.

PRAIRIE PANCAKES

(See recipe in Oklahoma Specialties Section)

FRENCH TOAST

4 eggs
1 cup milk
¼ teaspoon vanilla
1 teaspoon orange juice
1 tablespoon sugar

½ teaspoon salt
8–12 slices French bread,
   ¾-inch thick
4 tablespoons margarine
powdered sugar (optional)

Yield: 4–6 servings

Beat together eggs and next 5 ingredients. Arrange bread slices in 9 x 13-inch baking dish. Pour mixture over bread, turning so that each slice is coated with egg mixture. Cover tightly with plastic wrap and refrigerate overnight. Fry on hot griddle in margarine, turning once until golden brown on both sides. Sprinkle with powdered sugar if desired.

COWHAND SODA BISCUITS

2¼ cups unsifted flour
1 teaspoon baking soda
1 teaspoon salt
3 tablespoons shortening,
   cut into ½-inch pieces

1 cup buttermilk
½ pound of shortening for
   deep frying

Yield: 1 dozen

Combine the flour, baking soda and salt in a deep bowl. Add 3 tablespoons of shortening pieces and, with your fingertips, rub the flour and shortening together until they resemble flakes of coarse meal. Pour in the buttermilk and beat vigorously with a spoon to make a smooth dough. Over moderate heat, melt the remaining ½ pound of shortening in a Dutch oven or heavy casserole about 8 inches in diameter and 4 or 5 inches deep. Heat the shortening until hot, not smoking. To shape each biscuit, cut off about 2 tablespoons of the dough and, flouring your hand lightly as you proceed, roll the dough into balls about 1½-inches in diameter. Drop two or three biscuits at a time in the hot shortening, turning with a spoon to brown on all sides. When all the biscuits have been added to the pot, cover it tightly and fry for 4 minutes. Turn the biscuits over and fry an additional 4 minutes. Drain on paper towels and serve hot.

Note: Although this method of cooking biscuits isn't used much any longer, it was the only method pioneer women could use on the prairie.

MOM'S SAUSAGE GRAVY & COUNTRY FRESH BISCUITS

(See recipe in Oklahoma Specialties Section)

BUTTERMILK BISCUITS WITH CHOCOLATE GRAVY

Biscuits:
2 cups flour
1 teaspoon salt
2 teaspoons baking powder

½ teaspoon baking soda
¼ cup vegetable shortening
¾ – 1 cup buttermilk

Chocolate Gravy:
1 cup sugar
⅓ cup flour
1 heaping teaspoon cocoa
½ teaspoon salt

2 cups milk
½ cup butter
1 teaspoon vanilla extract

Yield: 1 dozen

Preheat oven to 450°. Sift flour, salt, baking powder, and soda into bowl. Cut in shortening until mixture resembles coarse meal. Pour buttermilk into flour mixture, slowly. Knead dough 10 to 15 times. On lightly floured surface, roll out to ½-inch thickness. Cut and bake on ungreased baking sheet for 10 to 15 minutes.

For gravy, combine sugar, flour, cocoa and salt in small bowl; mix well. Heat milk in 2–quart saucepan until lukewarm. Stir in dry ingredients. Cook until mixture is the consistency of gravy; stirring constantly. Do not boil. Remove to serving bowl. Stir in butter and vanilla. Serve with biscuits for breakfast.

BLUEBERRY BUTTERMILK BISCUITS

2 cups sifted flour
½ cup sugar
3 teaspoons baking powder
¼ teaspoon baking soda
1 teaspoon salt
⅓ cup vegetable shortening

1 teaspoon grated orange
  peel
1 egg, beaten
¾ cup buttermilk
½ cup blueberries, frozen

Topping:
2 – 3 tablespoons butter,
  melted
3 tablespoons sugar

¼ teaspoon cinnamon
⅛ teaspoon ground nutmeg

Yield: 1 dozen

Preheat oven to 400°. In a large bowl, combine first 5 ingredients. Cut in shortening until mixture resembles coarse meal. Add orange peel; mix lightly. Combine eggs and buttermilk. Add to flour mixture, stirring to blend. Add frozen blueberries and stir gently. Transfer dough to a lightly floured surface, knead gently 5 to 6 times. Pat dough to ½-inch thick. Cut with floured cutter. Bake on ungreased baking sheet 15 minutes or until lightly browned. Prepare topping in a small bowl, by combining melted butter, sugar, cinnamon and nutmeg. Brush tops of biscuits while warm.

GRAMMY'S BISCUITS

(See recipe in Oklahoma Specialties Section)

ORANGE MUFFINS

1 cup margarine, softened
1 cup sugar
2 eggs
1 teaspoon baking soda
1 cup buttermilk
2 cups sifted flour

2 tablespoons grated orange
    rind
½ cup golden raisins
    (optional)
juice of 2 oranges
1 cup brown sugar, packed

Yield: 1 dozen

Preheat oven to 400°. In a large bowl, cream together margarine and sugar; add eggs and beat until well mixed. In separate bowl, dissolve baking soda in buttermilk and add, alternating with flour, to the egg and margarine mixture. Add orange rind and raisins. Fill well–buttered muffin tins ⅔ full and bake for 20 to 25 minutes. For topping, mix together juice from oranges and brown sugar in a small bowl. Spoon generously over muffins while still hot and in tins. Remove from tins immediately.

HONEY CORN MUFFINS

1 cup yellow cornmeal
1 cup milk
¼ cup sour cream
1 egg
¼ cup honey

⅓ cup margarine, melted
⅓ cup sugar
1¼ cups flour
1 tablespoon baking powder

Yield: 1 dozen

Preheat oven to 400°. Beat together first 7 ingredients until blended. In separate bowl, stir together flour and baking powder; add, all at once to batter. Stir until well–blended; do not over mix. Divide batter between 12 paper–lined muffin cups and bake for 20–22 minutes or until cake tester, inserted in center comes out clean.

COTTAGE CHEESE MUFFINS

⅓ cup sugar
3 tablespoons margarine,
   softened
½ cup cottage cheese

1 teaspoon grated lemon
   peel
1 egg
1¾ cups biscuit baking mix
¼ cup milk

Yield: 1 dozen

Preheat oven to 375°. In a medium bowl, cream sugar with margarine. Gradually blend in cottage cheese, lemon peel and add egg; beat well. Stir in biscuit baking mix; slowly add milk and continue mixing until moist. Pour batter into ungreased 2–inch muffin cups. Bake for 15 to 18 minutes or until golden brown.

SIX WEEK RAISIN BRAN MUFFINS

5 cups flour
3 cups sugar
5 teaspoons baking soda
1½ teaspoons salt

7½ cups (15–ounces) bran
   cereal with raisins
1 quart buttermilk
1 cup vegetable oil
4 eggs, beaten

Yield: 4 dozen

Preheat oven to 400°. In extra large bowl, blend flour, sugar, baking soda and salt. Stir in cereal and mix until coated. Add buttermilk, oil and eggs; continue to blend until moist. Mixture may be stored in tightly covered container in refrigerator for up to six weeks. When ready for muffins, fill paper lined muffin tins ⅔ full and bake for 15–20 minutes. Muffins may also be frozen after baking.

ORANGE BOWKNOTS

Rolls:

1¼ cups milk, scalded
½ cup shortening
⅓ cup sugar
1 teaspoon salt
1 cake of yeast

2 eggs, well beaten
¼ cup orange juice
2 tablespoons grated orange peel
5 cups flour

Topping:

2 tablespoons orange juice
1 tablespoon grated orange peel

1 cup sifted powdered sugar

Yield: 2–3 dozen

Preheat oven to 400°. In a large bowl, combine milk, shortening, sugar and salt; cool to lukewarm. Soften yeast in this mixture. Add eggs, orange juice and orange peel and beat thoroughly. Add flour and mix to soft dough. Cover and let stand 10 minutes. Knead on lightly floured surface. Place in large greased bowl and let rise in a warm place approximately 2 hours or until dough doubles in bulk. Divide dough in half, punch down and let dough rest 10 minutes. Roll each half of dough onto floured surface into an approximate 10 x 14-inch rectangle. Dough should be ½-inch thick. Cut dough into 10-inch strips, ½-inch wide. Tie each into a knot. Arrange on a greased baking sheet; cover and let rise again until double in size. Bake in hot oven for 15 minutes. While in oven, prepare topping by blending orange juice, orange peel and powdered sugar together until smooth. Take bowknots out of oven and frost with topping while still warm.

PUMPKIN–PECAN TEA LOAF

Wonderful served toasted!

⅔ cup shortening
2⅔ cups sugar
4 eggs
1 16–ounce can pumpkin
⅔ cup water
2½ cups flour
2 teaspoons baking soda
1½ teaspoons salt

½ teaspoon baking powder
½ teaspoon ground
  cardamom, optional
1 teaspoon ground cloves,
  optional
1 teaspoon cinnamon
1 cup raisins
1 cup chopped pecans

Yield: 2 loaves

Preheat oven to 350°. Cream shortening and sugar until well-blended; beat in eggs. Add pumpkin and water; stir until well-blended. In separate bowl, stir together flour and next 6 ingredients until thoroughly blended. Gradually add dry ingredients to pumpkin mixture and stir well. Fold in raisins and pecans. Pour batter into 2 greased and floured 9 x 5-inch loaf pans. Bake for 1 hour and 15 minutes, or until bread begins to pull away from side of pans and wooden skewer inserted in center comes out clean. Allow bread to cool in pans for 10 minutes before turning out onto racks.

Note: Serve with soft cream cheese instead of butter.

APRICOT ALMOND BREAD

½ cup shortening
1¼ cups sugar
½ cup sour cream
2 large ripe bananas,
  mashed (1 cup)
2 cups flour
1 teaspoon baking soda

1 teaspoon baking powder
½ teaspoon salt
1 teaspoon cinnamon
1 cup chopped dried
  apricots
1 cup slivered almonds

Yield: 1 loaf

Preheat oven to 350°. In large bowl, cream together shortening, sugar, sour cream and mashed bananas. In separate bowl combine flour, baking soda, baking powder, salt and cinnamon. Gradually add to creamed mixture making sure all is moistened. Gently fold in apricots and almonds. Pour batter into 9 x 5-inch greased loaf pan and bake for 40 to 45 minutes or until cake tester comes out clean. Remove from pan and allow to cool. If using mini loaf pans, reduce baking time to 30 minutes.

CHERRY PECAN BREAD

Bread:

4 cups flour
2 teaspoons baking soda
1 teaspoon salt
1½ cups sugar
1 cup margarine
4 eggs

2 teaspoons vanilla
2 cups buttermilk
2 cups chopped maraschino
   cherries
2 cups chopped pecans

Glaze:

2 cups sifted powdered
   sugar

½ teaspoon vanilla
milk

Yield: 2 loaves

Preheat oven to 350°. In large mixing bowl, stir together flour, baking soda and salt; set aside. In separate bowl, cream together sugar, margarine, eggs and vanilla. Add flour mixture and buttermilk alternately to sugar mixture beating until just blended after each addition. Fold in cherries and pecans. Pour into 2, lightly greased 8½ x 4½-inch loaf pans. Bake for 60 minutes. Make glaze by combining powdered sugar, vanilla and enough milk to make consistency to drizzle. While bread is still warm, drizzle frosting over each loaf.

Note: Cherry juice can be substituted for milk when making glaze.

BEST BANANA NUT BREAD

1½ cups sugar
½ cup vegetable oil
2 eggs, slightly beaten
1½ cups flour
1 teaspoon soda

1 teaspoon salt
½ cup milk
3 bananas, mashed
1 teaspoon vanilla
2 cups chopped pecans

Yield: 2 loaves or 3 dozen muffins

Preheat oven to 350°. Gradually add sugar to oil; add eggs, combine well and set aside. In separate bowl, mix together flour, salt and soda, then add to sugar mixture, combining well. Gradually add milk and remaining ingredients and stir thoroughly. Pour into 2 greased 8½ x 4½-inch loaf pans or into muffin tins. Bake 60 minutes.

STRAWBERRY BREAD

2 cups frozen, unsweetened
   whole strawberries
2¼ cups sugar, divided
3 cups plus 2 tablespoons
   flour
1 tablespoon cinnamon

1 teaspoon salt
1 teaspoon baking soda
1¼ cups oil
4 eggs, beaten
1¼ cups chopped pecans

Yield: 2 loaves

Preheat oven to 350°. Place strawberries in medium bowl and sprinkle with ¼ cup sugar. Toss to coat and let stand until strawberries are thawed, then slice. Combine flour, remaining sugar, cinnamon, salt and baking soda in large bowl; mix well. Stir oil and eggs into strawberries; add strawberry mixture to flour mixture. Add in pecans and blend until dry ingredients are just moistened (do not over mix). Divide batter between 2, 4½ x 8½-inch greased and floured loaf pans. Bake 45–50 minutes. Allow bread to cool in pans for 10 minutes. Turn loaves out and allow to cool completely.

INDIAN FRY BREAD

(See recipe in Oklahoma Specialties Section)

ROSIE'S BUNS

2 packages yeast
2 cups lukewarm water
2 eggs
⅓ cup sugar

1 teaspoon salt
⅓ cup melted shortening,
   cooled
6½ cups flour

Yield: 3 dozen

Preheat oven to 350°. Dissolve yeast in warm water; let set 5 minutes. Add eggs, sugar, salt and shortening to yeast; beat well. Add flour to liquid until dough forms. Knead for 10 minutes on floured board. Let set in bowl 20 minutes, then make rolls and place in greased pan. Let rise until doubled. Bake for 15–20 minutes.

Note: Grated cheese or onion may be added before making into buns.

TERRITORIAL LIGHT BREAD

(See recipe in Oklahoma Specialties Section)

LESLIE'S LIGHT ROLLS

2 cups milk	1 teaspoon salt
3 tablespoons shortening	2 cakes of yeast
3 tablespoons sugar	7 cups flour

Yield: 3 dozen

Preheat oven to 350°. Scald milk and allow to cool until lukewarm. Add shortening, sugar, salt and yeast, allowing all to dissolve. Begin adding flour and mixing dough with hands. When dough no longer sticks to hands, knead until light and smooth, about 8 to 10 minutes. Place in greased bowl, turning to grease top. Cover let rise in warm place, free from draft, until doubled in bulk, about 1 hour. Punch dough down; turn out onto lightly floured board. Divide dough into 3 equal pieces.

Divide each piece into 12 equal parts. Shape each into a smooth round ball. Place in large greased muffin cups. Cover and let rise again. Bake until lightly golden, about 15 minutes.

Note: One of my favorite memories as a child was coming in after riding the school bus home. As soon as I would come in the front door, I would smell my mother's homemade bread rising. It seems that everyone says their mother was the best cook in the world, but I know without a doubt, that my mother's homemade bread and home-made noodles were the best in the world. In addition to enjoying her baked goods after they came out of the oven, I can remember begging my mom for what I nicknamed "gum". As my mother kneaded the dough, I would always pinch an inch off and enjoy it before it was cooked. —Jeanette Clemons

GARDEN PIZZA CRUST

3½ cups grated zucchini
3 eggs, beaten
⅓ cup flour
½ cup grated mozzarella
   cheese

½ cup grated Parmesan
   cheese
½ teaspoon basil
salt and pepper to taste

Yield: 1 crust

Preheat oven to 350°. Salt zucchini lightly and let set for 15 minutes. Squeeze out excess moisture and combine zucchini with all other ingredients and spread into oiled 9 x 13-inch pan. Bake 20–25 minutes until dry and firm. Brush crust with oil and broil until lightly browned. Top with pizza sauce and your favorite toppings and bake 20 minutes.

Note: Fridays are "Pizza Night" at our house and my girls and I, ever since they were very small, make pizza from scratch. We mix up the dough, (and play with some, too) and form it into a shape — sometimes a big heart, a snowman or even the state of Oklahoma! Then, together, we decorate it with pepperoni, cheese and olives. Kate and Alex love eating it almost as much as making it!! — Clara Tao Colvin

QUICK HERB ROLLS

½ cup margarine
1½ teaspoons parsley flakes
½ teaspoon dill weed
1 tablespoon onion flakes

2 tablespoons grated
   Parmesan cheese
1 10–ounce can refrigerator
   biscuits

Yield: 10 servings

Preheat oven to 425°. Melt margarine in 9 x 13 x 2-inch cake pan. Mix parsley flakes and next 3 ingredients together in the same pan and let stand 15 minutes. Cut each biscuit into fourths. Roll each biscuit piece in herb mixture to coat all sides. Arrange pieces in same pan and bake 12 to 15 minutes.

CHUNK OF CHEESE BREAD

1¾ cups water
½ cup cornmeal
2 teaspoons salt
½ cup molasses
2 tablespoons margarine

1 package dry yeast
½ cup warm water
4 – 4½ cups flour
1 pound Cheddar cheese, cut into ¼ to ½-inch cubes

Yield: 2 loaves

Preheat oven to 350°. In 2–quart saucepan, combine water, cornmeal and salt. Bring to a boil, stirring constantly. Cook until slightly thickened and remove from heat. Stir in molasses and margarine; cool to lukewarm. Soften yeast in ½ cup warm water in large mixing bowl and blend into cornmeal mixture. Gradually add flour to form stiff dough. Knead on well–floured surface until smooth and satiny, about 5 minutes. Place in large greased bowl and cover. Let rise in warm place until light and doubled in size, 1 to 1½ hours. Line 2, 8 or 9-inch round pans with a 14–inch square of foil, allowing edges to extend over pan; grease well. Place dough on surface sprinkled with cornmeal. Work cheese into dough ¼ at a time until cubes are evenly distributed. Divide dough into 2 parts. Shape each into loaves, covering cheese cubes; place into pans. Place pans in warm area and allow to rise until light and doubled in size, about 1 to 1½ hours. Bake 45 to 55 minutes until a deep golden brown.

BEAN BREAD

1 cup white cornmeal
2 eggs, well beaten
1 15–ounce can pinto beans, drained

¼ cup flour
⅓ cup bacon fat
½ teaspoon baking soda
¾ teaspoon salt

Yield: 1 loaf

Preheat oven to 350°. In large bowl, mix all ingredients together and bake in lightly greased 8½ x 4½-inch loaf pan for 1 hour.

DILLY BREAD

2½ – 3 cups flour, divided
2 tablespoons sugar
1 tablespoon instant minced
   onion
2 teaspoons dill seed
¼ teaspoon salt
¼ teaspoon baking soda

1 package dry yeast
1 cup creamed cottage
   cheese
¼ cup water
1 tablespoon margarine
1 egg
course salt, optional

Yield: 1 loaf

Preheat oven to 350°. In large bowl, combine 1 cup of the flour and the next 6 ingredients. In small saucepan, heat cottage cheese, water and margarine until mixture is warm. Add egg and warmed mixture to the flour mixture. With electric mixer, blend at lowest speed until moistened. Increase to medium speed and beat an additional 3 minutes. By hand, stir in 1½ to 2 cups flour to form a stiff dough. Cover and let rise in warm place until light and doubled in size, about 1 hour. Punch down batter. Turn into well–greased 8–inch round casserole dish. Cover and let rise in warm place an additional 30 to 45 minutes. Bake for 35 to 40 minutes or until golden brown. Brush with additional margarine and sprinkle with coarse salt if desired.

BEER BREAD

3 cups self–rising flour
¼ cup sugar

1 12–ounce can beer
1 stick margarine, melted

Yield: 1 loaf

Preheat oven to 370°. In a large bowl, mix together flour, sugar and beer; pour into greased 8½ x 4½ x 2½-inch loaf pan. Pour melted margarine over top and bake for 1 hour. When done, remove from pan and allow to cool on rack.

CHEDDAR BACON OLIVE BREAD

2½ cups flour
2½ tablespoons sugar
2 teaspoons baking powder
½ teaspoon baking soda
1 teaspoon salt
1 teaspoon dry mustard
generous pinch of cayenne
   pepper
¼ cup softened margarine

1 cup shredded sharp
   Cheddar cheese
1 egg
1 cup buttermilk
1 teaspoon Worcestershire
   sauce
1 cup pitted ripe olives,
   coarsely chopped
5 slices of crisp bacon,
   crumbled

Yield: 6–8 servings

Preheat oven to 375°. Mix together first seven ingredients. Cut in margarine with a fork until mixture resembles coarse meal. Stir in Cheddar cheese. In a small bowl, combine egg, buttermilk and Worcestershire sauce. Make a well in flour mixture and pour in liquid. Mix just until moistened. Stir in olives and bacon. Turn batter into greased 8½ x 4½ x 2½-inch loaf pan. Bake for 30–40 minutes. Turn out of pan and cool on wire rack. To make muffins, divide batter among 12 well–greased muffin pans. Bake for 20–25 minutes.

SESAME–SWISS CHEESE BREAD

2 cups sifted flour
3 tablespoons sugar
4 teaspoons baking powder
1½ teaspoons salt
1 cup shredded Swiss cheese
⅓ cup toasted sesame seeds

2 eggs, beaten
1¼ cups milk
¼ cup vegetable oil
½ teaspoon sesame seeds
   for top

Yield: 1 loaf

Preheat oven to 375°. In a large bowl, sift together flour, sugar, baking powder and salt. Stir in cheese and toasted sesame seeds. In separate bowl, blend together eggs, milk and oil. Add liquid all at once to flour mixture, stirring just until flour is moistened. Turn into greased 4½ x 8½-inch or 9 x 5 x 3-inch loaf pan. Sprinkle with ½ teaspoon sesame seeds. Bake for 65 to 70 minutes. Cool 15 minutes and remove from pan.

GOLDEN CHEESE LOAVES

2 cups flour
1 tablespoon sugar
3 teaspoons baking powder
2 teaspoons dry mustard
1 teaspoon salt
¼ cup margarine
½ cup shredded Cheddar
    cheese

2 tablespoons grated
    Parmesan cheese
1 cup milk
1 egg, beaten
½ teaspoon paprika
½ teaspoon onion salt

Yield: 1 loaf

Preheat oven to 375°. Combine flour and next 4 ingredients in large bowl; mix well. Cut in margarine until mixture resembles coarse meal. Toss in Cheddar and Parmesan cheeses. In separate small bowl, combine milk and egg. Add to dry mixture and stir with fork until moistened. Turn into 8½ x 4½ greased loaf pan. Sprinkle with paprika and onion salt. Bake for 50 minutes. Allow to cool 10 minutes in pan before turning onto rack to finish cooling.

ZUCCHINI BREAD

1 cup sugar
½ cup shortening
2 eggs
1 teaspoon vanilla
¼ teaspoon salt
1½ cups flour

2 teaspoons baking powder
¼ teaspoon cinnamon
1 cup raisins
¾ cup chopped pecans
1 cup grated zucchini squash

Yield: 1 loaf

Preheat oven to 350°. In large bowl, blend sugar, shortening, eggs and vanilla until thoroughly combined. In separate bowl, combine salt, flour, baking powder and cinnamon, mixing well. Combine the two mixtures and add raisins, nuts and zucchini. Thoroughly mix batter until all ingredients are moist. Pour batter into greased and floured 9 x 5-inch loaf pan and bake for 50 minutes.

POPPY SEED BREAD

Bread:

3 cups flour
1½ teaspoons salt
1½ teaspoons baking
   powder
2½ cups sugar
3 eggs, beaten
1 cup plus 1 tablespoon
   vegetable oil

1½ cups milk
1½ teaspoons almond
   extract
1½ teaspoons butter
   flavoring
1½ teaspoons vanilla
1½ tablespoons poppy seeds

Glaze:

¾ cup sugar
¼ cup orange juice
½ teaspoon almond extract
½ teaspoon butter flavoring

½ teaspoon vanilla
1 teaspoon margarine,
   melted

Yield: 2 loaves

Preheat oven to 350°. In large bowl combine flour and remaining bread ingredients, mixing well with electric mixer. Batter will be thin. Pour into 2, 8½ x 4½-inch loaf pans or 1 tube pan. Bake for 45 minutes. Prepare glaze by combining sugar and orange juice in medium saucepan over low heat, stirring until sugar dissolves. Add the remaining ingredients and pour over the hot loaves.

GRANDMA'S OATMEAL BREAD

1 quart boiling water	½ cup warm water
2 cups oats	1 teaspoon sugar
8 ounces black molasses	1 teaspoon salt
1 tablespoon shortening	9 cups flour
1 teaspoon salt	melted margarine
1 package dry yeast	

Yield: 1 loaf

Preheat oven to 350°. Combine boiling water with oats, molasses, shortening and salt. Allow mixture to cool to lukewarm. Dissolve yeast in warm water along with sugar and salt and add to oat mixture. Begin adding flour and working with dough until dough no longer sticks to hands. Knead about 5–8 minutes and then allow to rise in a warm spot 2 hours, until doubled. Punch down and place into 4 or 5-inch loaf pans. Allow to rise an additional 2 hours. Bake for 40 minutes. Remove hot bread from pans immediately and brush with melted margarine.

SWEET CORNBREAD

(See recipe in Oklahoma Specialties Section)

BUTTERMILK CORNBREAD

1 cup yellow cornmeal	¼ teaspoon baking soda
⅓ cup flour	1 egg, beaten
1 teaspoon baking powder	1 cup buttermilk
½ teaspoon salt	

Yield: 9 servings

Preheat oven to 400°. Combine dry ingredients in large mixing bowl. Add egg and buttermilk, mixing well. Pour batter into a well-greased 8-inch square pan. Bake for 20 minutes or until lightly browned. Cut into squares.

MEXICAN CORNBREAD

1 cup yellow cornmeal
⅓ cup flour
2 tablespoons sugar
1 teaspoon salt
2 teaspoons baking powder
½ teaspoon baking soda
2 eggs, beaten
1 cup buttermilk

½ cup vegetable oil
1 8¾-ounce can cream-style corn
⅓ cup chopped onion
2 tablespoons chopped green pepper
½ cup shredded Cheddar cheese

Yield: 8–10 servings

Preheat oven to 350°. In a large mixing bowl, combine first six ingredients. In a separate large bowl, combine remaining ingredients; add to dry ingredients and stir only until moistened. Pour into a greased 9–inch square baking pan or 10–inch heavy skillet. Bake for 30–35 minutes or until bread is golden brown and tests done.

CATTLE RUSTLER CORNBREAD

(See recipe in Oklahoma Specialties Section)

Note: For a sweet spread that is great on everything from muffins to toast, combine equal amounts of softened butter and honey, then add just a little vanilla extract. You'll want to keep a batch of this on hand to sweeten all your breads.

CAFE
OKLAHOMA

SIDE DISHES

COWBOYS – FAMOUS AND OTHERWISE

You could sum up the cowboy trade, and what became of it, in three names: Tom Mix, Bill Pickett, and Will Rogers. But let's use a fourth name – Jesse Chisholm – as a starting point.

Jesse Chisholm was a half-Indian trader who opened a trail across the Red River from Texas in 1867, crossing the Indian Territory – Oklahoma – north to Kansas. "Cowboying" as we think of it started here, on the long trail drives. The Chisholm was the most popular of several cattle trails which shared one purpose – to get cattle from the Texas rangelands, across Oklahoma, to the railheads of Kansas for shipment to the markets in the East.

It was more dangerous than glamorous – Jesse Chisholm himself is buried in central Oklahoma, on the trail that bears his name.

The average cowboy was in his early 20's, a proud and independent nomad who went from job to job, but never said he "worked" for anybody – he *rode* for the such-and-such "brand". It was said he had "a $10 horse, which he didn't own, and a $40 saddle, which he did." We think of him as white, but chances were just as good that he was black, a freed slave who'd come west, or Mexican, descended from the Mexican *vaqueros* who were the first cowboys. In Indian Territory, he was Native American, because the Indians had their own cattle ranches. Indian cattlemen regarded the Texas drovers as unwanted trespassers, and had the Cherokee Lighthorse Brigade to intercept them and charge a tariff for crossing Indian lands.

The cowboy trade in this form only lasted 20 or 30 years, until the railroads came and made it obsolete. But that was time enough: while most of the young men who rode the trails are unknown today, a few passed into American mythology.

Like Bill Pickett. Part Choctaw, part black, Pickett rode for the fabled 101 Ranch in northern Oklahoma. He was billed in the Ranch's Wild West shows as "greatest sweat-and-dirt cowhand that ever lived – bar none." Pickett was sensational. He invented the technique of "bulldogging" a galloping longhorn steer to earth by biting its lower lip, like a bulldog. In New York's Madison Square Garden, the big Texas steer he was chasing leaped the fence and thundered up into the grandstand, with Pickett and another cowboy in hot pursuit. Between the two of them, they finally maneuvered the steer back onto the arena floor, and the newspapers had a field day with their heroics – Pickett's and the other cowboy's, a young part-Cherokee named Will Rogers.

Will was another alumnus of the 101 Ranch, and while Pickett's talents involved physical prowess, Will's involved finesse – he first made his name by making an art form out of another workaday cowboy skill: roping. He was so amazing with a lariat that he went into show business as "The Cherokee Kid." Since trick roping is a, well, tricky business, he learned to cover his mistakes with his humor. When he'd fail in stepping through the spinning lariat, he'd cover it by saying, "Well, I got all my feet through but one." Or, if he botched the trick altogether, he'd comment, "I've only got enough jokes for one miss. I've either got to practice roping, or learn more jokes." The crowds loved him.

Like Will Rogers, there was a livestock foreman at the 101 Ranch who also passed into American mythology: Pennsylvania-born Thomas Edwin Mix. When he first arrived (after a stint as a bartender in the Territorial capital), the other cowboys had to help Tom Mix saddle a horse. By 1909, though, he was a good enough hand to take prizes in Arizona rodeos, and it was there that he came to the attention of Californians in the brand-new motion picture business. He became the biggest cowboy star of the 1920's, and created a flamboyant pattern for screen cowboys and country music stars for years to come. . .

The cattle drives and trail hands have vanished, but the mystique surrounding the cowboy life endures.

Maybe Will Rogers said it best: "I have always regretted that I didn't live about thirty or forty years earlier, and in the same old country – the Indian Territory. I would have liked to have gotten there ahead of the barbed wire fence . . . I wish I could have lived my whole life then and drank out of a gourd instead of a paper envelope."

SOONER BE SOUP

1½ pounds of 10 or 15
   dried bean soup mixture
1½ pounds ham pieces
½ clove garlic, minced
2 32–ounce cans tomatoes
1 medium onion, chopped
2–3 jalapeño peppers,
   chopped

¼ cup chopped celery
½ teaspoon coarse black
   pepper
½ teaspoon cumin seed
1 teaspoon cilantro
2 carrots, cleaned and
   halved
juice of 1 lemon

Yield: 8 servings

Rinse and sort bean mixture. In a large bowl, cover beans with water and refrigerate 3 hours. Pour off liquid and transfer beans to Dutch oven. Add remaining ingredients to beans and cover entire mixture with water. Over high heat, bring mixture to rolling boil; reduce heat and allow to simmer 4 hours, stirring occasionally. Additional water may be added as necessary. Prior to serving, remove and discard carrots as they have been added to absorb the natural starch.

Note: Serve with a tossed salad and cornbread for a complete meal.

MEXICAN TACO SOUP

A family favorite!

1 pound ground beef
1 medium onion, chopped
1 15–ounce can white
   northern beans
1 15–ounce can pinto beans
1 15–ounce can kidney
   beans
1 15–ounce can black beans
   (optional)

1 1.25–ounce package taco
   seasoning
1 2–ounce package dry
   ranch dressing mix
1 30–ounce can tomatoes,
   chopped
tortilla chips
Cheddar cheese to garnish

Yield: 8 servings

In Dutch oven, brown ground beef and onion; drain. Add remaining ingredients and heat thoroughly. Cover and allow mixture to heat. Serve over corn chips or tortilla chips and top with cheese.

Note: Do not drain beans. A complete meal in 30 minutes.

TORTILLA SOUP

1 medium onion, chopped
2 cloves garlic, minced
2 tablespoons vegetable oil
2 16-ounce cans stewed
  tomatoes
1 10¾-ounce can tomato
  soup
1 14½-ounce can chicken
  broth
1 14½-ounce can beef broth
1 10-ounce can tomatoes
  with green chilies

1 4-ounce can chopped
  green chilies
1½ cups water
1 teaspoon salt
1 teaspoon sugar
½ teaspoon lemon pepper
1 teaspoon Tabasco sauce
2 teaspoons Worcestershire
  sauce
tortilla chips
Cheddar cheese, grated
1 avocado, chopped

Yield: 8–10 servings

Sauté onion and garlic in vegetable oil in Dutch oven or large soup pot. Add remaining 12 ingredients and bring to a boil. Reduce heat and allow to simmer for 1 hour. To serve, place chips, cheese and avocado in individual bowl and pour soup over ingredients.

Note: For a meatier soup add chicken fajita meat in bowls with other ingredients.

FIRESIDE SOUP

1 pound lean ground beef
1 medium onion, chopped
½ large green bell pepper,
  chopped
1 clove garlic, crushed
1 16-ounce can tomatoes
1 8-ounce can tomato sauce
1 10¾-ounce can beef
  consommé

1 tablespoon Worcestershire
  sauce
½ teaspoon salt
½ teaspoon pepper
½ soup can red wine or
  water
1 15½-ounce can red kidney
  beans, drained
½ head cabbage, chopped

Yield: 5 servings

In large Dutch oven, sauté ground beef until brown; drain. Add onion, green pepper and garlic; cook for 15–20 minutes. Add all other ingredients except cabbage; cover and simmer for 1 hour. Uncover, add cabbage and simmer an additional 30 minutes. Soup will thicken when lid is removed.

Note: Serve with garlic bread and you have a meal.

BLACK BEAN SOUP

3 cups dried black beans
10 cups water
1 teaspoon salt
1 cup chopped celery
1 cup chopped onion
1 cup chopped green bell
    pepper
1 cup sliced carrots
2 teaspoons dried basil
2 teaspoons dried oregano
1 teaspoon black pepper

½ teaspoon ground cumin
¼–½ teaspoon ground red
    pepper
4 cloves garlic, minced
1 bay leaf
2 14½–ounce cans, (no salt
    added) whole tomatoes,
    undrained and chopped
1 11–ounce can white corn
1 8–ounce can, no salt
    added, tomato sauce

Yield: 4½ quarts

Sort and wash beans; place in a large Dutch oven or stock pot. Add water and salt; bring to a boil and cook 1 minute. Remove from heat, cover and let stand 1 hour. (Do not drain beans). Add celery and next 10 ingredients to beans. Bring mixture to a boil; cover, reduce heat and simmer 1½ hours or until beans are tender. Add tomatoes, corn and tomato sauce; stir well. Bring to a boil; reduce heat, and simmer, uncovered 30 minutes. Discard bay leaf before serving.

BROCCOLI CHEESE SOUP

2 tablespoons margarine
1 medium onion, chopped
6 cups chicken broth
1 10–ounce package fine egg
    noodles
2 10–ounce packages frozen
    chopped broccoli

1 1–pound box Velveeta,
    cubed
1 8–ounce jar jalapeño
    Cheez Whiz
1 teaspoon garlic powder
6 cups milk
1 teaspoon salt
¼ teaspoon pepper

Yield: 10–12 servings

Melt margarine in large Dutch oven. Sauté onions 3 minutes; add broth and bring to a boil. Slowly add egg noodles and salt, so mixture continues to boil. Cook uncovered 3 minutes. Stir in broccoli and garlic powder and continue cooking for 4 minutes. Reduce heat and stir in both types of cheese and pepper, stirring constantly until cheese melts; do not allow soup to return to boiling.

CREAM OF POTATO SOUP

6–8 potatoes, peeled and
   chopped
6 slices bacon
2 cups chopped celery
1 medium onion, chopped

2 quarts half-and-half cream
2 teaspoons salt
pepper to taste
1 teaspoon thyme

Yield: 4 servings

In large kettle, cover potatoes with water and boil. While potatoes are cooking, cut up bacon into 1–inch pieces and fry. When done, drain bacon well on paper towels and reserve bacon drippings. In drippings, sauté celery and onions; remove from skillet and drain. When potatoes are tender, drain them well and slightly mash. Add bacon, celery, onions and remaining ingredients to potatoes and simmer over low heat for 45 minutes.

Note: Milk may be substituted for half-and-half.

I will always remember the "get–well" potato soup my mother always prepared when I was not feeling well. Mother, Beryl Hudspeth Cothran, is 85 years old now and has lived in Atoka County all of her life. She was a wonderful cook and even today when I forget an ingredient in an old recipe, I will call her and she always remembers. I still love potato soup, and when I'm sick, this is the medicine that makes me feel better, no matter what the ailment might be.——Linda Croak

POTATO–CORN CHOWDER

2–3 large potatoes, peeled
   and diced
1 pound bacon, diced
2 small onions, diced
1 17–ounce can corn,
   drained or (16–ounce bag
   of frozen corn)

1 quart milk
salt and pepper to taste
1 4–ounce can chopped
   green chilies, undrained
   (optional)

Yield: 8 servings

In Dutch oven, boil potatoes in small amount of water (cover by ½ inch) until tender; drain and return to Dutch oven. In a skillet, fry diced bacon and onions until browned; drain and add to potatoes. Add remaining ingredients and allow to simmer for 1 to 1½ hours, stirring frequently, so chowder won't burn.

CLAM CHOWDER

3 10¾–ounce cans cream of
   potato soup
1 10¾–ounce can cream of
   celery soup

3 10⅓–ounce cans New
   England clam chowder
2 7½–ounce cans clams with
   juice
1½ pints whipping cream

Yield: 8–10 servings

Combine all ingredients in a heavy pot. Simmer over low heat, stirring until hot.

CRANBERRY SALAD

A must for your Thanksgiving or Christmas meal!

1 pound fresh cranberries
1½ cups sugar
1 pound seedless red
   grapes, chopped in half
2 cups chopped pecans

3 cups miniature
   marshmallows
1 cup whipping cream,
   whipped

Yield: 10–12 servings

Place rinsed cranberries in food processor and lightly chop. Transfer cranberries to bowl and mix with sugar. Cover bowl and allow to set in refrigerator overnight. Before serving, add chopped grapes, pecans and marshmallows to cranberry mixture and fold in whipped cream. Serve cold.

FIREHOUSE SPECIAL

A meal in itself!

1 head of lettuce, chopped
1 large tomato, chopped
2 15–ounce cans ranch style
   beans, drained
2 small purple onions,
   chopped

1 15–ounce can sliced black
   olives, drained
Cheddar cheese, shredded
1 16–ounce bottle creamy
   Italian dressing
3 cups slightly crushed corn
   chips

Yield: 4-6 servings

In 13 x 9 x 2-inch dish, layer each of the ingredients, except corn chips, in the order listed. Allow to refrigerate 30 minutes before serving. (Seasoned meat may be added, if desired.) Add chips just before serving.

Note: Submitted by our local fire–fighting chefs! Wonderful!

123

PRETZEL SALAD

2 cups coarsely crushed
   pretzels
¾ cup margarine, melted
3 teaspoons sugar
1 8-ounce package cream
   cheese, softened
1 cup sugar

1 9-ounce container frozen
   whipped topping
3 3-ounce boxes strawberry
   gelatin
2 cups boiling water
2 10-ounce packages frozen
   strawberries

Yield: 12 servings

Preheat oven to 400°. Mix together first 3 ingredients and press into a
13 x 9 x 2-inch baking pan. Bake 8 minutes, making sure not to over-
bake. In separate bowl, combine softened cream cheese, sugar and
whipped topping. Spread mixture over cooled pretzel crust. Mix together
strawberry gelatin with boiling water and frozen strawberries. Allow to
stand 10 minutes to thaw strawberries. Pour gelatin over cream cheese
layer. Refrigerate until gelatin is set. Cut into squares to serve.

*Note: One day, while in elementary school, my younger brother de-
cided to make dessert for the family for our evening meal. Seeing
this as positive behavior, mom kicked us out of the kitchen so Chris
could be "creative". That evening, after the dinner dishes were cleared,
Chris proudly served jello for dessert. As it was one of our favorites,
all of us took a huge spoonful in anticipation of our favorite fruit
flavor. We were in for quite a surprise!!! I gagged terribly, my older
brother spit the jello out as soon as it hit his tongue, and my poor
sister fared worse, having to excuse herself to the restroom. After
years of watching my mom cook, Chris thought salt was put in everything—and the more the better!! To this day, I take a tiny taste of any
jello dish before eating the rest.—Eileen Wilson*

MACHO SALAD

1 pound ground chuck
1 1¼–ounce package taco
   seasoning
1 medium head of lettuce
4 ounces Cheddar cheese,
   grated
½ cup chopped onion
2 medium tomatoes, diced

1 15–ounce can chili beans
   in sauce
½ 9–ounce bag nacho
   flavored tortilla chips
½ 9–ounce bag taco flavored
   tortilla chips
1 8–ounce bottle Catalina
   dressing
salt and pepper to taste

Yield: 4–6 servings

Brown ground chuck with taco seasoning and drain. In large bowl, tear lettuce into bite–size pieces. Layer the remaining ingredients in order, topping with the Catalina dressing. Toss gently. Add salt and pepper to taste, and serve immediately.

CAESAR SALAD

1 bud garlic
½ teaspoon salt
¼ teaspoon freshly ground
   pepper
4–6 anchovy fillets
1–1½ tablespoons vinegar
3 tablespoons oil
½ teaspoon dry mustard

1 teaspoon Worcestershire
   sauce
juice of ½ lemon
1 head Romaine lettuce
1 coddled egg
3–4 tablespoons grated
   Parmesan cheese
1 cup croutons

Yield: 6–8 servings

In a large bowl, preferably an unfinished wooden bowl, rub garlic bud around the bowl, mashing thoroughly with back of spoon. Add salt, pepper and anchovy fillets; continue to stir and mash around entire bowl until mixture is a smooth paste. Add vinegar, oil, dry mustard, Worcestershire sauce and lemon juice; mix all thoroughly. Shake washed lettuce in a large cloth to remove all moisture. Add lettuce, torn into bite–size pieces, to bowl and toss well. Break egg over lettuce and toss again. Sprinkle Parmesan cheese and croutons over salad, gently toss again and serve immediately.

Note: Anchovy paste can be used in place of anchovy fillets. The dressing can also be prepared in advance and refrigerated in a covered jar until time to serve.

CHICKEN POPPY SEED SALAD

Salad:

4 whole chicken breasts, cooked

1 cup green seedless grapes, halved

1 cup seedless red grapes, halved

1 11-ounce can mandarin oranges (drained)

2 avocados, peeled and chunked

1 small red onion, thinly sliced

1 head red or green cabbage, shredded

Dressing:

¾ cup sugar

1 teaspoon dry mustard

1 teaspoon salt

⅓ cup vinegar

1½ tablespoons onion juice

1 cup vegetable oil

3 tablespoons poppy seeds

Yield: 8 servings

For salad, chop cooked chicken into large chunks. In large bowl, add chicken, grapes, oranges, avocados and red onion; toss gently. Serve over shredded cabbage. For dressing, combine all ingredients, except poppy seeds, into blender and mix well. Stir poppy seeds into dressing mixture and pour over salad.

CHICKEN SALAD SUPREME

2½ cups chopped cooked chicken

1 cup diced celery

1 cup sliced seedless green grapes

½ cup slivered almonds

2 tablespoons minced parsley

1 teaspoon salt

1 cup mayonnaise

½ cup whipping cream, whipped

black olives to garnish

Yield: 6–8 servings

Combine chicken and next 5 ingredients in large bowl. Top with mayonnaise and whipped whipping cream, tossing to coat salad. Garnish with olives and serve chilled.

 *Side Dishes*

BARBECUE PIG IN THE GREENS
(See recipe in Oklahoma Specialties Section)

REUBEN SALAD
A great combination for a salad!

Dressing:
2 cups sour cream
½ cup chili sauce
4 tablespoons sliced green
   onion

2 tablespoons sugar
½ teaspoon salt

Salad:
1 16–ounce can sauerkraut
¼ cup chopped dill pickle
¼ cup snipped parsley
6 cups torn lettuce, divided

½ pound thinly sliced
   cooked corned beef
1½ cups (6 ounces) grated
   Swiss cheese
rye bread croutons

Yield: 6 servings

Prepare dressing in a small bowl by combining sour cream, chili sauce, onion, sugar, and salt. Refrigerate. Combine sauerkraut, dill pickle and parsley in medium bowl and set aside. In large salad bowl, layer half of the torn lettuce, sauerkraut mixture, corned beef and cheese. Top with half of the dressing. Repeat layers ending by spreading the remaining dressing on top. Cover and refrigerate at least 2 hours. Top with rye bread croutons just before serving.

EXOTIC LUNCHEON SALAD

2 quarts coarsely chopped
   cooked chicken
1 20–ounce can sliced water
   chestnuts, drained
2 pounds seedless grapes
2 cups sliced celery
2½ cups slivered, toasted
   almonds, divided

3 cups mayonnaise
1 tablespoon curry powder
2 tablespoons soy sauce
2 tablespoons fresh lemon
   juice, optional
Boston or Bibb lettuce
1 29–ounce can pineapple
   chunks, drained, optional

Yield: 12 servings

In large container, mix chicken, water chestnuts, grapes, celery and 2 cups of the toasted almonds. In separate bowl, combine mayonnaise with curry powder, soy sauce and lemon juice, if desired. Add to chicken mixture and chill several hours or overnight. Spoon into nests of lettuce and sprinkle with remaining nuts. Pineapple may be added to salad or used to garnish.

SPINACH SALAD & DRESSING

Salad:
1 large bunch fresh spinach,
   cleaned and drained
1 medium red onion, sliced
   & separated into rings
4 hard–boiled eggs, sliced

6 slices bacon, crisply
   cooked and crumbled
½ pound fresh mushrooms,
   cleaned and sliced

Dressing:
½ cup salad oil
¾ cup sugar
⅓ cup ketchup
¼ cup red wine vinegar

2 tablespoons
   Worcestershire sauce
1 tablespoon prepared
   mustard (optional)
salt and pepper to taste

Yield: 4–6 servings

In large bowl, tear spinach into bite–size pieces. Top with remaining salad ingredients and set aside. Combine all dressing ingredients into quart–size jar and shake well until sugar is dissolved. When ready to serve, pour dressing over salad and toss well.

SANTA BARBARA SALAD

A wonderfully refreshing salad!

Salad:
1 bunch red leaf lettuce
1 bunch green leaf lettuce
2 medium avocados, peeled
   and chopped

1 medium red onion,
   chopped
2 11–ounce cans mandarin
   orange slices, drained
1 cup sliced almonds

Dressing:
1 cup vegetable oil
1 cup vinegar
½ cup sugar
1 clove garlic, minced

½ teaspoon fresh lemon
   juice
1 teaspoon dill weed

Yield: 6 servings

Wash and drain lettuce. In a large bowl tear lettuce into bite–size pieces and add remaining salad ingredients. Mix vegetable oil with remaining 5 ingredients in jar and shake well. Pour over salad, toss and serve chilled.

NAPPA SALAD

A wonderful salad to serve with soup.

Salad:
1 head nappa cabbage,
   chopped
5 green onions, chopped
2 3–ounce packages Ramen
   noodles

1 cup coarsely chopped
   pecans
½ cup sunflower seeds
¼ cup margarine

Dressing:
1 cup sugar
1 teaspoon soy sauce

1 cup vegetable oil
½ cup vinegar

Yield: 8–10 servings

Combine cabbage and onions in bowl and toss well. Add Ramen noodles that have been lightly browned under broiler. Sauté pecans and sunflower seeds in margarine and mix with cabbage. Make dressing by mixing sugar and remaining 3 ingredients. Pour dressing over salad just before serving. Toss thoroughly!

Note: The Ramen noodles are packaged with a sauce. It is not needed for this recipe.

STRAWBERRY SPINACH SALAD

1 quart strawberries,
  cleaned and sliced

1 pound fresh spinach,
  cleaned and torn into
  bite-size pieces

Dressing:
2 tablespoons poppy seed
2 tablespoons sesame seed
½ cup cooking oil

½ cup sugar
¼ cup vinegar
¼ teaspoon paprika

Yield: 6 servings

In large salad bowl, combine spinach and strawberries and gently toss. For dressing, combine all ingredients in pint jar and shake well. Pour dressing over salad, toss well and allow to chill in refrigerator at least 2 hours. Before serving, toss salad again to distribute dressing.

COLESLAW ON THE LITE SIDE

2 cups finely shredded green
  cabbage (approximately
  ¼ head)
¼ cup finely shredded
  purple cabbage

½ small white onion, finely
  chopped
1 small carrot, grated
ice cubes

Dressing:
¼ cup plain non–fat yogurt
2 tablespoons reduced
  calorie mayonnaise
¼ teaspoon dry mustard

dash black pepper
¼ teaspoon celery seed
4 packages artificial
  sweetener

Yield: 8 servings

In a large bowl, combine shredded green and purple cabbage, onion, carrot and several ice cubes and set in refrigerator for 30 minutes. In a small bowl, prepare dressing by combining remaining ingredients and mix well. Remove salad from refrigerator, rinse and drain thoroughly and toss with dressing. Serve chilled.

COLD RICE AND BEAN SALAD

Salad:

3 cups cold cooked rice
1 15–ounce can pinto beans, rinsed and drained
1 15–ounce can black beans, rinsed and drained
1 10–ounce package frozen peas, thawed

1 cup sliced celery
1 medium red onion, chopped
2 4–ounce cans diced green chilies, drained
½ cup snipped cilantro

Dressing:

⅓ cup white wine vinegar
¼ cup olive or vegetable oil
2 tablespoons water

¾ teaspoons salt
½ teaspoon garlic powder
½ teaspoon pepper

Yield: 15 servings

In a 2½–quart covered container, combine all salad ingredients and mix well. Prepare dressing in a screw–top jar by combining all ingredients and shaking well to mix. Add dressing to the rice mixture; toss gently to mix. Cover and chill for up to 24 hours before serving.

CRUNCHY RICE SALAD

A different salad with an Oriental touch!

1 cup uncooked long–grain rice
1 16–ounce can mandarin orange slices, drained
1 cup chopped green onions
1 cup diagonally sliced celery
1 8–ounce can sliced water chestnuts, drained

1 cup thinly sliced fresh mushrooms (or 3½–ounce can sliced mushrooms, drained)
¼ cup rice vinegar
¼ cup vegetable oil
¼ cup soy sauce
lettuce leaves

Yield: 10–12 servings

Cook rice according to package directions, omitting salt. Allow to cool. Combine cooled rice and next 5 ingredients in large bowl. In a small bowl, combine vinegar, oil and soy sauce, mix well and pour over rice mixture. Toss lightly, cover and chill thoroughly. To serve, line glass bowl with lettuce leaves and fill with salad, or serve individually on lettuce leaves.

CURRIED RICE SALAD

Great compliment to a summer buffet!

1½ cups cooked, long–grain
   rice
¼ cup minced onion
1 tablespoon vinegar
2 tablespoons vegetable oil
½ teaspoon salt

½ teaspoon curry powder
1 cup diced celery
1 10–ounce package frozen
   peas, thawed
¾ cup mayonnaise

Yield: 6–8 servings

Combine cooked rice and next five ingredients and refrigerate at least three hours. Add celery and peas and top with mayonnaise mixing all well. Cover and refrigerate an additional hour before serving.

CORNBREAD SALAD

(See recipe in Oklahoma Specialties Section)

PASTA SALAD AL PESTO

1 pound rotini pasta
½ cup sour cream
½ cup cream
2 teaspoons dried sweet
   basil flakes

½ cup grated Parmesan
   cheese
2 cloves garlic, minced
4 tablespoons pine nuts

Yield: 4–6 servings

In Dutch oven, cook pasta in boiling salted water until tender. Drain and rinse with cold water and transfer to large bowl. Combine the remaining ingredients in a food processor and blend until pine nuts are pureed. Pour dressing over cooked pasta and toss to blend. Refrigerate until serving time.

ANTIPASTO PASTA SALAD

From Oklahoma's Italian community!

Salad:
1 16–ounce package egg noodles
1 12–ounce package spinach noodles
1 tablespoon olive oil
8–10 green onions, chopped

2 15½–ounce cans pitted black olives, coarsely chopped
2½ cups grated Parmesan cheese (fresh, if possible)
1½ pounds Genoa Salami, cut into ¼-inch x 1½-inch strips

Dressing:
¾ cup red wine vinegar
3 teaspoons salt
½ teaspoon freshly ground pepper
4 teaspoons Dijon mustard
1½ teaspoons tarragon

1½ teaspoons basil
1½ teaspoons thyme
3 cloves garlic, crushed
1⅛ cups virgin olive oil
1⅛ cups vegetable oil

Yield: 8 servings

Cook egg and spinach noodles in boiling salted water according to package directions, just until tender. Drain, rinse and toss with olive oil. Place cooked noodles into very large mixing bowl. Add green onions, olives, and salami and sprinkle all with Parmesan cheese. While noodles are cooking, prepare dressing by whisking vinegar and salt together until salt is dissolved. Whisk in remaining ingredients except oil. When salt is totally dissolved, drizzle oil into vinegar mixture and continue to whisk until oil is combined. Pour dressing over salad mixture and gently toss.

MEDITERRANEAN PASTA

8–ounces spiral pasta (about 3 cups)
2 cups partially peeled, sliced and halved cucumbers

1 cup cherry tomato quarters
½ cup sliced and halved yellow squash
¼ cup diced celery
¼ cup sliced black olives

Dressing:
¾ teaspoon dill weed
¾ cup creamy cucumber dressing
½ cup non–fat plain yogurt

1 teaspoon lemon juice
salt and pepper to taste
crumbled Feta cheese

Yield: 4–6 servings

Cook pasta according to package directions, rinse with cold water and drain well. In large bowl, toss pasta, cucumber, tomatoes, squash, celery and black olives. In separate bowl, mix dill weed, dressing, yogurt, lemon juice, salt and pepper and blend well. Pour dressing over pasta mixture, toss to mix, cover and chill. Sprinkle with Feta cheese before serving.

CAULIFLOWER SALAD

Great served with ham or turkey!

1 head of cauliflower
1 15–ounce can sliced black olives, drained

2 bunches green onions, washed and chopped with tops
1 cup real mayonnaise

Yield: 8 servings

Wash cauliflower and break into small pieces. Add black olives, green onions and mayonnaise. Toss well, cover and refrigerate 6–8 hours before serving.

BLACK–EYED PEA SALAD

(See recipe in Oklahoma Specialties Section)

RAW VEGETABLE SALAD

2 bunches broccoli
1 head cauliflower
½ red onion, chopped
½ cup honey
½ cup wine vinegar
¾ teaspoon celery seeds

½ teaspoon sesame seeds
1 16–ounce bottle Zesty
   Italian Dressing
sugar to taste
1 medium tomato, diced
   (optional)

Yield: 8 servings

In a medium bowl, separate broccoli and cauliflower into bite-size pieces and mix with onion. Mix honey and next 5 ingredients well and pour over vegetables. Allow to refrigerate overnight. Tomatoes, if used, should be added just before serving.

BROCCOLI BACON SALAD

Salad:
2 bunches fresh broccoli
¾ pound bacon, fried and
   crumbled

1 red onion, chopped
1 cup raisins (optional)

Dressing:
1 cup real mayonnaise
½ cup sugar

2 tablespoons vinegar

Yield: 6–8 servings

Break broccoli into bite–size pieces, rinse and allow to drain well. Transfer drained broccoli to a large bowl and add bacon, onion and raisins. For dressing, in a small bowl combine mayonnaise, sugar and vinegar and toss with broccoli mixture. Cover and allow to refrigerate at least 2 hours.

FARMER'S SALAD

1 medium white onion, diced
1 medium green pepper, diced
2 medium cucumbers, peeled and diced
½ teaspoon salt

¼ teaspoon pepper
2 tablespoons sugar
white vinegar
3 medium tomatoes, seeded and diced
6 lettuce leaves

Yield: 6 servings

In large bowl, combine diced onion, green pepper and cucumbers; sprinkle with salt, pepper and sugar. Toss well to distribute seasonings. Cover mixture and refrigerate 30 minutes to allow vegetables to "crisp". Just prior to serving, add enough white vinegar to cover vegetables and toss. Add diced tomatoes, gently toss again and serve on lettuce leaf.

OKLAHOMA SLAW

(See recipe in Oklahoma Specialties Section)

CABBAGE ONION SALAD

Salad:
1 head cabbage, shredded

2 large onions, sliced thin and separated into rings

Dressing:
1 cup sugar
1 cup vinegar
¼ teaspoon pepper
1 teaspoon salt

1 teaspoon celery seed
1 teaspoon dry mustard
1 cup vegetable oil

Yield: 6 servings

Alternate shredded cabbage and onion slices in large bowl with onion for top layer and set aside. For dressing, bring sugar, vinegar and dry seasonings to a boil in a medium saucepan. Take off heat and add vegetable oil. Drip hot dressing mixture over cabbage and onions. Do not stir. Cover and refrigerate 24 hours before serving.

Note: Best if red cabbage and white onions are used together or white cabbage and red onions.

AVOCADO SALAD

Great as a Mexican dinner side dish!

1 head iceberg lettuce, finely
   chopped
3 green onions, chopped
½ small red onion, chopped
2 stalks celery, chopped
2 avocados, peeled and cut
   into bite size pieces

2 tablespoons fresh lemon
   juice
2 tablespoons mayonnaise
garlic salt and pepper to
   taste

Yield: 4–6 servings

Combine lettuce and next 4 ingredients and toss well. Sprinkle all with lemon juice and stir in mayonnaise. Add garlic salt and pepper to taste. Cover and keep in refrigerator until served.

OKRA SALAD

(See recipe in Oklahoma Specialties Section)

OLIVE SALAD

1 6–ounce can black olives,
   drained
1 8–ounce jar green olives,
   drained

3 celery stalks
2 small cucumbers, peeled
2 small, firm tomatoes,
   seeded

Yield: 6–8 servings

Finely chop all ingredients and combine in medium size bowl with tight–fitting lid. Allow salad to chill at least 30 minutes prior to serving. Dressing will form from the juices of the chopped vegetables.

OLD STAND–BY POTATO SALAD

(See recipe in Oklahoma Specialties Section)

PAWNEE BILL POTATO SALAD

(See recipe in Oklahoma Specialties Section)

PAWHUSKA POTATO SALAD

(See recipe in Oklahoma Specialties Section)

SOUR CREAM CORN SALAD

A crisp summer favorite!

2 17–ounce cans whole corn,
    drained
½ cup chopped onions
1 cup diced, unpeeled
    cucumbers
1 cup diced celery
2 tomatoes, seeded and
    diced

1 cup sour cream
1 teaspoon salt
1 teaspoon garlic salt
¾ cup salad dressing
2 tablespoons sugar
¼ cup vinegar
1 teaspoon prepared
    mustard

Yield: 12 servings

In a large mixing bowl, toss all vegetables. In a separate small bowl, make dressing by combining remaining ingredients and mixing well. Pour dressing over vegetables, toss and allow to refrigerate at least 4 hours. The flavor improves overnight.

GREEN BEAN AND RED ONION SALAD WITH DILLED DRESSING

Salad:

1 1-pound package frozen whole green beans

½ pound mushrooms, cleaned and sliced

1 medium red onion, thinly sliced

Dressing:

⅓ cup vegetable oil

4 tablespoons red wine vinegar

2 medium green onions, cut into fourths

2 tablespoons chopped parsley

½ teaspoon dill weed

1 teaspoon Dijon mustard

1 teaspoon honey

salt and pepper to taste

Yield: 6 servings

Prepare frozen beans by cooking in boiling water for 5 minutes, or just until tender; drain. In 9 x 13-inch baking dish, layer green beans, mushrooms and onion slices. In food processor, blend the dressing ingredients until green onions are pureed. Pour dressing over the vegetables and refrigerate at least 4 hours before servings.

FRESH CORN FRITTERS

1 cup self-rising flour

2 teaspoons sugar

1 teaspoon salt

½ teaspoon garlic powder

½ teaspoon pepper

3 eggs, beaten

1½ cups fresh corn cut from the cob (about 3 ears)

½ cup milk

2 teaspoons oil

vegetable oil

Yields 2½ dozen

Combine first 5 ingredients in a large mixing bowl; mix well and set aside. Thoroughly combine eggs, corn, milk and 2 teaspoons vegetable oil. Stir corn mixture into dry ingredients until moistened. Drop mixture by heaping teaspoonfuls into hot vegetable oil. Allow fritters to cook until golden, turning once.

LAYERED BROCCOLI CASSEROLE

3 10–ounce packages frozen
   chopped broccoli, thawed
   and drained
½ cup chopped green onions
1 cup grated Swiss cheese
2 eggs
1 cup sour cream

½ teaspoon dill weed
2 tablespoons lemon juice
¼ cup grated Parmesan
   cheese
¼ cup buttery cracker
   crumbs

Yield: 6–8 servings

Preheat oven to 350°. In a lightly greased 9 x 9-inch baking dish, evenly spread the chopped broccoli. Top with layer of onions and Swiss cheese. Beat together eggs, sour cream, dill weed and lemon juice until blended and pour over the cheese. Combine Parmesan cheese and cracker crumbs and sprinkle over the entire dish. Bake for 35 minutes or until lightly browned.

ITALIAN GREEN BEANS WITH POTATOES AND ONIONS

Great for a dinner buffet!

2 large potatoes, peeled and
   diced
1 10½–ounce can chicken
   broth
1 small onion, minced
1 1–pound can stewed
   tomatoes, chopped (do
   not drain)

2 10–ounce packages frozen
   Italian green beans
1 teaspoon oil (optional)
salt and pepper to taste
6 strips bacon, cooked crisp,
   drained and crumbled

Yield: 6–8 servings

In Dutch oven, place first 7 ingredients and simmer, covered, for about 30 minutes or until potatoes are tender. Sprinkle top with crumbled bacon before serving.

DALE'S FOURTH OF JULY BEANS

(See recipe in Oklahoma Specialties Section)

HONEY BAKED BEANS

3 16–ounce cans pork and
    beans
6 strips bacon, cooked crisp,
    drained and crumbled
1 cup brown sugar, firmly
    packed

2 tablespoons chili powder
½ cup chili sauce
⅓ cup finely chopped onions
¾ cup sour cream
1 cup grated Cheddar cheese
¼ cup chopped green onions

Yield: 10 servings

Preheat oven to 350°. Combine first 6 ingredients in ovenproof casserole and stir until thoroughly mixed. Cover and bake 1½ hours or until mixture is thickened. Stir together sour cream, Cheddar cheese and green onions until blended. Spread mixture over beans and return to oven, uncovered, for an additional 15 minutes or until cheese is melted.

WILD BILL'S BAKED BEANS

(See recipe in Oklahoma Specialties Section)

CARROTS GLAZED WITH MAPLE BUTTER

2 pounds baby carrots
¼ cup margarine
¼ cup maple syrup

½ cup golden raisins
    (optional)
salt to taste

Yield: 8–10 servings

Prepare baby carrots by cooking in boiling salted water until tender; drain and set aside. In a 12–inch skillet, heat together margarine and maple syrup. Add carrots and cook for 5 minutes, stirring continuously. Add the raisins and continue cooking for 5 minutes, or until carrots are lightly browned and glazed.

COPPER CARROTS

3 20–ounce cans sliced
  carrots, drained
1 medium green pepper,
  chopped
1 medium white onion,
  chopped

1 10¾–ounce can tomato
  soup
¼ cup vegetable oil
½ cup sugar
½ cup white vinegar
1 teaspoon pepper

Yield: 6–8 servings

In large bowl, combine vegetables and toss. In a small bowl, make dressing by combining tomato soup and next 4 ingredients and mix well. Pour over vegetables, cover and refrigerate overnight, stirring occasionally. Serve cold.

Note: May also chop carrots and use as a dip with chips.

ASPARAGUS CASSEROLE

1½ packages round buttery
  crackers, crushed
2 cups grated Cheddar
  cheese

2 19–ounce cans asparagus
  spears, drained, reserving
  juice
1 10¾–ounce can cream of
  mushroom soup

Yield: 6 servings

Preheat oven to 350°. In a medium bowl, combine cracker crumbs and cheese; place half of mixture in bottom of 8 x 8-inch casserole dish. Arrange asparagus spears on top of cracker mixture. Combine mushroom soup and juice from asparagus and pour over spears. Top with remaining cheese and cracker mixture. Bake 30 minutes until bubbly.

FETTUCCINE ASPARAGUS

1 10–ounce package frozen
   asparagus or 1 large
   bunch fresh asparagus
1 pound fettuccine pasta
1 tablespoon olive oil
dash of salt
½ cup margarine

2 eggs, beaten
1 pint sour cream or plain
   yogurt
½ pound fresh Parmesan
   cheese, grated
fresh basil and chives to
   taste

Yield: 8 servings

Parboil asparagus until tender. Slice on the diagonal into bite–size pieces and set aside. Cook pasta in large pot of boiling water to which olive oil and salt have been added. Cook pasta just until tender and drain thoroughly. Melt margarine in pasta pot. Remove from heat and return pasta to pot immediately adding the eggs, sour cream and cheese. Stir and lift from the bottom until the mixture is smooth. Gently fold in most of the asparagus and fresh spices. Place in pre–warmed serving dish and top with remaining asparagus and spices.

CHEESE GRITS

(See recipe in Oklahoma Specialties Section)

SCALLOPED CORN CASSEROLE

1 16–ounce can cream style
   corn
2 eggs, beaten
½ cup cracker crumbs
¼ cup margarine, melted
¼ cup milk
¼ cup shredded carrots
1 teaspoon salt

1½ teaspoons chopped
   sweet green peppers
¼ cup chopped celery
1 tablespoon chopped onion
½ teaspoon sugar
½ cup shredded Cheddar
   cheese

Yield: 4–6 servings

Preheat oven to 350°. In large mixing bowl combine all ingredients except cheese and pour into 2–quart baking dish that has been sprayed with non–stick vegetable spray. Top corn mixture with shredded cheese and bake 40–50 minutes.

GRILLED HERB CORN

½ cup of butter, softened
2 tablespoons minced fresh
   parsley
2 tablespoons minced fresh
   chives

1 teaspoon dried thyme
½ teaspoon salt
¼ teaspoon cayenne pepper
8 ears sweet corn, husked

Yield: 8 servings

In a small bowl, combine first 6 ingredients. Spread 1 tablespoon over each ear of corn. Wrap corn individually in heavy–duty foil. Grill, covered, over medium coals for 15 minutes, turning frequently.

CORN BAKE

2 eggs, beaten
1½ cups sour cream
1 10–ounce package frozen
   corn kernels, thawed
½ cup fresh white bread
   crumbs
1 4–ounce can chopped
   green chilies, drained

1 teaspoon finely chopped
   jalapeño peppers
1 teaspoon salt
¼ teaspoon pepper
8–ounces Monterey Jack
   cheese cut in ¾-inch
   cubes
½ cup (2 ounces) shredded
   Cheddar cheese

Yield: 8–10 servings

Preheat oven to 350°. Grease 10–inch quiche pan or 8 x 8-inch baking dish. Combine eggs and sour cream in large bowl. Mix in corn, bread crumbs, chilies, jalapeño peppers, salt and pepper. Stir in Monterey Jack cheese and pour into prepared dish. Bake for 35–40 minutes until knife inserted in center comes out clean. Sprinkle with Cheddar cheese for last 5 minutes of baking. Let dish stand on wire rack for 10 minutes to cool prior to cutting into wedges or squares to serve.

CABBAGE CASSEROLE

1 head cabbage, chopped
4 slices bacon, cooked crisp
   and crumbled
3 eggs
1 cup milk
2 teaspoons prepared
   mustard

1 teaspoon salt
½ teaspoon black pepper
½ cup butter flavored
   crackers, crushed
   (optional)

Yield: 4–6 servings

Preheat oven to 350°. Boil cabbage in small amount of water until cabbage is crisp (about 10 minutes); drain. Toss cabbage with bacon pieces and set aside. In separate bowl beat together eggs and milk; add mustard, salt, and pepper and mix thoroughly. Pour mixture over cabbage and bacon, tossing all gently to coat well. Turn mixture into 9 x 9-inch dish and top with cracker crumbs. Bake for 45–60 minutes, until filling is set and crumbs are lightly browned.

CAULIFLOWER GRATIN WITH CHILIES AND CHEESE

1 large head cauliflower
1½ cups (6–ounces)
   shredded Monterey Jack
   cheese
1 4–ounce can chopped
   green chilies, drained
½ cup diced onion

½ teaspoon salt
¼ teaspoon pepper
2 tablespoons margarine
   melted
½ cup fine, dry bread
   crumbs

Yield: 6–8 servings

Preheat oven to 350°. Remove larger outer leaves and stalk of cauliflower. Break cauliflower into florets and rinse well. Place in 3–quart saucepan and cook in small amount of boiling water 10–12 minutes or until tender; drain. In large bowl combine cheese and next 4 ingredients; stir well. Add cauliflower and toss gently. Spoon into a 2–quart baking dish that has been prepared with non–stick vegetable spray. In small bowl pour melted margarine over bread crumbs, tossing to coat. Sprinkle over casserole and bake for 25–30 minutes or until lightly browned.

YELLOW SQUASH CASSEROLE

1½ pounds yellow squash, sliced
2 small onions, grated
4 small carrots, grated
1 4–ounce jar pimientos, drained
1 stick margarine, melted

1 16–ounce package herb-seasoned stuffing mix
1 cup sour cream
1 10¾–ounce can cream of chicken soup
1 teaspoon Accent
1 teaspoon coarsely ground black pepper

Yields 6–8 servings

Preheat oven to 350°. Steam yellow squash until tender; drain and slightly mash. Add grated onion, carrots and pimientos to squash and set aside. Pour melted margarine over stuffing mix to coat evenly. Add ½ of stuffing mix and remaining ingredients to vegetables, gently stirring until combined. Coat 9 x 9-inch baking dish with non–stick vegetable spray. Layer remaining stuffing mixture on bottom of dish, reserving a handful to sprinkle on top. Add vegetable mixture and sprinkle with reserved dressing. Bake for 30 minutes.

HOMINY–SQUASH CASSEROLE

1 15½–ounce cans hominy, drained
1 8–ounce carton sour cream
1 pound Monterey Jack cheese, cubed
1 4–ounce can chopped green chilies, drained
1 teaspoon salt

1 pound yellow squash, cut into ½-inch slices (may use frozen)
1 large onion, chopped
1 stick margarine
1 cup Cheddar cheese, shredded
1 cup bread crumbs

Yield: 6 servings

Preheat oven to 350°. Mix together hominy and next 4 ingredients and set aside. In medium saucepan, heat squash and onion in margarine until margarine is melted and squash becomes tender. Combine both mixtures and place in prepared 9 x 13 x 2-inch baking dish. Top with Cheddar cheese and bread crumbs and bake for 45 minutes.

SPICY HOMINY CASSEROLE

1 small onion, chopped
½ cup chopped celery
2 tablespoons margarine
2 15½–ounce cans hominy
1 10¾–ounce can cream of
   mushroom soup

1 10¾–ounce can cream of
   celery soup
½ pound jalapeño Cheddar
   cheese, grated

Yield: 6 servings

Preheat oven to 350°. In large saucepan or skillet, sauté onion and celery in margarine until vegetables are crisp. Add first can of hominy, juice and all. Drain second can of hominy and add to mixture along with soups; blend well. Pour mixture into lightly greased 2–quart baking dish and top with cheese. Bake 10 to 15 minutes until bubbly.

FRIED OKRA

(See recipe in Oklahoma Specialties Section)

OKRA FRITTERS

(See recipe in Oklahoma Specialties Section)

HONEY BAKED ONIONS

8 medium onions, peeled
4 tablespoons margarine,
   melted
4 tablespoons honey

2 tablespoons tomato sauce
¼ cup chicken broth
¼ teaspoon paprika
salt to taste

Yield: 8 servings

Preheat oven to 350°. Cut onions in half crosswise and place, cut side down in a 9 x 13-inch pan. Stir together remaining ingredients and pour over onions. Cover pan tightly with foil and bake 1 hour or until onions are tender.

EGGPLANT PARMESAN

2 medium eggplants
1 cup flour
1 egg, beaten
1 cup seasoned bread
   crumbs
olive oil
½ pound mozzarella cheese,
   sliced

2 8–ounce cans tomato
   sauce
1 teaspoon oregano
salt and pepper to taste
1 cup freshly grated
   Parmesan cheese

Yield: 4–6 servings

Preheat oven to 400°. Slice cleaned, unpeeled eggplant into ¾-inch slices. Dip each slice first in flour, then in egg and then in bread crumbs to coat. Sauté each slice in small amount of hot olive oil, a few at a time, until they are lightly browned on both sides, adding additional oil if needed. Arrange browned slices in a 9 x 13 x 2-inch baking dish and place a slice of mozzarella cheese on each piece. Pour tomato sauce and spices evenly over each slice and sprinkle top with grated Parmesan cheese. Bake for 15–20 minutes.

PAN FRIED TATERS

(See recipe in Oklahoma Specialties Section)

CHEESE PACKED POTATOES

10 small potatoes, baked
2 cups cottage cheese
1 teaspoon garlic salt
2 tablespoons margarine
1½ cups chopped onions

1 cup chopped fresh
   mushrooms
1 clove garlic, minced
8–10 ounces Cheddar
   cheese, shredded
¼ cup chopped fresh chives

Yield: 20 servings

Preheat oven to 375°. Cut potatoes in half lengthwise. Scoop out potato halves, leaving ½-inch of potato on skins and discard. Scoop out remaining potato pulp and place in a large bowl. Add cottage cheese and garlic salt. Stir until well–blended; set aside. In a 10–inch skillet, melt margarine. Add onions, mushrooms and minced garlic; cook until well–blended. Spoon mixture into potato skins and place on greased baking sheet. Sprinkle top of potatoes with shredded cheese and chives. Bake 8–10 minutes. Serve warm.

SUNSHINE POTATOES

6 medium potatoes
1 10¾–ounce can cream of
   chicken soup
2 tablespoons margarine
1 8–ounce carton sour cream

3 tablespoons chopped
   green onions
1½–2 cups grated Old
   English cheese
salt and pepper to taste

Yield: 8–10 servings

Preheat oven to 350°. In large pan, boil potatoes in skins for 15 minutes or until completely done. Cool, peel and grate cooked potatoes in large bowl. In medium saucepan, over low heat, combine soup and margarine and heat until margarine is melted. Take off heat and blend in sour cream, onions and cheese, mixing well. Pour heated mixture over grated potatoes, adding salt and pepper to taste. Toss lightly until mixed. Pour into buttered 9 x 13-inch baking dish. Bake 45–60 minutes.

Note: May substitute frozen hash browns for potatoes. Can refrigerate overnight and then bake.

POTATOES, HONEY!

2½ pounds new potatoes,
   quartered
½ cup butter
¼ cup water

3 tablespoons honey
½ teaspoon salt
¼ teaspoon pepper

Yield: 6–8 servings

In a large saucepan or Dutch oven, cover potatoes with water. Bring to a boil and cook until potatoes are tender; drain and set aside. In same pan, melt butter; stir in water, honey, salt and pepper. Return ½ of potatoes to pan, tossing to thoroughly coat potatoes with honey mixture. Gently remove potatoes from mixture and transfer to serving dish; cover to keep warm. Add remaining potatoes to honey mixture and repeat procedure. Serve warm.

ROAST POTATOES AND ONIONS

4 medium potatoes,
  unpeeled and diced
1 medium onion, chopped
2 tablespoons paprika

6 tablespoons margarine,
  melted
salt to taste

Yield: 4 servings

Preheat oven to 350°. In a 9 x 13-inch pan, toss all ingredients together until nicely combined. Bake for about 40 minutes, turning occasionally, until potatoes are tender.

SPICED SWEET POTATOES WITH CINNAMON, HONEY AND WALNUTS

1 1-pound, 12-ounce can
  sweet potatoes, drained
  and mashed
¼ cup margarine, softened
¼ cup cream
⅓ cup maple syrup

1 teaspoon pumpkin pie
  spice
½ cup chopped walnuts
salt to taste
walnuts

Yield: 6 servings

Preheat oven to 325°. Combine all ingredients in an 8 x 8-inch casserole and bake approximately 1 hour or until heated thoroughly. Sprinkle top with extra chopped walnuts.

MALLOW YAMS

2 medium apples, sliced
⅓ cup chopped pecans
½ cup packed brown sugar
½ teaspoon cinnamon

2 17-ounce cans chunk
  sweet potatoes, drained
¼ cup margarine
miniature marshmallows

Yield: 6–8 servings

Preheat oven to 350°. Toss sliced apples with pecans and set aside. Mix brown sugar and cinnamon together and sprinkle over sliced apples. Alternate layers of apple mixture and sweet potatoes in deep casserole dish. Dot with margarine, cover and bake 35 to 40 minutes. Remove cover, sprinkle with marshmallows and return to oven until marshmallows brown slightly.

SWEET POTATO CHIPS

4 medium sweet potatoes,
   peeled (approximately 2
   pounds)
½ teaspoon salt
½ teaspoon freshly ground
   pepper

2 teaspoons sugar
1 tablespoon fresh lemon
   juice
4 tablespoons margarine,
   melted

Yield: 8 servings

Preheat oven to 250°. Very thinly slice sweet potatoes (¹⁄₁₆ to ⅛-inch thick), rinse in cold water. Drain and dry well with paper towels. Transfer to a large bowl and add the salt, pepper, sugar, lemon juice and margarine. Toss to coat well. Layer the potatoes in a large ovenproof skillet; mounding them slightly in the center. Pour in any liquid from the bowl. Cover tightly with foil and bake for 50 minutes or until tender. Serve straight from the skillet.

SWEET POTATO PRALINE CASSEROLE

3 cups mashed sweet
   potatoes
1¼ sticks margarine, melted
   and divided
1 cup sugar
½ teaspoon salt

2 eggs, beaten
¼ cup milk
½ teaspoon vanilla
1 cup packed brown sugar
½ cup flour
1 cup chopped pecans

Yield: 8 servings

Preheat oven to 350°. Combine sweet potatoes with ¼ stick of melted margarine. Add sugar and next 4 ingredients, mixing well. Pour into 9 x 13-inch baking dish that has been prepared with non–stick vegetable spray. For topping, mix remaining margarine, brown sugar, flour and pecans; layer over sweet potato mixture. Bake 35 minutes.

LUSCIOUS LIMAS

4 10-ounce packages frozen Fordhook limas
8 slices bacon, cooked
1 medium onion, chopped

2 4½-ounce jars button mushrooms, drained
1 cup sugar

Yield: 9 servings

Prepare limas in Dutch oven according to package directions. While limas are cooking, in separate pan, fry bacon until crisp, reserving drippings. Crumble bacon and add to limas. In bacon drippings, sauté chopped onions and mushrooms until onions are transparent. Remove onions and mushrooms from drippings and add to limas; stir in sugar and combine all well. Reduce heat, cover pan and continue cooking slowly from 30–45 minutes. While cooking, keep bean liquid about ¾ total level of mixture. Uncover beans and allow liquid to cook down to about ¼ level. Add additional sugar if needed.

ROUND UP RICE

A wonderfully rich change from potatoes!

4 cups cooked long-grain rice, divided
1 pound Monterey Jack cheese, grated
2 4-ounce cans mild chopped green chilies, drained

1 16-ounce carton French onion dip
1½ cups (6 ounces) grated colby cheese

Yield: 8–10 servings

Place 2 cups of cooked rice in 2-quart casserole dish that has been sprayed with non-stick vegetable spray. Layer ½ of the grated Monterey Jack cheese on top of rice. Spread green chilies and French onion dip on top of cheese. Add remaining Monterey Jack cheese on top of dip. Finish with remaining rice. Bake for 30 to 40 minutes. Turn oven off. Top with colby cheese and return to warm oven until cheese melts. Serve warm.

CHEESE ALMOND RICE

1½ cups sliced mushrooms (canned)
3 teaspoons chopped onion
½ cup chopped or slivered almonds
1½ cups shredded Cheddar cheese

2 cups regular long–grain rice
¼ teaspoon pepper
3 tablespoons chopped parsley
4 beef bouillon cubes
6 tablespoons soy sauce
salt to taste

Yield: 12 servings

Preheat oven to 375°. Drain mushrooms, reserving liquid. Combine mushrooms with onion, almonds, cheese, uncooked rice, pepper and parsley in 3–quart casserole. Add water to mushroom liquid to make 5 cups of liquid. Heat to simmering; add bouillon cubes and soy sauce to boiling liquid. Stir until cubes are dissolved. Pour over casserole mix. Cover and bake for 45–60 minutes.

RICE PUDDING

1 cup rice
2 cups boiling water
1 teaspoon vanilla
2 cups milk

3 eggs, beaten
¾ cup sugar
¼ cup butter, melted
1 cup raisins, optional

Yield: 8–10 servings

Preheat oven to 350°. Bring water to a boil, add rice. Reduce heat, cover and simmer for 10 minutes (until water is absorbed). In a large bowl, mix remaining ingredients, toss in rice. Transfer mixture to a 13 x 9 x 2–inch casserole dish. Bake for 30–40 minutes or until top is golden.

Note: This may also be served as a dessert or with sausage and cinnamon rolls for a delicious breakfast/brunch.

MACARONI & CHEESE

A favorite for the kids!

1 8–ounce package elbow
   macaroni
¾ teaspoon salt
1¼ cups grated Velveeta

2 tablespoons margarine
2 cups milk
¾ teaspoon pepper

Yield: 6–8 servings

Preheat oven to 350°. Cook macaroni in boiling water and salt according to package instructions. After cooking, place in colander, rinse with cold water and drain well. In a 13 x 9 x 2-inch buttered baking dish, layer ½ of the macaroni and ½ of the cheese, dotting the top with margarine. Repeat layers. Heat milk until warm and pour over the top layer. Pepper all and bake 40 minutes stirring as needed when mixture begins to bubble.

Note: Macaroni and cheese, as well as grilled cheese sandwiches have been a life saver for me as a mother of young children. When my daughter was a toddler, she would call grilled cheese sandwiches, "girl cheese sandwiches". When her little brother started eating solid food, we ordered a grilled cheese sandwich at a local restaurant. Katey was quick to correct our order — since the sandwich was for her brother, he needed a "boy cheese sandwich"! — Pam Dimski

MOM'S MUSHROOM AND SAUSAGE STUFFING

A change from traditional stuffing!

1 pound ground sausage
1 16–ounce package
  cornbread stuffing mix
1 14½–ounce can chicken
  broth
1 stick margarine

1½ medium onions, chopped
3–4 celery stalks, chopped
2 8–ounce packages of fresh
  mushrooms, cleaned and
  sliced

Yield: 8-10 servings

Preheat oven to 350°. In 10–inch skillet, brown sausage, drain and set aside. Melt margarine in skillet and sauté onion and celery until crisp. Add sliced mushrooms and continue cooking until onions are transparent. In large bowl, mix cornbread stuffing mix with sausage, onion, celery and mushrooms. Pour broth over entire mixture and turn into 13 x 9-inch baking dish prepared with non–stick vegetable spray. Bake 30–45 minutes.

SCALLOPED PINEAPPLE

Great served with ham or pork roast

2 cups sugar
1 cup margarine
3 eggs

1 20–ounce can pineapple
  chunks, drained
4 cups bread chunks
2 tablespoons milk

Yield: 6 servings

Preheat oven to 325°. Cream together sugar and margarine until fluffy. Add eggs and continue to blend until thoroughly combined. By hand, gently fold in pineapple and bread chunks. Moisten with milk. Turn into 8 x 8-inch glass baking dish and bake one hour.

Note: This can also be used as a hot dessert served with whipped cream.

155

CREAMY DILL SAUCE

Even kids will eat their vegetables with this on top!

3 tablespoons margarine or butter
3 tablespoons flour
2 cups milk

1 tablespoon chicken–flavor instant bouillon or 3 chicken–flavor bouillon cubes
2 teaspoons fresh lemon juice
¾ teaspoon dill weed

Yield: 2 cups

In medium saucepan, melt margarine; stir in flour until smooth. Gradually add milk, then bouillon, lemon juice and dill weed. Cook and stir until slightly thickened. Serve with hot steamed fresh vegetables. Refrigerate leftovers.

Note: My poor mother had her hands quite full trying to please 5 children for dinner each evening. One day, mom got completely fed up with the 5 of us saying, "I don't like that" to the vegetables and food she served at dinner. Much to our surprise, my cool, calm and collected mom simply announced that from now on, if any of us complained about the dinner menu, we would get a double serving and remain at the table until our double helping was gone. After about a week of sitting at the table until bedtime, or finishing a double helping of VEGETABLES, we finally wised up. It was too bad that "Mom's Rule" didn't count with desserts!!—Eileen Wilson

CAFE
OKLAHOMA

MAIN DISHES

ROUTE 66: MAIN STREET OKLAHOMA

They used to call it "The Mother Road" and "Main Street U.S.A.," and that says a lot about Route 66.

It was a great deal more than just pavement (in fact, for the first ten years or so of its history, it wasn't even *that*). It represented an era, and nowhere more so than in Oklahoma. Overall, Route 66 began in Chicago, swept down south through the Midwest and into Oklahoma, making a turn due west at Oklahoma City and stretching from there to the California coast.

If this were, say, 1947, and you were traveling south on Route 66, the first thing you'd encounter crossing the Oklahoma border is "The Everlasting Hills of Oklahoma," as the country song of the day went. By now the road was all paved and conditions weren't so rough – at least you didn't have to carry camping gear as they did during the '20's and '30's. Now there were tourist courts in all the towns to put you up for the night. Sure, a few places still made you furnish your own food and cooking utensils, but mostly you could count on finding a good roadhouse or a hometown cafe along the way. They specialized in "wagon wheel" hamburgers, and chicken-fried steaks smothered in cream gravy – an honest-to-goodness delicacy in Oklahoma.

The road took you through Claremore – Will Rogers used to say that he had been born between Claremore and Oologah, "before there was a town at either place". Route 66 was a two-lane road with a speed limit of 65, which meant that oncoming trucks bore down on you head-on, and passed on your left with a rush of wind and just a few feet to spare. It made you think twice about resting your elbow on the car's window ledge, even though most people did it anyway.

Tulsa is next – The Oil Capital of the World, and for a long time home to Bob Wills and "Western Swing." You could listen in on the radio – Bob and Johnnie Lee Wills, or maybe even Gene Autry or another of the big country stars. For that matter, as long as you were in Tulsa, you might go see the performance live at the legendary Cain's Ballroom, famed for its spring-loaded hardwood dance floor.

And speaking of the radio, turn it on and you might hear Bobby Troup's smash hit "Get Your Kicks On Route 66" - the highway had become more than a highway.

Through Kellyville, Bristow and Stroud, the land starts leveling and the woods start thinning until the highway carries you into Oklahoma City – "Oklahoma City looks mighty pretty," goes the song – and the road bends toward the west. This was the highway that carried so many west during the Great Depression, although many more stayed behind to work for the WPA – it was they who turned Route 66 into a ribbon of pavement during the 1930's. Oil country – you can tell it by the hundreds of derricks surrounding you as you drive Route 66 through the city, west.

Through El Reno, Weatherford, Clinton, Elk City, the rolling land becomes flat at the Texas border on the west side of Oklahoma where Route 66 exits the state. But you'll go through miles and hours of cattle, wheat and oil before you ever reach Texas.

If Oklahoma contributed anything to the lore of Route 66, it was hospitality. It seemed like the folks here always had the time to help. At least that much hasn't changed. When the Interstate Highway System opened, passing *by* towns rather than *through* them, there was nowhere for Route 66 to go except into legend. But the traveler crossing Oklahoma lost something with its passing – contact with the people who lived along the road.

And that's what Route 66 had really been all about from the start – people.

There're still pieces of it intact – marked by replicas of the familiar "US 66" emblem, designating it as a "historic highway" by act of the Oklahoma legislature. But the things that made Route 66 what it was still remain – the friendliness, the hospitality, the willingness to give a stranger an even break.

It's still there. But you'll have to get off the Interstate to rediscover it.

BRIGHT-EYED BREAKFAST

4 tablespoons margarine, divided
3 tablespoons flour
¾ teaspoon salt
1½ cups evaporated milk
½ cup water
1½ cups shredded Cheddar cheese

1 cup sliced fresh mushrooms
¼ cup chopped onion
12 eggs, beaten
1 cup buttered fresh bread crumbs

Yield: 8–10 servings

Preheat oven to 350°. Melt 2 tablespoons of margarine in medium sauce-pan. Blend in flour and salt. Gradually add evaporated milk and water. Cook over medium heat, stirring constantly, until mixture just comes to boil and thickens. Remove from heat. Add cheese and stir until melted. Cover and set aside. Melt remaining 2 tablespoons butter in large skillet. Sauté mushrooms and onions until all liquid has evaporated. Add eggs and continue cooking until it is set. Fold eggs into cheese sauce. Pour all into 9 x 13-inch baking dish. Sprinkle bread crumbs over mixture. Cover and refrigerate overnight. Bake uncovered for 20 to 25 minutes.

GOOD MORNIN' OKLAHOMA BRUNCH

(See recipe in Oklahoma Specialties Section)

BANDANA BRUNCH

1 teaspoon salt
½ cup flour
1 teaspoon baking powder
10 eggs, well beaten
2 cups cottage cheese

1 pound Monterey Jack cheese, grated
½ cup margarine, melted
1 4-ounce can chopped green chilies, drained

Yield: 8–10 servings

Preheat oven to 350°. In large bowl combine salt, flour and baking powder. Beat in eggs. Add cottage cheese and next 3 ingredients. Pour into greased 9 x 13-inch baking dish. Bake 25 to 30 minutes. Serve warm.

BLACK MESA BREAKFAST

(See recipe in Oklahoma Specialties Section)

HOPPEL POPPEL

8 ounces sausage
5 medium potatoes, peeled
    and chopped
¼ cup chopped onions

¼ cup chopped green bell
    pepper
6 eggs, beaten
salt and pepper to taste
1 cup shredded colby cheese

Yield: 6–8 servings

Brown sausage in skillet, stirring until crumbly. Remove sausage with slotted spoon, reserving drippings. Cook potatoes, onion and green pepper in drippings until tender; remove from heat. Add eggs, sausage, salt and pepper. Stir until eggs are soft–set. Sprinkle with cheese. Let stand covered for 5 minutes or until cheese melts. Serve with toast or biscuits. May substitute bacon or ham for sausage.

QUICK BREAKFAST PIZZA

1 pound pork sausage
1 can refrigerator crescent
    rolls
1 cup frozen hashbrown
    potatoes, thawed

1 cup shredded Cheddar
    cheese
5 eggs
¼ cup milk
½ teaspoon salt
½ teaspoon pepper

Yield: 8 servings

Preheat oven to 375°. Cook and crumble sausage until browned; drain fat. Separate dough into 8 triangles and place on ungreased 12–inch pizza pan. Press into pan and up sides to form crust. Seal perforations. Spoon sausage evenly over crust and top with hashbrown potatoes and cheese. Beat together eggs, milk and spices. Pour mixture over pizza and bake 25 to 30 minutes.

QUICHE ME QUICK

½ pound sausage
3 eggs
½ teaspoon salt
½ pint whipping cream
1 10-inch deep dish pastry
   shell

¼ cup chopped onion
¼ cup chopped bell pepper
1 cup shredded Swiss cheese
1 cup shredded Cheddar
   cheese

Yield: 6-8 servings

Preheat oven to 350°. Brown and crumble sausage; drain and set aside. Whisk together eggs, salt and whipping cream until thoroughly blended. Cover bottom of pastry shell with sausage; top with onion and bell pepper. Toss cheeses together and sprinkle over meat. Pour egg and whipping cream mixture over all. Bake for 45 minutes. Allow to cool before cutting to serve.

BRUNCH SPINACH QUICHE

1 8-ounce package light
   cream cheese, cubed
1 cup 2% milk
4 eggs, beaten
¼ cup chopped onion
1 tablespoon margarine
1 cup finely chopped ham or
   bacon bits

4-ounces frozen chopped
   spinach; thawed and
   squeezed dry
¼ cup chopped pimiento
¼ cup finely chopped sweet
   red pepper
dash black pepper
1 10-inch prepared pie crust

Yield: 8 servings

Preheat oven to 350°. Combine cream cheese and milk in small saucepan over low heat; stir until smooth. Gradually add cream cheese mixture to eggs and mix until well-blended. Sauté onions in margarine and add with ham, spinach, pimiento and peppers to egg mixture; thoroughly blend. Pour into pastry shell and bake 35 to 40 minutes or until set.

Note: A combination of melons (honeydew, watermelon, cantaloupe or any regional varieties) cut into different shapes makes a charming accompaniment to many brunch dishes. For a distinctive touch, top each serving with a splash of champagne.

TENDERLOIN OF BEEF IN WINE SAUCE

5–6 pound beef tenderloin
olive oil
salt, pepper and garlic
   powder to taste
4 tablespoons margarine
½ cup chopped green onions

4 ounces sliced fresh
   mushrooms
1 cup claret wine
1 cup beef consommé
3 teaspoons cornstarch
1 tablespoon lemon juice

Yield: 10 servings

Preheat oven to 350°. Rub tenderloin with olive oil and seasonings to desired taste. Bake, uncovered, in shallow pan for 45 minutes or until meat thermometer registers desired doneness. In medium pan, melt margarine; sauté onions and sliced mushrooms until tender. Add wine and simmer until reduced by half. In small bowl, combine beef consommé and cornstarch, mixing well. Pour broth into pan containing other ingredients and simmer until thickened. Just before serving, add lemon juice and pan drippings from meat. Serve sauce poured over sliced beef.

BEEF TENDERLOIN WITH PEPPERCORNS

Tender and tasty!

1 5–6 pound beef tenderloin
   (trimmed)
3½ tablespoons Dijon
   mustard
1 tablespoon dried whole
   sage
1½ tablespoons green
   peppercorns, drained

1½ tablespoons whole black
   peppercorns, ground and
   divided
1½ tablespoons whole white
   peppercorns, ground and
   divided
3 tablespoons butter,
   softened

Yield: 10–12 servings

Preheat oven to 425°. Cut tenderloin lengthwise to within ½-inch of one long edge, leaving edge intact. Open tenderloin out flat. Place heavy-duty plastic wrap on tenderloin; pound meat to flatten slightly. Remove wrap; spread meat with mustard. Sprinkle with sage, green pepper corns, and ½ tablespoon each of black and white ground peppercorns. Fold one side of tenderloin back over and tie securely with heavy string at 3-inch intervals. Spread butter over outside and sprinkle with remaining ground peppercorns. Place tenderloin on a rack in a roasting pan; insert meat thermometer into thickest portion of tenderloin. Bake 30 to 45 minutes or until meat thermometer registers 140° (rare) or 160° (medium). Let stand 10 minutes before slicing.

TWO STEP TENDERLOIN WITH A KICK

(See recipe in Oklahoma Specialties Section)

BEEF TENDERLOIN DELUXE

Great flavor and so tender!

3–4 pound beef tenderloin
½ cup chopped onions
1½ teaspoons margarine,
   melted
1 cup dry sherry

3 tablespoons soy sauce
2 tablespoons dry mustard
⅛ teaspoon salt
⅛ teaspoon pepper

Yield: 6–8 servings

Preheat oven to 400°. Trim excess fat from tenderloin. Place meat in a large shallow baking pan; bake, for 10 minutes. In medium pan, melt margarine and sauté onions until tender; add remaining ingredients. Bring to a boil, stirring occasionally; pour sauce over meat. Reduce oven temperature to 325° and bake 35 minutes or until a meat thermometer reads 140° to 170°. Baste often with drippings. Slice and serve with drippings.

SOUR CREAM TENDERLOIN

4 beef tenderloin fillets (filet
   mignon)
or boneless ribeye, cut 1 –
   1½-inches thick
1 tablespoon margarine
⅓ teaspoon salt or meat
   seasoning

pepper to taste
1 cup canned sliced
   mushrooms
½ cup sour cream
¼ cup port red wine

Yield: 4 servings

In large frying pan, fry fillets in margarine about 3 minutes on each side for rare, 5 minutes per side for medium or 8 to 10 minutes for medium well. Transfer fillets to serving dish and keep warm. Add remaining ingredients to pan drippings, stirring to blend well until mixture is hot. Pour sauce over fillets to serve.

FILET MIGNON

4 2-inch thick fillets
1 teaspoon seasoned salt
½ teaspoon coarse black
  pepper

¼ cup butter
4 small onions, peeled,
  halved
1 cup red wine

Yield: 4 servings

Rub steaks with seasoned salt and pepper. Melt butter in heavy frying pan. Add steaks and brown on both sides. Reduce heat to simmer. Add onions and wine. Cover skillet tightly and allow steaks to simmer for 30 minutes.

BLUE RIBBON BRISKET

(See recipe in Oklahoma Specialties Section)

DOWN HOME BRISKET

3½ – 4 pound trimmed beef
  brisket
4–5 cups brewed coffee

1 4–ounce bottle liquid
  smoke
1 tablespoon onion powder
1 tablespoon garlic powder

Yield: 8 servings

Preheat oven to 325°. Line a 9 x 13-inch baking pan with aluminum foil, allowing foil to generously hang over ends and sides of pan. Place brisket in prepared pan and pour coffee over meat. In separate bowl, combine liquid smoke, onion powder and garlic powder; pour over brisket. Fold foil over brisket and crimp to seal. Bake for 6–8 hours. Turn every 2 hours and check liquid; if liquid is needed, add coffee.

BEEF POT ROAST IN BEER

3–4 pound beef rump roast
¼ cup, plus 2 tablespoons
    flour, divided
1 teaspoon salt
dash pepper
2 tablespoons shortening
1 12–ounce can beer,
    divided

2 bay leaves
6 small white onions,
    quartered
4 medium carrots
½ cup cold water
2 tablespoons ketchup

Yield: 6–8 servings

Coat roast with 2 tablespoons of flour and season with salt and pepper. In Dutch oven or large covered skillet, brown roast on all sides in hot shortening. Add ½ cup of the beer, bay leaves, onions and carrots. Cover and cook 1 to 1½ hours over low heat until meat and vegetables are tender; remove to heated platter. Skim fat from pan juices. To the pan, add enough of the remaining beer to make 1½ cups of liquid. In separate container, thoroughly combine cold water and ¼ cup flour; slowly stir into pan juices with ketchup. Cook and stir until thickened, allow to simmer 2–3 additional minutes. Pour mixture over sliced beef to serve.

BARBECUE BEEF RIBS

(See recipe in Oklahoma Specialties)

HICKORY RIBS

(See recipe in Oklahoma Specialties)

KRAUT BISCUITS

1 package frozen dinner rolls (12)	2 tablespoons chili powder
1½ pounds hamburger	1 teaspoon garlic salt
1 head cabbage, shredded	1 teaspoon salt
	1 teaspoon pepper

Yield: 12 rolls

Let rolls rise halfway according to package directions. In a large skillet, brown hamburger meat (do not drain). Add cabbage and seasonings. Cook until cabbage is tender and clear. Roll out individual dinner rolls. Put heaping tablespoon of meat mixture on dough and fold dough to form biscuit. Place filled rolls in a lightly greased 9 x 13-inch pan and let rise again for 30 minutes. Bake according to dinner roll directions.

COWBOY BEDROLL

1 2–pound round steak	½ teaspoon dried oregano, crushed
1 pound bulk Italian sausage	½ teaspoon garlic salt
½ cup sliced green onions	1 16–ounce can Italian style tomato sauce
½ cup canned, sliced mushrooms	
½ teaspoon tarragon leaves	

Yield: 6–8 servings

Preheat oven to 325°. Trim all fat from steak. Evenly spread sausage in layer over steak. Top evenly with green onions, mushrooms and seasonings. Roll up steak and secure with string or skewers. Place roll in baking dish and top with tomato sauce. Cover and bake 1½ – 2 hours. Slice to serve.

CHICKEN FRIED STEAK AND GRAVY

(See recipe in Oklahoma Specialties Section)

BOOT-SCOOTIN' STEAK

1 ½ pounds flank steak
1 cup vegetable oil
½ cup firmly packed brown
   sugar

½ cup soy sauce
¼ cup red wine
1 tablespoon minced garlic
1 teaspoon ground ginger

Yield: 6 servings

Trim excess fat from steak; score steak on both sides in 1½-inch squares. Place steak in a large shallow dish or zip–top heavy duty plastic bag. In a small bowl combine oil and remaining ingredients, stirring well. Pour over steak. Cover or seal; marinate in refrigerator overnight turning occasionally. Drain steak, reserving marinade. Grill, covered, over medium coals (300° to 400°) 6 to 8 minutes on each side or to desired degree of doneness, basting twice with marinade. Discard remaining marinade. To serve, slice steak across the grain into thin slices.

BEST OF THE WEST BURRITOS

½ cup chopped green bell
   pepper
½ cup chopped onion
2 tablespoons vegetable oil
1 pound ground beef
½ teaspoon cumin
½ teaspoon salt
½ teaspoon garlic powder
½ teaspoon oregano
½ teaspoon dry mustard
1 tablespoon chili powder

2 tablespoons picante sauce
1 8–ounce can tomato sauce
1 15–ounce can pinto beans,
   drained and mashed
1 4–ounce can chopped
   green chilies, drained
8–ounces Cheddar cheese,
   grated
6–8 flour tortillas
sour cream & salsa
   (optional)

Yield: 6–8 servings

In a large pan, sauté pepper and onion in oil until tender. Add ground beef and cook until browned; drain. Add remaining ingredients except cheese and tortillas. Continue to cook 10 minutes or until seasonings blend. Thoroughly mix in cheese and remove from heat. Place 2 to 3 tablespoons of meat mixture on tortilla, fold up bottom and wrap sides around tightly; repeat with remaining tortillas. Delicious with sour cream and salsa.

CORNMEAL WAFFLES & CHILI

Great quick dinner for a cold winter night!

Chili:
8 ounces ground beef
1 16–ounce jar thick &
   chunky salsa

1 15–ounce can pinto beans,
   drained & rinsed

Waffles:
½ cup cornmeal
½ cup flour
¼ cup sugar
1 teaspoon baking powder
½ teaspoon baking soda

½ teaspoon salt
1 cup buttermilk
1 large egg
3 tablespoons vegetable oil

Toppings:
sour cream, chopped
   cilantro, black olives,
   shredded Cheddar
   cheese

Yield: 4 servings

For chili, brown meat in a medium–size skillet about 5 minutes, stirring to break up chunks. Drain off all fat. Stir in salsa and beans; bring to a simmer. Cover mixture and allow to cook 25–30 minutes, stirring occasionally, while preparing waffles. To make the waffles, in a medium bowl combine cornmeal, flour, sugar, baking powder, baking soda and salt; mixing well. Add buttermilk, egg and oil and combine thoroughly. Heat and grease waffle iron according to individual directions. Pour in appropriate amount of batter and spread to edges. Close and cook until iron opens easily. To serve, spoon chili on waffles and top with an assortment of your favorite toppings.

COWHAND CHILI & RICE

(See recipe in Oklahoma Specialties)

HUNGARIAN GULYAS

2 large red onions, sliced
1 medium green pepper,
   chopped
¼ cup margarine
2 pounds lean stewing beef,
   cut in 1–inch cubes

1 tablespoon paprika
¼ cup tomato paste
½ cup dry red wine
2 cups beef broth
salt to taste
4–6 cups egg noodles

Yield: 4–6 servings

In a large skillet, sauté onions and green peppers in margarine until tender. Add meat and brown. Mix in paprika, tomato paste, wine and beef broth to cover meat. Add salt to taste. Cover and simmer slowly, 3 hours or until meat is tender. Add more broth if liquid is needed. When meat is tender, remove cover. Continue cooking until goulash thickens slightly. Serve over hot noodles.

EASY LASAGNA

1 pound ground beef
1 32–ounce jar thick
   spaghetti sauce
1 cup water
2 cups small curd cottage
   cheese
12–ounces mozzarella
   cheese, shredded

½ cup grated Parmesan
   cheese
2 eggs, beaten
¼ cup chopped parsley
1 teaspoon salt
¼ teaspoon pepper
8 ounces lasagna noodles,
   uncooked

Yield: 8 servings

Preheat oven to 350°. In large pan brown ground beef; drain. Add sauce and water to beef and simmer 15 minutes; set aside. For cheese filling, combine remaining ingredients, except lasagna noodles. Pour 1 cup of sauce mixture on bottom of 13 x 9 x 2-inch baking pan. Layer 3 pieces of uncooked lasagna over sauce. Lasagna noodles will expand to fill space. Cover noodles with 1½ cups of sauce mixture, then half of the cheese filling. Repeat layer of lasagna, sauce and cheese filling. Top with layer of lasagna and remaining sauce. Cover with aluminum foil and bake 55 to 60 minutes. Remove foil, return to oven and allow to bake an additional 10 minutes. For ease in serving, allow lasagna to cool 10 minutes before cutting.

PICADILLO

1 pound ground beef
2 tablespoons vegetable oil
1 medium onion, chopped
1 medium bell pepper,
    chopped
1 8–ounce can tomato sauce
2 bay leaves
¼ teaspoon onion powder

¼ teaspoon garlic powder
½ teaspoon oregano
½ cup sliced green olives
1 tablespoon vinegar
1 tablespoon flavor enhancer
4 cups cooked rice
1 15–ounce can black beans,
    drained

Yield: 4 servings

Brown ground beef, drain off fat and set aside. In same pan, add oil and sauté onions and bell peppers until tender. Add remaining ingredients and simmer 20 to 30 minutes. Return ground beef to above mixture to heat; stir occasionally. Remove bay leaves. Serve on a bed of black beans and rice.

TEX–MEX MEAT LOAF

1½ pounds lean ground beef
1 16–ounce can pinto beans,
    drained and rinsed
1 cup picante sauce, divided
1 medium onion, chopped
1 clove garlic, minced

½ cup dry bread crumbs
2 eggs
1½ teaspoons cumin
¾ teaspoon salt
2 tablespoons brown sugar

Yield: 4–6 servings

Preheat oven to 350°. In large bowl, combine meat, beans, ½ cup picante sauce, onion, garlic, bread crumbs, eggs, cumin and salt, mixing well with hands. Press mixture into 9 x 5-inch loaf pan. Bake for 1 hour. Carefully pour off and discard drippings. Combine remaining ½ cup picante sauce and brown sugar; mix well. Spread sauce over top of meat loaf and continue baking 15 minutes. Allow to stand 10 minutes before slicing.

INDIAN TACOS

(See recipe in Oklahoma Specialties Section)

MINI LOAVES ITALIANO

A nice change from plain meat loaf!

1 pound lean ground beef
1 teaspoon basil
¼ teaspoon garlic powder
¼ teaspoon fennel
½ teaspoon oregano,
   crushed

¼ teaspoon brown sugar
8 ounces, no–salt added
   tomato sauce
2 ounces, mozzarella cheese,
   grated

Yield: 4 servings

Preheat oven to 350°. Combine meat with basil, garlic powder, fennel, oregano and brown sugar in a bowl. Mix well and shape into 4 small loaves. Bake 30 minutes. Remove from oven, top with tomato sauce and cheese and return to oven 4–6 minutes or until cheese melts.

SOUTHWEST LASAGNA

1½ pounds ground beef
1½ teaspoons ground cumin
1 tablespoon chili powder
¼ teaspoon garlic powder
¼ teaspoon red pepper
1 teaspoon salt
1 teaspoon black pepper
1 16–ounce can tomatoes,
   chopped
10–12 corn tortillas
2 cups small curd cottage
   cheese, drained

1 cup grated Monterey Jack
   cheese with peppers
1 egg
½ cup grated Cheddar
   cheese
2 cups shredded lettuce
½ cup finely chopped
   tomatoes
¼ cup sliced black olives
3 green onions, chopped

Yield: 6–8 servings

Preheat oven to 350°. In a large skillet brown ground beef and drain. To meat, add ground cumin and next 6 ingredients; heat thoroughly. Cover the bottom and sides of 9 x 13-inch greased baking dish with part of the tortillas. Pour in beef mixture, and layer top with remaining tortillas. In separate bowl, combine cottage cheese, Monterey Jack cheese and egg; pour over second tortilla layer. Bake for 30 minutes. Make a diagonal stripe across the center of the casserole with the grated Cheddar cheese. Working from the cheese to outer corners, make diagonal strips of lettuce, tomatoes, olives and end in corners with chopped green onions.

MEAT LOAF DIJONNAISE

Meat Loaf:
1½ pounds lean ground beef
1 cup fresh bread crumbs
2 eggs
2 tablespoons grated
   Parmesan cheese
1 small onion, grated

⅓ cup tomato sauce
1 tablespoon Dijon mustard
1 teaspoon sweet basil
   flakes
salt and pepper to taste

Topping:
1 tablespoon Dijon mustard
⅔ cup tomato sauce

1 tablespoon grated
   Parmesan cheese

Yield: 6 servings

Preheat oven to 350°. In a large bowl, combine first 9 ingredients and mix until well–blended. Pack mixture into a 9 x 5-inch loaf pan. To top the meat loaf, spread on Dijon mustard, cover with tomato sauce and sprinkle with Parmesan cheese. Bake for 1 hour or until meat is cooked throughly.

FIESTA BAKE

1 pound ground beef
1 1¼–ounce package taco
   seasoning
¾ cup water
1 cup chopped onion
1¾ – 2 cups flour, divided
1 package quick rise yeast

1 tablespoon sugar
2 teaspoons finely chopped
   onion
¾ teaspoon salt
⅔ cup warm water
2 tablespoons vegetable oil
½ cup crushed corn chips

Yield: 4 servings

Preheat oven to 375°. Brown ground beef in a large skillet; drain. Add taco seasoning, water and chopped onion to ground beef and allow to simmer 20 minutes; set aside. In medium bowl, combine 1 cup flour, yeast, sugar, onion and salt; mix well. Add very warm water (120°–130°) and oil to mixture. Mix by hand until almost smooth. Stir in corn chips and enough of the remaining flour to make a stiff dough. Spread in well–greased 9 x 9 x 2-inch pan, pressing halfway up the sides of the dish; cover and let rise in warm place 10–15 minutes. Spread meat filling over crust and bake for 35 minutes or until crust is golden brown.

Note: Can be topped with sour cream, grated cheese, chopped tomatoes or any of your favorite taco toppings.

VOLTURO MEAT SAUCE

An heirloom recipe!

1 cup chopped onion
4 cloves garlic
½ cup water
1½ pounds lean ground
   meat
3 tablespoons oil
¼ – ½ cup chopped fresh
   parsley
2 teaspoons garlic salt

1 teaspoon black pepper
½ teaspoon cinnamon
3 10¾–ounce cans tomato
   puree
1 12–ounce can tomato
   paste
1 cup tomato juice
boiling water

Yield: 4 servings

In container of blender, place onions, garlic and water. Blend until all pieces are thoroughly minced; set aside. In Dutch oven, brown ground beef just until color changes. Drain off fat and set meat aside. In same pot, pour oil in pan and tilt to cover bottom. To oil add chopped parsley, garlic salt, black pepper, cinnamon and onion/garlic mixture. Turn to high heat and stir constantly until onions turn translucent. Add ground meat to mixture and reduce to medium heat. Add tomato puree, tomato paste and tomato juice; add enough water to puree and paste cans to rinse and add to mixture. Stir entire mixture thoroughly and return heat to high until mixture begins to boil. Cover Dutch oven, turn heat to low and allow to simmer approximately 2 hours until mixture cooks down and is very thick. Stir frequently during cooking time so sauce will not burn. After sauce has cooked down, add enough boiling water to bring it back up to the original level. Repeat the process and allow sauce to cook down again or at least 1 hour until sauce reaches right consistency for serving. The more times the mixture is cooked down, the richer the sauce is. Serve with Perfect Spaghetti.

Note: This is an old Volturo family recipe and all the measurements are approximate. My grandmother Volturo would wake me at 3 o'clock in the morning so we could start the sauce and let it cook all day. The aroma was wonderful! As I've learned through the years, the only way to produce a sauce that suits your taste is to experiment with measurements until you get the taste you want. Of course, I'll never be able to duplicate Grandma Volturo's!— Rita White

PERFECT SPAGHETTI

4 quarts water
3 teaspoons salt

1 teaspoon oil
16 ounces spaghetti noodles

Yield: 4 servings

In large pot, bring water, salt and oil to a rapid boil. Gently place spaghetti into boiling pot, stirring it around as it softens. Do not cover the pot. Using a long fork, stir the spaghetti frequently to keep it from sticking together or to the bottom of the pot. Keep the water boiling throughout the entire cooking time. Cook the spaghetti approximately 8 minutes or until tender. There should be a trace of firmness in the spaghetti. Drain. To serve spaghetti, place a small amount of drained spaghetti in the bottom of a large bowl. Cover with a layer of meat sauce. Repeat spaghetti and sauce layers until all spaghetti or sauce is used. Sprinkle top with grated Parmesan or Romano cheese.

TEX MEX STUFFED POTATOES

4 large potatoes
1 pound lean, ground beef
1 1.1-ounce package taco
  seasoning
1 tablespoon tomato paste
½ cup bottled salsa

2 tablespoons no-fat sour
  cream
1 ounce sharp Cheddar
  cheese, shredded
3 cups shredded lettuce
3 tomatoes, cubed

Yield: 4 servings

Preheat oven to 350°. Wrap potatoes in foil and bake 1½ hours or until soft. Allow potatoes to cool, then slice in half lengthwise. Scoop out half the pulp from each piece and set aside. Meanwhile, in 12-inch frying pan, cook ground beef until browned. Drain off all fat, then add taco seasoning, mix and cook 1 minute. Stir in reserved potato pulp, tomato paste, salsa and sour cream. Stuff the shells with prepared meat filling. Place on baking sheet and sprinkle with shredded cheese. Broil in oven 6–8 minutes until cheese is melted. Serve with lettuce and tomatoes.

THICK BEEF STEW

3 pounds stew meat
2 cups sliced carrots
1½ large onions, chopped
6 large potatoes, peeled and
  chopped
2 cups chopped celery
1½ teaspoons salt

1½ teaspoons pepper
2 10¾-ounce cans cream of
  mushroom soup
1 soup can water
2 bay leaves
1 cup Burgundy wine
  (optional)

Yield: 10 servings

In Dutch oven, brown stew meat and drain. Add remaining ingredients except the burgundy. Simmer over low heat for 5 hours, stirring occasionally. Add Burgundy last 30 minutes of cooking.

Note: This recipe can easily be used in a crock pot.

SWEET AND SOUR BEEF STEW

2 pounds beef, cubed
2 tablespoons vegetable oil
1 cup ketchup
½ cup packed brown sugar
½ cup red wine
1 tablespoon Worcestershire
  sauce

1 small onion, chopped
2 cups water
4 large carrots, cleaned and
  chopped
4 large potatoes, peeled and
  chopped
4 small onions, chopped

Yield: 4 servings

In Dutch oven, brown beef in oil and drain off excess oil. Combine ketchup and next 5 ingredients and pour over beef. Allow to simmer 30 minutes, stirring occasionally. Add chopped carrots, and cook 1 hour. Add potatoes and onions, cover and cook until tender. Remove cover and cook until stock thickens.

STEW WITH A KICK

Great for the football crowd!

1 large onion, chopped
2 large carrots, sliced
½ cup chopped celery
2 jalapeño peppers, sliced
½ clove garlic, minced
½ teaspoon dried cilantro
½ teaspoon ground cumin
2 pounds round steak, cubed

1 14–ounce can low salt beef broth
2 14–ounce cans tomato sauce (no salt)
1 14–ounce can tomatoes
2 medium zucchini, cubed
4 large potatoes, chopped
1 cup frozen corn

Yield: 8–10 servings

Combine all ingredients except the corn in a large crock pot; mix well. Cook on high setting 5 to 7 hours, stirring occasionally. Add corn the last hour of cooking; turn crock pot to low setting for the remaining hour.

Note: A meal in itself, serve with cornbread or garlic toast.

GREEN CHILE CHILI

1½ – 2 pounds ground meat (beef, venison or pork)
2 onions, finely chopped
⅛ teaspoon cayenne
⅛ teaspoon crushed red pepper
½ teaspoon garlic powder
1 tablespoon oregano
1½ teaspoons cilantro
1 teaspoon cumin

2-3 tablespoons chili powder
1 teaspoon salt
1 teaspoon black pepper
1 7–ounce can chopped green chilies
3 cups fresh tomato wedges
2 jalapeño peppers
1 12–ounce can of beer, divided
2-3 tablespoons cornmeal

Yield: 6–8 servings

Brown and drain ground meat. Add chopped onions, herbs and spices and cook until onions are clear and soft. Stir in chopped green chilies. In blender, puree tomato wedges with jalapeño peppers and add to meat mixture. Stir in 1 cup of beer, cover and allow to simmer at least 1 hour, stirring occasionally. At end of hour, add remaining beer. For texture, sprinkle cornmeal, one tablespoon at a time over chili, and stir well to avoid lumps. After adding cornmeal, simmer at least 5 additional minutes.

Note: This recipe is easily freezable and can be microwaved to warm. Serve with Mexican Cornbread for a complete meal.

176

BLACK BEAN CHILI

2 pounds dried black beans
8 cups water
salt to taste
1 pound sirloin tips
2 tablespoons
   Worcestershire sauce
1 pound smoked sausage,
   chopped
2 bunches green onions,
   chopped and divided
1 green bell pepper,
   chopped

3 jalapeño peppers, chopped
1 4–ounce can chopped
   green chilies
1 16–ounce can stewed
   tomatoes
3 tablespoons summer
   savory
3 tablespoons bouquet garni
3 tablespoons Greek
   seasoning
3 tablespoons chili powder

Yield: 12 servings

Soak beans covered in water in large saucepan overnight; drain. Add 8 cups water and bring to a boil. Reduce heat and allow to simmer 45 minutes. Add salt to taste and cook an additional 15 minutes. Brown sirloin tips in Worcestershire sauce in nonstick skillet; add to beans. Add sausage, half of the green onions, green pepper, jalapeño peppers and green chilies; mix well. Stir in tomatoes, savory, bouquet garni, Greek seasoning and chili powder. Continue to simmer, covered for 3 hours or until done to taste.

Note: Great topped with shredded cheese and chopped onion!

RED DIRT CHILI

(See recipe in Oklahoma Specialties Section)

VENISON STEW

2 tablespoons vegetable oil
2 pounds venison stew meat
3 large onions, coarsely
   chopped
2 garlic cloves, crushed
1 tablespoon Worcestershire
   sauce
1 bay leaf
1 teaspoon dried oregano
1 tablespoon salt

1 teaspoon pepper
3 cups water
7 potatoes, peeled and
   quartered
1 pound carrots, cut into
   1–inch pieces
¼ cup all–purpose flour
¼ cup cold water
bottled browning sauce,
   optional

Yield: 8–10 servings

Heat oil in a Dutch oven and brown meat. Add onions, garlic, Worcestershire sauce, bay leaf, oregano, salt, pepper and water. Simmer, covered 1½ to 2 hours or until meat is tender. Add potatoes and carrots and continue to cook until vegetables are tender, about 30–45 minutes. Mix together flour and water; stir into stew. Cook and stir until thickened and bubbly. Add browning sauce if desired. Remove bay leaf before serving.

VINITA VENISON CASSEROLE

2 pounds venison loin
red wine to cover meat
2 tablespoons olive oil
2 tablespoons butter
4 tablespoons flour
3 cups beef bouillon
1 4–ounce can mushrooms

1 teaspoon chopped onions
1 teaspoon salt
1 pinch cayenne
1 teaspoon pepper
1 tablespoon parsley
2 tablespoons sherry

Yield: 4–6 servings

Soak venison in red wine overnight. Brown cubed venison in skillet in olive oil and butter. Mix flour into ½ cup bouillon to serve as thickening; add to remaining 2½ cups bouillon and pour over meat. Add remaining ingredients, except sherry, to pan; cover and let simmer one hour or until tender. Add sherry to casserole just before serving.

QUAIL OR PHEASANT IN CREAM

2 pheasants or 4 quail
  (whole or breasts)
bacon strips
4 tablespoons butter
8 shallots, chopped

cognac
salt and pepper
2 cups chicken broth
1 cup heavy cream
¼ cup horseradish

Yield: 4 servings

Preheat oven to 350°. Cover pheasant or quail breasts with strips of bacon and tie them securely. Brown in an iron skillet with butter and shallots. Pour a little cognac over the top and ignite. Salt and pepper the pieces, add broth and cook uncovered for ½ hour, basting frequently with the juice. Combine cream and horseradish and pour over birds. Let this cook another 20 minutes, continuing to baste in the sauce. Season to taste. Serve on a platter with the sauce poured on the top.

ROAST LEG OF LAMB

1 5–pound leg of lamb
6 cloves garlic, crushed
3 – 4 tablespoons dried
  rosemary

salt and pepper to taste
several sprigs of fresh
  rosemary

Yield: 8 servings

Preheat oven to 450°. Rub lamb with mixture of garlic, dried rosemary, salt and pepper. Place meat in roasting pan and lay sprigs of fresh rosemary on top. Brown in hot oven for 15 minutes. Reduce oven temperature to 350° and roast for approximately 1½ hours (10 minutes per pound).

VEGETABLE LASAGNA

3 cups sliced zucchini
2 cups (8 ounces) sliced
  mushrooms
1 cup chopped onion
3 cloves garlic, finely
  chopped
1 tablespoon olive oil
1 26–ounce jar prepared
  spaghetti sauce
1 teaspoon oregano leaves

1 16–ounce container non-
  fat cottage cheese
1½ cups grated Parmesan
  cheese
8 ounces lasagna noodles,
  uncooked
2½ cups (10 ounces)
  shredded mozzarella
  cheese

Yield: 8–10 servings

Preheat oven to 350°. In large skillet, cook vegetables and garlic in oil until tender. Stir in spaghetti sauce and oregano and allow to simmer 15 minutes. In separate bowl, combine cottage cheese and Parmesan cheese and set aside. In 13 x 9-inch baking dish, layer ½ each of the noodles, sauce, cottage cheese and mozzarella cheese. Repeat layers. Cover dish and bake 45 minutes; uncover and allow to bake an additional 15 minutes. Let lasagna cool 20 minutes prior to serving.

ROASTED VEGETABLES AND PASTA

6 ounces wide egg noodles,
  uncooked
1 1.1-ounce package dry
  onion soup mix
1½ teaspoons dried thyme
½ cup olive oil, divided
2 carrots, cut into 1–inch
  slices
1 eggplant, cut into 1–inch
  pieces

1 medium zucchini, cut into
  1–inch slices
½ pound fresh mushrooms,
  halved
¼ cup white wine vinegar
⅓ cup pine nuts or slivered
  almonds, toasted
freshly ground pepper

Yield: 4–6 servings

Preheat oven to 450°. Cook noodles according to package directions, omitting salt and oil. Drain. Rinse and drain again; place in a large bowl and set aside. In a large bowl combine onion soup mix and thyme; stir in ¼ cup olive oil. Add carrots, eggplant, zucchini and mushrooms, tossing to coat. Spread evenly into a 15 x 10 x 1-inch jelly roll pan. Bake for 20 minutes, stirring after 10 minutes. Stir into noodles. Combine remaining ¼ cup olive oil, white wine vinegar, and nuts. Pour over noodle mixture, tossing to coat; sprinkle with pepper. Serve immediately.

LASAGNA ROLLS WITH SPINACH AND CHEESE

More festive than traditional lasagna.

1 16–ounce package lasagna
noodles
2 10–ounce packages frozen
chopped spinach, thawed
and thoroughly drained
1 pound ricotta cheese
1 8–ounce package cream
cheese, at room
temperature

1 cup grated Parmesan
cheese
8 ounces mozzarella cheese,
coarsely grated
½ teaspoon sweet basil
flakes
¼ teaspoon oregano flakes
1 30–ounce jar prepared
spaghetti sauce

Yield: 5–6 servings

Preheat oven to 350°. Cook lasagna noodles in boiling, salted water until tender, but firm; set aside. In a large bowl, beat together remaining ingredients, except spaghetti sauce, until blended. To prepare rolls, lay out each lasagna noodle and spoon about ½ cup filling on the top, spreading the length of each noodle. Beginning with the end, roll up noodle and secure with toothpick, if necessary. Continue with remaining noodles and place in a 9 x 13-inch baking dish, coiled side up. Pour spaghetti sauce evenly over the top of the noodles and sprinkle with additional Parmesan cheese. Bake for 30–45 minutes or until mozzarella cheese is melted.

PASTA PRIMAVERA

12 ounces spaghetti or
linguine
2 cups small broccoli pieces
2 tablespoons olive oil
12 ounces small fresh
mushrooms, cleaned and
halved
1 small onion, minced
1 small carrot, cut into
matchstick strips
1 small red pepper, cut into
¼-inch strips

1 12–ounce can evaporated
skim milk
2 teaspoons chicken flavor
instant bouillon
1¼ teaspoons cornstarch
½ teaspoon salt
1 medium tomato, seeded
and diced
2 tablespoons grated
Parmesan cheese
2 tablespoons minced
parsley

Yield: 6 servings

In 4–quart saucepan, prepare pasta as label directs, drain. Return pasta to pan to keep warm. While pasta is cooking, in 2-quart saucepan over high heat, cook broccoli pieces in 1 inch boiling water. Reduce heat to low; cover and simmer 2 to 3 minutes, stirring occasionally, until broccoli is tender–crisp; drain. While broccoli is cooking, in 12–inch skillet over high heat, in olive oil, cook mushrooms, onions and carrots, stirring frequently until vegetables are golden and tender–crisp. Add red pepper strips and cook, stirring until vegetables are tender. In 2 cup measuring cup, with fork, mix evaporated skim milk, chicken bouillon, cornstarch and salt. Into vegetable mixture in skillet, stir evaporated milk mixture. Over high heat, heat to boiling and allow to boil 1 minute. Add diced tomato, Parmesan cheese, parsley, broccoli and pasta, tossing to coat evenly; heat thoroughly and serve.

RED PORK CHILI

1½ pounds lean boneless
   pork, cubed
3 tablespoons shortening

2 cups Fresh Red Chili
   Sauce (see following
   recipe)
3 cups freshly cooked rice

Yield: 4 servings

Pat the pork cubes dry with paper towels. In a heavy 12-inch skillet, melt the shortening over moderate heat until very hot, but not smoking. Brown the pork in the hot shortening, turning the cubes frequently and cooking them evenly without burning. Stir in the red chili sauce and bring to a boil over high heat. Reduce heat to low and simmer, partially covered for 35 to 40 minutes until the pork is done. Transfer the pork chili to a heated bowl and serve at once, accompanied by the rice.

FRESH RED CHILI SAUCE

½ pound fresh hot red
   chilies, stemmed, seeded
   and coarsely chopped
1 cup boiling water
½ cup coarsely chopped
   onions

¼ cup vegetable oil
2 tablespoons coarsely
   chopped garlic
2 teaspoons dried oregano
2 teaspoons salt

Yield: 2 cups

Combine the chilies and boiling water in a bowl and let them steep for about 10 minutes. Transfer the mixture to an electric blender and blend at high speed for 30 seconds. Turn off the blender, scrape down the sides with a rubber spatula and add the onions, oil, garlic, oregano and salt. Blend until the chili sauce is reduced to a smooth puree, then taste for seasoning.

Note: Use as base for Red Pork Chili or as accompaniment for tacos and enchiladas.

CHALLEUPAHA'S

3-4 pound pork loin roast, fat trimmed

1-1½ pounds dried pinto beans, rinsed

2 garlic cloves, crushed

2½ tablespoons chili powder

1½ tablespoons cumin seed

1½ tablespoons oregano

1½ tablespoons Tabasco sauce

corn tortilla chips

Garnish:

1 head lettuce, shredded

2-3 tomatoes, chopped

1 onion, chopped

grated Cheddar cheese

Tabasco sauce

Yield: 15 servings

Preheat oven to 250°. Place pork roast in Dutch oven; cover with water. Place beans and spices with pork, cover and bake 8 hours, stirring every 2-3 hours. When meat is tender, remove any bones; shred meat and return to bean mixture. Serve over corn tortilla chips and garnish with lettuce, tomatoes, onions and Tabasco.

ALL AMERICAN RIBS WITH HONEY BARBECUE SAUCE

3 - 4 pounds country-style pork ribs

salt, pepper and garlic powder, to taste

Honey Barbecue Sauce:

1 cup ketchup

1 cup chili sauce

½ cup honey

½ cup brown sugar

2 teaspoons dry mustard

¼ cup vinegar

¼ teaspoon cayenne pepper

¼ cup margarine

Yield: 4-6 servings

Preheat oven to 350°. Lay ribs in a 12 x 16-inch roasting pan and sprinkle with salt, pepper and garlic powder to taste. Place in oven and bake 45 minutes. At end of cooking time, remove ribs from pan and drain off all rendered fat; return ribs to pan. Prepare barbecue sauce by stirring together all ingredients until blended. Baste ribs with sauce and return to oven. Continue baking and basting until ribs are tender and highly glazed, turning ribs over as necessary. Any unused sauce can be stored in the refrigerator several weeks.

184

TRAIL BOSS PORK

Great served on toasted pita bread!

1 cup chopped onion
1 cup chopped carrot
⅔ cup water
½ cup ketchup
4 tablespoons vinegar
2 tablespoons
    Worcestershire sauce
2 teaspoons brown sugar

2 teaspoons chili powder
½ teaspoon pepper
4 cups bite–sized cooked
    pork
1 cup sliced celery
3 teaspoons cornstarch
1 tablespoon water
4 cups cooked rice

Yield: 4 servings

In medium–size saucepan, stir together first nine ingredients. Bring mixture to a boil and reduce heat; cover and allow to simmer 5 – 10 minutes. Stir in pork and celery and simmer, covered, until heated thoroughly. In small jar with lid, shake together cornstarch and water until combined. Pour into meat mixture and allow to cook until thickened and bubbly, stirring occasionally. Serve with cooked rice.

ITALIAN PORK SANDWICHES

1 pound lean ground pork
    loin
¼ cup dry Italian bread
    crumbs
¼ cup chopped onion
¼ cup prepared spaghetti
    sauce

2 teaspoons dried basil
    leaves
1 egg
6 slices Italian bread
1 6½–ounce jar marinated
    artichoke hearts, drained
    and chopped
½ cup red bell pepper

Yield: 6 servings

Heat grill. In a small bowl, combine pork, bread crumbs, onion, spaghetti sauce, basil and egg; mix well. Shape into 6, oblong patties. When ready to grill, oil grill rack. Place patties on gas grill over medium heat or on charcoal grill 4 to 6 inches from medium coals. Cook 10 to 15 minutes or until patties are no longer pink, turning once, halfway through cooking. Place on bread slices. Top with artichoke hearts and red bell pepper.

POLITICALLY CORRECT HAM LOAF

(See recipe in Oklahoma Specialties Section)

ITALIAN ROAST PORK WITH WINE SAUCE

2 tablespoons minced garlic
1 tablespoon fennel seeds,
   crushed
1¼ teaspoons salt
½ teaspoon freshly ground
   pepper

4 tablespoons olive oil,
   divided
1 3–4 pound boneless pork
   loin
1 tablespoon margarine

Wine Sauce:
¾ cup dry white wine
¾ cup water

½ teaspoon fennel seeds,
   crushed

Yield: 10 servings

Combine garlic, fennel, salt, pepper and 2 tablespoons oil in a cup. Rub over meat, wrap in foil and refrigerate 4 hours or overnight. One hour before roasting, remove pork from refrigerator. Preheat oven to 400°. Heat 2 tablespoons oil and margarine in roasting pan over medium–high heat. Add pork and cook, turning until browned on all sides. Transfer to oven. Roast, turning pork halfway through, until meat thermometer inserted in thickest part of meat registers 160°, approximately 45–55 minutes. Transfer roast to platter; keep warm. Let stand 10 minutes before slicing. For wine sauce, add wine, water and fennel to roasting pan; bring to a boil, scraping up browned bits on bottom of pan. Reduce heat and simmer 5 minutes. Strain through sieve and skim off fat. Serve over sliced pork.

PIG OUT LOAF

1½ pounds ground pork
1½ pounds ground ham
1 egg, beaten
½ cup pineapple juice
1 cup cracker crumbs

salt and pepper to taste
¼ cup chopped onions
⅛ cup brown sugar, packed
3 pineapple rings

Mustard Glaze:
½ cup brown sugar, packed
½ teaspoon dry mustard

2 tablespoons pineapple
   juice

Yield: 4–6 servings

Preheat oven to 350°. Combine all loaf ingredients together, mixing well with hands. Press mixture into a 9 x 5 x 3-inch loaf pan and top with pineapple rings. Bake for 1½ hours. Make mustard glaze by combining brown sugar, dry mustard, and pineapple juice. Spoon glaze over loaf during the last 30 minutes of cooking. Allow to cool before slicing.

GRAM'S STUFFED CABBAGE ROLLS

1 2–pound head green
   cabbage
1½ cups water
1 pound pork sausage,
   browned
1 cup long grain rice
   (cooked 10 minutes)
½ teaspoon cinnamon

1 teaspoon salt
pepper to taste
⅛ teaspoon allspice
⅛ teaspoon clove
3 tablespoons melted
   margarine
1 32–ounce can whole
   tomatoes

Yield: 4–6 servings

Core and trim cabbage. In Dutch oven bring water to a rolling boil and place in whole head of cabbage for wilting to make leaves easy to roll. Turn cabbage frequently, and allow to boil 5 minutes or until tender, but still sturdy. Remove cabbage and allow to drain and cool. Separate leaves and cut any coarse ribs enough to make rolling easy; set aside. With hands, combine sausage and rice with remaining ingredients, except tomatoes, until seasoning is thoroughly blended. Place 1 heaping tablespoon of meat mixture onto large cabbage leaf. Roll toward the core end of leaf, tucking in the sides; secure each with toothpick. In Dutch oven, line bottom of pan with 2–3 cabbage leaves; layer cabbage rolls on top. Pour canned tomatoes over cabbage rolls to cover, breaking apart tomatoes to release juice. If necessary, additional water may be added to cover rolls. Cover pan and allow rolls to steam in juice for 45 minutes.

Note: Growing up in Elk City, my family lived across the street from my grandparents, Ernest and Jessie Jones. My brother, sister and I spent a lot of time with my grandparents and we shared many meals. No meal was quite as special as our birthday dinners, when we got to pick out our favorite dish. I always asked for these cabbage rolls and Polka Dot Salad. On birthdays we wouldn't eat in the kitchen, but we would eat at the big table in the dining room. Since this was Gram's "good table" we had to be extra careful to protect it — special pads and her best tablecloths. The chairs to the table had needlepoint seats that my mother, sister and I helped grandmother make. On these special days we would set the table with Gram's china dishes and the silver ware she kept in the special wooden box with the soft lining. I'm glad that grandmother took such good care of her "good table" — it now has a special place in my home and the needlepoint seats are now pillows I've shared with my mother and sister. — Diane Joy–Sisemore

HAM AND ASPARAGUS PASTA

¾ pound fresh asparagus
  spears
or 10–ounce package frozen
  cut asparagus
2 14½–ounce cans low
  sodium stewed tomatoes
1 tablespoon dried parsley
  flakes
½ teaspoon dried basil,
  crushed
½ teaspoon dried oregano,
  crushed

⅛ teaspoon ground red
  pepper (optional)
1 cup evaporated skim milk
10 ounces multicolored
  pasta
6 ounces lean, fully cooked
  ham, cut into bite–size
  strips
1 small red or green pepper,
  cut into thin strips

Yield: 4 servings

If using fresh asparagus, snap off and discard the woody bases. Bias–slice asparagus into 1–inch pieces (or thaw and drain the frozen cut asparagus). Set aside. For sauce, in a medium saucepan, combine stewed tomatoes, parsley, basil, oregano and ground red pepper, if desired. Bring to a boil; reduce heat and simmer sauce, uncovered, about 15 minutes or until reduced to 2½ cups, stirring occasionally. Add the evaporated milk all at once, stirring constantly. Heat mixture thoroughly; do not boil. Meanwhile, prepare pasta according to package directions, except, add the asparagus, ham and sweet pepper to the boiling water during the last 4 minutes of cooking time. Drain pasta and vegetables and serve with sauce.

HONEY BAKED HAM WITH CINNAMON APPLE RINGS

A boost for the traditional baked ham.

1 12–pound (bone in) ready–to–eat picnic ham
whole cloves
3 tablespoons Dijon mustard
1 cup packed brown sugar
1 cup honey, divided

1½ teaspoons cinnamon, divided
2¼ cups apple juice, divided
3 apples, cored and sliced into rings
⅛ teaspoon nutmeg
1 cup finely chopped pecans

Yield: 8 – 10 servings

Preheat oven to 325°. Prepare ham by removing the skin and all but a thin layer of fat. Score surface of ham in a diamond pattern, without cutting into the meat. Place a whole clove in half of the diamonds. Brush the top of the ham with Dijon mustard and place in appropriate size roasting pan. Combine brown sugar with ½ cup honey and 1 teaspoon of the cinnamon and spread mixture over the ham. Pour 1½ cups of the apple juice into the pan and bake for 1½ hours, basting occasionally with pan juices. While ham is baking, lay apple rings in a 9 x 13-inch pan. Combine remaining honey, apple juice, cinnamon and nutmeg, and drizzle over the apples. Bake for 20 minutes, sprinkle top with pecans and continue baking for 10 minutes. Serve ham surrounded with apple rings.

Note: Apples can be prepared earlier in the day and heated just before serving.

CHICKEN ON THE BRICKS

(See recipe in Oklahoma Specialties Section)

CHICKEN IN LEMON SAUCE

8 boneless chicken breasts,
  split and skinned
1 cup flour
salt and pepper to taste
½ cup margarine

1 garlic clove, minced
½ cup fresh lemon juice
⅓ cup minced fresh parsley
lemon slices for garnish

Yield: 6–8 servings

Pound chicken thinly, coat with flour and season with salt and pepper to taste. Over medium heat, melt margarine in large skillet and sauté garlic gently. Add chicken breasts, cooking until browned. Remove chicken to serving platter and keep warm. Pour lemon juice into skillet and stir, mixing with the drippings; allow to boil one minute or until slightly thickened. Stir in parsley and pour sauce over chicken to serve. May use lemon slices to garnish.

OLD FASHIONED CHICKEN–N–DUMPLINGS

(See recipe in Oklahoma Specialties Section)

THREE CHEESE CHICKEN

½ cup part skim ricotta
  cheese
¼ cup shredded mozzarella
  cheese
4 tablespoons Parmesan
  cheese, divided

1 tablespoon bread crumbs
½ teaspoon basil
2 chicken breasts, split and
  boned

Yield: 2 servings

Preheat oven to 350°. Combine ricotta, mozzarella, 2 tablespoons Parmesan cheese, bread crumbs and basil in a small bowl. Carefully separate skin from each chicken breast, leaving one side of skin attached. Spoon half of cheese mixture between skin and flesh of each breast half. Pull skin edges under breast; secure with wooden toothpicks. Place chicken, skin side up in shallow baking pan. Bake uncovered about 35 minutes or until chicken is cooked thoroughly and golden brown. Sprinkle with remaining Parmesan cheese just before serving.

Note: To save calories, cholesterol and fat, remove the skin prior to serving. The chicken can be prepared, stuffed and frozen.

PINEAPPLE CHICKEN

4 boneless, skinless chicken
  breasts
⅓ cup low calorie Italian
  salad dressing
1 20–ounce can crushed
  pineapple, drained,
  reserving liquid

2 tablespoons brown sugar
½ teaspoon ground ginger
⅓ cup chopped green
  pepper
¼ cup slivered almonds
1 tablespoon cornstarch

Yield: 4 servings

Flatten chicken breasts slightly with a mallet. Marinate chicken breasts in Italian dressing, pineapple juice, brown sugar and ginger in the refrigerator overnight. Preheat oven to 375°. In a small bowl, combine crushed pineapple, green pepper and almonds. Remove chicken from marinade and spoon pineapple mixture evenly on each chicken breast. Roll chicken up, secure with toothpicks and place seam side down in a baking dish sprayed with non–stick vegetable spray. Pour ¼ cup of marinade over chicken. Cover and bake for 35 minutes. Remove chicken to a platter. In a small pan, combine remaining marinade and chicken dish drippings with cornstarch and cook for 2 minutes until thick. Pour over chicken to serve.

CHICKEN TACOS

1 cup chopped onion
1 clove garlic, minced
2 cups chopped, cooked
  chicken
1 8–ounce can tomato sauce
1 4–ounce can chopped
  green chilies, drained

12 taco shells
2 – 3 cups shredded lettuce
1 – 2 medium tomatoes,
  chopped
2 ounces Monterey Jack
  cheese, shredded

Yield: 6 servings

Spray skillet with non–stick vegetable spray. Over medium heat, add onion and garlic to skillet and allow to cook until tender. Stir in chicken, tomato sauce and green chilies; heat thoroughly. Divide chicken mixture between taco shells. Top with lettuce, tomatoes and cheese.

Note: If you prefer, warm shells in oven while preparing chicken mixture. Also, salsa and low fat yogurt may be added for a slightly different taste, yet keeping the recipe low in calories.

CHICKEN BURROS

Terrific served with no–fat refried beans!

8 6–inch flour tortillas
1 small onion, sliced and
   separated into rings
2 cloves garlic, minced
1 medium green pepper, cut
   into bite–size pieces
1 tablespoon cooking oil

10 ounces boned, skinless
   chicken breasts, cut into
   thin strips
½ cup salsa
2 – 3 cups shredded lettuce
½ cup plain low–fat yogurt
1 – 2 green onions, sliced

Yield: 4 servings

Preheat oven to 300°. Wrap tortillas in foil and place in oven for 10-12 minutes. While tortillas are warming, spray 12–inch skillet with non–stick vegetable spray. Add onion and garlic; stir–fry for 2 minutes. Add green pepper, oil and chicken and continue to stir–fry for additional 2-4 minutes or until chicken begins to lose pink color. Return vegetables to skillet and add salsa. Cook and stir until heated thoroughly. To serve, divide chicken mixture evenly among tortillas. Top with shredded lettuce, yogurt and green onions. Roll up tortillas and enjoy.

CHICKEN FLAUTAS

Great as main dish or as an appetizer served with dips!

2 cups finely shredded
   cooked chicken
⅔ cup chunky style salsa
¼ cup green onion slices
½ teaspoon ground cumin
¼ teaspoon salt

vegetable oil
32 corn tortillas
2 cups (8 ounces) shredded
   Cheddar or Monterey
   Jack cheese

Yield: 8 servings

Preheat oven to 400°. Combine chicken, salsa, onion, cumin and salt; mix well. Heat about ½ inch of oil in small skillet until hot, but not smoking. Quickly fry each tortilla in oil to soften, about 2 seconds on each side. Drain on paper towels. Spoon 1 tablespoon chicken mixture and 1 tablespoon cheese down center of each tortilla. Roll tightly and secure with wooden pick. Place seam–side down on baking sheet. Bake 18 – 20 minutes or until crisp. Serve warm with guacamole, queso, sour cream or additional salsa.

CHICKEN IN SOUR CREAM

2 cups sour cream
1/4 cup lemon juice
4 tablespoons
   Worcestershire sauce
2 tablespoons celery salt
2 teaspoons paprika

1 clove garlic, crushed
2 teaspoons black pepper
6–8 boneless chicken breasts
2 cups fine bread crumbs
1/2 cup melted margarine

Yield: 6–8 servings

Combine sour cream with the next 6 ingredients and mix well. Pour sauce over chicken breasts, cover, and allow to marinate overnight in refrigerator. When ready to cook, preheat oven to 350°. Discard marinade and roll each chicken breast in bread crumbs and place in 9 x 13-inch glass pan. Pour melted margarine over top of chicken. Bake uncovered for 45 to 55 minutes.

Note: Great with Cheese Almond Rice. They can bake at the same time. Add a salad and bread – a great, easy dinner.

SWEET & SOUR GRILLED CHICKEN

Quick, easy & great!

3 tablespoons orange juice
1 tablespoon reduced
   sodium soy sauce
1 tablespoon honey
1 teaspoon lemon–pepper
   seasoning

1/2 teaspoon ground ginger
1/8 teaspoon garlic powder
2–4 skinless, boneless
   chicken breasts

Yield: 2–4 servings

In a shallow dish combine orange juice, soy sauce, honey, lemon–pepper seasoning, ginger and garlic powder. Set aside. Place chicken breasts, between two sheets of plastic wrap. Pound each with a meat mallet until 1/2–inch thick, place in marinade. Cover and refrigerate 4 to 6 hours or overnight. Remove chicken from marinade. Place chicken on grill directly over medium heat. Grill about 10–15 minutes or until tender. Continue brushing with marinade as chicken cooks.

GRILLED BBQ CHICKEN

1 cup vinegar
¼ cup vegetable oil
2 tablespoons salt
½ teaspoon poultry
   seasoning

1 egg
½ teaspoon pepper
½ cup barbecue sauce
5 chicken halves

Yield: 6–8 servings

Make marinade by combining all ingredients except chicken. Place chicken in sealed container; cover with marinade and allow to chill at least 1 hour. Charcoal chicken about 45 minutes, basting with mixture every 15 minutes.

OVEN BARBECUED CHICKEN

(See recipe in Oklahoma Specialties Section)

ONION CRUSTED CHICKEN

4–6 skinless & boneless
   chicken breasts
salt and pepper to taste
1 stick margarine, melted
1 teaspoon dry mustard

1 tablespoon Worcestershire
   sauce
2 2.8–ounce cans fried onion
   rings, crushed

Yield: 4–6 servings

Preheat oven to 350°. Flatten chicken breasts slightly with mallet or edge of plate. Season to taste with salt and pepper. Into melted margarine, combine dry mustard and Worcestershire sauce. Dip chicken pieces in margarine mixture, then roll in onion ring crumbs, making sure to cover thoroughly. Place chicken in buttered 9 x 13-inch pan and top with remaining crumbs. Drizzle any remaining margarine over top. Bake for 30–40 minutes or until chicken is thoroughly cooked.

SOUTH OF THE BORDER STIR FRY

1 pound boneless, skinless
   chicken breasts
2 tablespoons chili powder
2 tablespoons Mexican
   seasoning
2 teaspoons cornstarch
½ cup chicken broth
2 tablespoons olive oil,
   divided

1 cup canned or frozen
   whole kernel corn,
   drained
2 medium tomatoes, seeded
   and diced
1 cup canned black beans,
   drained
½ teaspoon salt

Yield: 4 servings

Cut chicken into thin strips; toss with mixture of chili powder and Mexican seasoning, coating well. Allow to stand 15 minutes. Combine cornstarch and chicken broth; mix well and set aside. In preheated 12–inch skillet, pour 1 tablespoon olive oil, tilting to coat bottom and sides. Allow oil to heat for 2–3 minutes. Add chicken pieces, stir–frying 3–4 minutes or until done. Remove chicken from skillet and set aside. Pour remaining olive oil into skillet and add corn and tomatoes; stir–fry 2 minutes. Return chicken to skillet and add broth mixture, beans and salt; cook, stirring constantly, until thickened. Serve with tortilla chips.

CHICKEN CORDON BLEU

4 boneless skinless chicken
   breasts
1 teaspoon salt
4 thin slices ham
4 thin slices Swiss cheese

1 beaten egg
1 cup bread crumbs
2 tablespoons vegetable oil
1 cup white or red wine

Yield: 4 servings

Preheat oven to 350°. Hammer breasts until ¼-inch thick; sprinkle with salt. Cover each breast with ham and cheese slice (moved to one end) and roll. Dip in egg, roll in bread crumbs and sauté in hot oil until evenly browned. Place browned chicken breasts in 8 x 8-inch baking dish and chill at least 1 hour. Remove from refrigerator, pour wine over chicken, cover and bake 45 minutes.

CILANTRO CHICKEN AND FETTUCCINE

Chicken:
10–12 boneless, skinless
chicken breast halves
salt and pepper to taste
1¼ cups coarsely chopped
fresh cilantro

¼ cup flour
4 teaspoons margarine
¼ cup chicken stock

Cilantro Sauce:
1½ cups grated Parmesan
cheese
2 cloves garlic, peeled
¼ cup softened margarine

1¼ cups coarsely chopped
fresh cilantro
1 cup olive oil

Fettuccine:
1½ pounds fettuccine
noodles
4–6 tablespoons margarine

1¾ cups piñon nuts (pine
nuts)
¼ cup grated Parmesan
cheese

Yield: 10–12 servings

Season chicken with salt and pepper. Roll chicken pieces in light coating of flour and cilantro. Melt margarine in 12-inch skillet. Add chicken breasts and brown lightly on all sides. Add chicken stock, cover pan and allow to simmer 10 minutes. While chicken is simmering, prepare cilantro sauce by placing Parmesan cheese and garlic in bowl of food processor. Blend until paste forms. Add softened margarine and 1¼ cups cilantro; slowly pour olive oil through mixture and continue to process until mixture is creamy. Set aside. Cook fettuccine noodles according to package directions; drain and place on large platter. Toss fettuccine with margarine, pine nuts and Parmesan cheese. Add cilantro sauce, reserving some to use over chicken. Place chicken on second serving platter and sprinkle lightly with any remaining cilantro. Serve with fettuccine.

ITALIAN CHICKEN

A wonderfully different chicken recipe!

1 large chicken, cut up
1 16–ounce package mild
  Italian sausage links
1 medium onion, chopped
1 small red pepper, coarsely
  chopped

1 small green pepper,
  coarsely chopped
6 – 12 small red potatoes,
  whole

Yield: 4–6 servings

Preheat oven to 350°. Place chicken pieces in 9 x 9-inch, lightly greased baking dish; cover and bake 15 minutes. Remove from oven and add sausage links that have been cut into 1-inch pieces, and all remaining ingredients. Return to oven and bake an additional 1½ hours or until chicken is thoroughly cooked.

Note: The sausage gives this recipe a very unusual flavor. Tomato wedges can also be added if desired.

CHICKEN BROCCOLI STIR FRY

2 chicken breasts, skinned
  and boned
3 tablespoons cornstarch
4 tablespoons soy sauce
2 tablespoons vegetable oil
½ pound broccoli, broken
  into small pieces

1 medium onion, sliced
¼ pound mushrooms, sliced
2 cups fresh bean sprouts
  (optional)
1 cup chicken broth
4 cups cooked white rice

Yield: 4 servings

Slice chicken breasts into thin strips and set aside. Combine cornstarch and soy sauce in small bowl; stir until thoroughly combined. Pour sauce over chicken strips and toss to coat well. Allow to stand 15 minutes. Heat oil in wok (or skillet) over high heat. Add chicken and stir fry until browned. Remove chicken from wok. Add broccoli and onions to wok; turn to medium and stir fry 2 minutes. Add mushrooms and bean sprouts; return chicken to wok and stir in chicken broth; skim top of broth to remove fat. Cover and cook for 5 minutes or until vegetables are crisp and tender. Serve with rice.

HONEY MUSTARD GLAZED CHICKEN

½ cup Dijon mustard
¼ cup honey
2 tablespoons lemon juice
1 clove garlic, crushed

¼ teaspoon tarragon leaves
1 fryer chicken, cut up
parsley sprigs for garnish

Yield: 4 servings

In small bowl, mix mustard, honey, lemon juice, garlic and tarragon. Grill or broil chicken about 45 minutes turning occasionally and brushing with mustard mixture frequently.

FRIED CHICKEN, HONEY!

4 boneless, skinless chicken
    breasts, thawed
1 cup flour
½ cup cornflake crumbs
½ cup bread crumbs
1 teaspoon poultry
    seasoning

½ teaspoon garlic powder
½ teaspoon ground black
    pepper
enough honey to coat
    chicken strips

Yield: 2–4 servings

Cut each chicken breast, across the grain into four strips. Mix flour, cornflakes, bread crumbs, poultry seasoning, garlic and black pepper together in a pie dish. Dip each chicken strip into honey, then into crumb mixture. Deep fry at 375° for 2–3 minutes.

Note: As early as I can remember, my grandma and grandpa lived on a farm in Ripley, Oklahoma. I was not more than 3 or 4 years old when I remember my grandma gathering bread crumbs in her apron. I loved to follow her outside to the chicken coop where she would call the chickens over, and I would get to help her drop the bread crumbs to feed the chickens. For some reason, Grandma always seemed to get very "friendly" with the fattest hen of the bunch. Before dinner later in the evening, I remember watching Grandma cleaning the chicken and preparing it for dinner, but years passed before I realized that Grandma didn't buy her chicken at the store. She was becoming "friendly" with the fattest hen for a very special reason — that hen was going to be the evening meal! — Jeanette Clemons

SOUTHERN FRIED CHICKEN

(See recipe in Oklahoma Specialties Section)

CHICKEN IN THE PASTA

Great with turkey, too!

¼ cup chopped onion
1 tablespoon margarine
1 10¾–ounce can cream of
   chicken soup
¾ cup milk
4 ounces sour cream

2 ounces chopped green
   chilies
2 cups chopped cooked
   chicken
8 ounces spaghetti, cooked
1 cup grated Cheddar cheese
pinch of salt

Yield: 6–8 servings

Preheat oven to 350°. In small skillet, sauté chopped onion in margarine until tender. In large bowl, combine sautéd onion with remaining ingredients, except cheese, and pour into greased 9 x 9-inch baking dish. Bake, covered, 20 to 25 minutes. Sprinkle grated cheese on top and return to oven for 5 minutes or until cheese melts.

CHICKEN KABOBS

6 boneless, skinless chicken
   breast halves
2 large green peppers, cut
   into 1½–inch pieces
2 large onions, cut into 18
   wedges

18 medium fresh
   mushrooms
1 8–ounce bottle Italian
   salad dressing
¼ cup soy sauce
¼ cup Worcestershire sauce
2 tablespoons lemon juice

Yield: 6 servings

Cut each chicken breast into three lengthwise strips. Place chicken and remaining ingredients in a glass bowl and stir to coat. Cover and refrigerate 4 hours, stirring occasionally. Remove chicken and vegetables, reserving marinade. Alternately place chicken and vegetables on 18 short skewers. Grill over medium–hot coals, turning and basting with marinade, for 12–15 minutes or until chicken juices run clear.

CHICKEN ENCHILADAS

¼ cup margarine
¼ cup all–purpose flour
1 14–ounce can reduced salt
chicken broth
¾ cup water
1 8–ounce carton lite sour
cream
1 4–ounce can chopped
green chilies
1 4–ounce can chopped
jalapeño peppers

1½ cups shredded, cooked
chicken
1 tablespoon onion powder
8 corn tortillas
1 cup Monterey Jack cheese
shredded
1 cup Cheddar cheese
shredded
chopped fresh parsley
picante sauce
guacamole, optional

Yield: 5–6 servings

Preheat oven to 350°. Melt margarine in medium–sized, heavy sauce-pan over low heat; add flour, stir until smooth. Cook 1 minute. Gradually add broth and water; continue to heat and stir until thickened. Stir in sour cream, green chilies, peppers and onion and blend well. Pour half of sour cream sauce into lightly greased 10 x 13 x 2-inch baking dish, set remaining sauce aside. Heat tortillas in the oven, wrapped in foil, at 300° to soften. Place 2 tablespoons each of chicken and each cheese on tortilla; roll up and place seam down in baking dish. Pour remaining sauce over top. Bake uncovered for 20–25 minutes. Sprinkle any re-maining cheese on top and bake an additional 5 minutes. Garnish with parsley and serve with picante sauce.

SKEWERED COCONUT CHICKEN

8–10 boneless, skinless
chicken breasts
1 cup coconut milk
1 tablespoon brown sugar
1 teaspoon lime juice

1 tablespoon soy sauce
½ teaspoon cayenne pepper
½ teaspoon freshly grated
ginger

Yield: 8 servings

Preheat coals on grill, about 300–400°. Cut chicken breasts into 1 inch strips. In a large mixing bowl, combine remaining ingredients and stir thoroughly. Add chicken strips; toss and allow to marinate at least 1 hour prior to grilling. Thread strips on skewers and grill 3–5 minutes. Brush with marinade, turn and grill an additional 3–5 minutes.

CHICKEN NUGGETS WITH ROYALTY SAUCE

A big hit with the kids!

Nuggets:

6 whole, boneless, skinless
   chicken breasts
2 eggs, beaten
1 cup water
1 cup flour

3 tablespoons sesame seed
1½ teaspoons salt
1 teaspoon Accent
vegetable oil

Royalty Sauce:

1 cup ketchup
½ teaspoon dry mustard
1 tablespoon brown sugar

2 tablespoons vinegar
3 tablespoons margarine

Yield: 4 servings

Cut chicken breasts into 1 by 1½-inch pieces and set aside while making batter. Mix eggs and water; add flour, sesame seed, salt and Accent to make batter. Heat vegetable oil in frying pan, filling pan no more than ⅓ full. Dip chicken pieces into batter; drain off excess batter. Add nuggets to hot oil. Fry 5–8 minutes or until golden brown on both sides and fork can be inserted with ease. Drain on paper towels. While chicken is cooking, make sauce by combining all ingredients in small saucepan on top of stove; cook over low heat 4–5 minutes, stirring frequently. Serve Royalty Sauce as dip for nuggets.

CHICKEN CASHEW CASSEROLE

1 tablespoon margarine
1 5½–ounce can chow mein
   noodles, divided
1 10¾–ounce can cream of
   mushroom soup
¼ cup water

1 cup diced celery
¼ pound cashews
1 cup cooked, diced white
   chicken meat
¼ cup chopped onion
salt and pepper to taste

Yield: 4 servings

Preheat oven to 325°. Melt margarine in 8 x 8-inch glass baking dish. Pour half of chow mein noodles in melted butter. In separate bowl, mix mushroom soup with remaining ingredients and pour over noodles. Sprinkle with remaining noodles and bake 35 minutes.

AZTEC CASSEROLE

1 10¾-ounce can cream of mushroom soup
1 10¾-ounce can cream of chicken soup
1 7-ounce can green salsa sauce or 7-ounce can chopped green chilies (undrained)
¾ cup milk

12 corn tortillas, cut into 1-inch squares
4 boneless and skinless chicken breasts, cooked and cubed
1 small onion, minced
½ pound Monterey Jack cheese, grated
½ pound Cheddar cheese, grated

Yield: 8 servings

In a medium bowl, combine soups, salsa and milk for sauce and set aside. Spray 9 x 13-inch baking dish with non–stick vegetable spray. Alternate layers in dish beginning with a small amount of sauce, tortillas, chicken chunks, onion, sauce and cheeses. Repeat layers, cover and refrigerate overnight to soak and set mixture. Bake in oven preheated to 325° for 1 – 1½ hours or until bubbly.

CHICKEN CASSEROLE

1 8-ounce package seasoned stuffing mix
½ cup margarine, melted
1 10¾-ounce can cream of chicken soup
1 10¾-ounce can cream of celery soup

1 5-ounce can evaporated milk
1 cup chicken broth
2 cups diced cooked chicken
1½ cups frozen English peas
2 tablespoons finely chopped celery
2 tablespoons minced onions

Yield: 8–10 servings

Preheat oven to 350°. Mix stuffing and margarine together in small mixing bowl. Spread half of the stuffing mixture on the bottom of a 9 x 13-inch casserole dish. Mix together the remaining ingredients and pour over stuffing layer. Top with remaining stuffing and bake 30 minutes, uncovered. Allow to stand 10 to 20 minutes before serving.

BRUNSWICK STEW

Grandmother's fool–proof cure for any ailment!

2 – 3 pounds frying chicken, cut up
2 teaspoons salt
2 teaspoons pepper
1 tablespoon Worcestershire sauce
2 cups dry white wine
1 cup diced onions

1 cup chopped celery
2 cups lima beans
2 16–ounce cans whole tomatoes
4 tablespoons flour
1 stick butter, melted
4 cups frozen corn

Yield: 6 servings

Place chicken in large pot and add 3 quarts of cold water. Bring to a boil, reduce to simmer, and cook for 1 hour. Skim off all fat. Add salt, pepper, Worcestershire sauce, white wine and vegetables, except corn. Cover and simmer 30 minutes. Blend flour and butter together, and add slowly, stirring to thicken broth. Add corn and cook 10 minutes longer.

CHICKEN GUMBO

½ cup chopped onion
½ cup slivered green pepper
1 cup chopped celery
1 tablespoon margarine
3 cups chicken broth
2 cups canned or peeled fresh tomatoes
1 bay leaf
¼ teaspoon thyme
1 cup sliced okra (fresh or frozen)

2 tablespoons chopped parsley
¼ teaspoon Tabasco sauce
½ teaspoon gumbo filé
salt to taste
3 cups cooked chicken pieces
6 cups cooked rice
lemon slices

Yield: 6 servings

In Dutch oven, sauté onion, green pepper and celery in margarine until soft. Add remaining ingredients except chicken, rice and lemon slices and allow to simmer 30 minutes. Add chicken pieces and heat thoroughly. Serve as a main dish over rice. Always serve with a slice of lemon whether used as a soup or entree.

Note: Recipe can be varied by adding whole cooked shrimp, chopped ham or both.

CROCK POT CHICKEN CURRY

2 whole chicken breasts,
  boned
½ cup margarine
½ cup flour
1½ teaspoons salt
dash pepper
2½ cups milk

¼ cup dry sherry (optional)
2 green onions with tops,
  finely chopped
1 teaspoon curry powder
3 cups cooked white rice or
  saffron rice

Yield: 2–4 servings

Cut chicken into bite–size pieces and set aside. In medium saucepan, melt margarine; blend in flour, salt and pepper, stirring until smooth. Gradually add milk and continue to stir until thickened. Pour mixture into crock pot set on low setting. Stir chicken, sherry, onions and curry powder into crock pot, cover, and cook 4 to 6 hours; taste for seasoning. If necessary, thicken with paste made of water and flour before serving. Serve over rice.

Note: Good to prepare on Sunday morning before church.

SOUTHWEST CHICKEN CHILI

¼ cup olive oil
8 medium garlic cloves,
  minced
2 large onions, chopped
4 medium red peppers,
  chopped
2 medium bell peppers,
  chopped
3 tablespoons chili powder
2 teaspoons cumin
¼ teaspoon cayenne pepper
1 28–ounce can tomatoes

2 13¾–ounce cans chicken
  broth
2 pounds boneless chicken
  breasts, cooked and
  diced
2 19–ounce cans kidney
  beans, drained
1 12–ounce jar salsa
1 10–ounce package frozen
  corn
1 teaspoon black pepper
salt to taste

Yield: 6 servings

Pour olive oil in large pan or Dutch oven. Sauté garlic, onion and peppers over high heat. Add chili powder, cumin and cayenne pepper; allow to cook 1 minute, stirring constantly. Add canned tomatoes, breaking them up with a spoon. Add chicken broth, reduce heat to medium low, and allow to simmer 15 minutes. Add remaining ingredients, cover pan and increase heat until mixture begins to boil. Reduce heat, and allow chili to simmer 30 minutes. Add black pepper and salt to taste.

SUSAN'S MEATLESS CHILI

(See recipe in Oklahoma Specialties Section)

WHITE CHILI

1 pound large white beans
6 cups chicken broth
2 cloves garlic, minced
2 medium onions, chopped,
    divided
2 tablespoons oil
2 4–ounce cans chopped
    green chilies

2 teaspoons ground cumin
1½ teaspoons dried oregano
¼ teaspoon ground cloves
¼ teaspoon cayenne pepper
4 cups diced cooked chicken
    breasts
3 cups grated Monterey Jack
    cheese

Yield: 6 servings

Combine beans, chicken broth, garlic and half the onions in a large soup pot and bring to a boil. Reduce heat and simmer until beans are very soft, approximately 3–4 hours. Add more chicken broth if necessary. In a separate skillet, sauté remaining onions in oil until tender. Add chilies and seasonings and mix thoroughly. Add to bean mixture. Add chicken and continue to simmer one hour. Serve topped with grated cheese.

Note: For a buffet, serve with some or all of the following condiments: chopped tomatoes, chopped parsley, chopped ripe olives, guacamole, chopped scallions, sour cream, crumbled tortilla chips or salsa.

JOE'S GREEN CHILI STEW

(See recipe in Oklahoma Specialties Section)

CORNISH HEN WITH
ALMOND RICE STUFFING

2 tablespoons slivered
  almonds
2 tablespoons finely
  chopped onion
⅓ cup uncooked long grain
  rice
3 tablespoons margarine
1 cup water

1 chicken bouillon cube
1 teaspoon lemon juice
½ teaspoon salt
1 3-ounce can chopped
  mushrooms, drained
2 1-pound Cornish hens
½ cup melted margarine

Yield: 2 servings

Preheat oven to 350°. In small saucepan, cook almonds, onion and rice in melted margarine until onions are tender. Add water, bouillon, lemon juice and salt. Cover and continue to cook approximately 20 minutes or until rice is done. Stir mushrooms into rice mixture and set aside. Thoroughly clean hens; salt and pepper inside and outside. Stuff birds with rice. Bake for approximately 1½ hours until golden brown and tender. While hens are cooking, brush with melted margarine every 15 minutes.

GRILLED TURKEY BREAST

A wonderful twist for turkey!

5 pound turkey breast
2 cups white sauterne or
  Chablis wine
1 cup peanut oil

1 cup soy sauce
2 lemons, sliced
2 cloves garlic

Yield: 10-12 servings

With turkey still slightly frozen, slice into small strips. In large pan or dish with cover, combine remaining ingredients and mix well. Place raw turkey strips in mixture and allow to marinate in refrigerator for 5 to 6 hours. Cook turkey strips over hot grill for 5 minutes.

Note: This makes turkey taste like nothing you've ever had before!

OLD OKLAHOMA CAT FISH FRY

(See recipe in Oklahoma Specialties Section)

OVEN-FRIED CATFISH SANDWICHES

A "Lake Weekend" specialty!

8 catfish fillets
salt and pepper to taste
2 cups finely crushed
  cornflakes
1 cup grated Parmesan
  cheese
1½ teaspoons paprika
½ teaspoon garlic salt
¼ teaspoon ground red
  pepper

4 egg whites
8 large sandwich buns
1 cup fat-free Thousand
  Island salad dressing
8 slices mozzarella cheese
16 slices bacon, cooked &
  drained
tomato slices
lettuce leaves

Yield: 8 servings

Preheat oven to 400°. Cut catfish fillets to make 8 sandwich size pieces. Sprinkle catfish with salt and pepper. In a medium bowl combine cornflake crumbs, Parmesan cheese, paprika, garlic salt and red pepper. In shallow bowl, beat egg whites until foamy. Dip each catfish piece into egg whites and coat with cereal crumb mixture. Place in a 9 x 13-inch baking dish that has been prepared with non-stick cooking spray. Bake 25 to 30 minutes, until fish flakes easily. Wrap sandwich buns in aluminum foil and place in oven during last 5 minutes of baking. To assemble, spread salad dressing evenly over both halves of bun. Place 1 piece of catfish, 1 slice of cheese, 2 bacon slices, tomato and lettuce on bottom of each bun. Replace top of bun and enjoy.

LOW FAT FISH "FRY"

1 egg white
⅓ cup dried bread crumbs
2 tablespoons grated
   Parmesan cheese

¾ teaspoon dried basil
¼ teaspoon pepper
½ teaspoon salt
4 6-ounce fish fillets

Tartar Sauce:
½ cup nonfat mayonnaise-
   type salad dressing
¼ cup finely chopped dill
   pickles
1 tablespoon chopped
   parsley
2 teaspoons lemon juice

1½ teaspoons Tabasco
   sauce
¼ teaspoon salt
Basil sprigs and lemon
   wedge for garnish –
   beautiful!

Yield: 4 servings

Preheat oven to 450°. In pie plate, with fork, beat egg white slightly; set aside. On wax paper, mix bread crumbs, Parmesan cheese, dried basil, pepper and salt. Dip fish fillets in egg white, then bread crumb mixture to coat. Place fillets on ungreased cookie sheet; bake 10–12 minutes without turning fish, or until fish flakes easily when tested with a fork. After this point, if you prefer a golden brown bread coating, broil the fish at the closest position to the heat source for 2 minutes. While fish is baking, combine all sauce ingredients in small bowl and mix well. Spoon sauce on fish fillets to serve.

Note: Fish Fries at our house when I was growing up always brought in both relatives and neighbors alike. All day Saturday was spent cleaning house and completing the last of the many chores by mopping and waxing the kitchen floor. Late in the afternoon after a long day of fishing, my father would proudly parade his large stringer of fish, first outside to all the neighbor kids playing baseball in the front yard, then through the house to the kitchen sink. Even the dripping fish didn't seem to bother me too much because I knew a giant fish fry was quickly approaching. Any relatives who happened to be visiting, couldn't resist the temptation to stay for dinner and Dad always invited anyone else who enjoyed a good ole' fashioned fish fry. It was usually summertime, when all the garden vegetables were the freshest. Home–grown tomatoes, sweet onions, fried okra and fried potatoes with more fish than we could eat, helped make Saturday nights in Oklahoma a life–long memory. — Jeanette Clemons

COUBILLION (KOO–BEE–ON)

A great way to serve the catch of the day!

4 tablespoons vegetable oil
1 medium onion, chopped
2 celery stalks, chopped
1 small bell pepper, chopped
salt & pepper to taste
1 teaspoon garlic powder

3 8–ounce cans tomato
  sauce
4 ounces white cooking wine
1 bay leaf
8–10 fish fillets
cooked rice

Yield: 8 servings

In electric skillet, pour in oil, and make a roux by sautéing vegetables with the seasonings until very brown, but being careful not to allow vegetables to burn. Add tomato sauce, cooking wine and bay leaf; cover, turn skillet on low and allow to simmer for 30 minutes. Add fish fillets, cover and allow to cook an additional 30 minutes or until flaky. Remove bay leaf and serve over cooked rice.

Note: This recipe is great using bass or crappie. Instead of using whole fillets, try cutting them into bite–size pieces.

SEAFOOD AND SUMMER VEGETABLES

1 tablespoon vegetable oil
4 small new potatoes, sliced
½ red onion, sliced
½ teaspoon white pepper
½ teaspoon thyme
¼ teaspoon salt
¼ teaspoon garlic powder
4 lemon slices

1 pound perch or haddock
1 medium zucchini, thinly
  sliced
1 medium green pepper,
  chopped
1 medium tomato, chopped
¼ cup white wine

Yield: 4–6 servings

Preheat oven to 375°. In skillet, heat oil, sliced potatoes, onion, and seasonings. Cover and cook 15 minutes, stirring occasionally. Meanwhile, place lemon slices in a 9 x 9-inch baking dish. Place fish over lemon slices and top with zucchini, green pepper and tomatoes; pour on wine. Spoon potato mixture with liquid over tomatoes. Cover and bake 25 minutes.

CATFISH BEER BATTER

1 cup flour	1 teaspoon soda
1 egg	dash of garlic powder
1 cup beer	

Yield: 1½ cups batter

Beat all ingredients together in medium size bowl. Batter will be thin. Season catfish with salt and pepper before dipping into batter. Fry in hot oil until golden brown and fish will flake with a fork.

Note: This recipe is easily doubled or tripled for larger groups.

FLOUNDER STUFFED WITH CRABMEAT

¼ cup chopped onion	½ cup saltine cracker
¼ cup margarine	crumbs
1 3–ounce can mushrooms,	2 tablespoons parsley
drained, reserving liquid	½ teaspoon salt
1 7½–ounce can crabmeat	8 flounder fillets

Sauce:

3 tablespoons margarine	⅓ cup dry white wine
3 tablespoons flour	1 cup shredded Swiss cheese
¼ teaspoon salt	½ teaspoon paprika
1–1½ cups milk	

Yield: 6–8 servings

Preheat oven to 400°. To prepare stuffing, in a small skillet, cook onion in margarine until tender. Stir in drained mushrooms, crabmeat, cracker crumbs, parsley and salt, and combine well. To stuff fillets, place flounder fillets skin side down; spread even amount of stuffing mixture in middle of fillets. Bring both ends of fish up and overlap. Place each stuffed fillet, seam side down in a 12 x 7 x 2-inch baking dish. To prepare sauce, melt butter in small saucepan; blend in flour and salt. Add enough milk to mushroom juice to make 1½ cups of liquid and add to mixture along with white wine. Cook sauce until thickened. Pour evenly over fillets. Bake for 25 minutes and remove from oven. Sprinkle cheese and paprika over fillets and return to oven for an additional 10 minutes or until cheese is melted.

CRAB VERMICELLI

2 6–ounce packages frozen
   king crab
¾ cup margarine, divided
2 tablespoons olive oil
5 large shallots, sliced
½ cup chopped parsley

1 2–ounce jar chopped
   pimiento, drained
2 tablespoons lemon juice
½ teaspoon Italian seasoning
1 pound vermicelli
croutons
grated Parmesan cheese

Yield: 4–6 servings

Thaw crab meat, reserving liquid. Heat ½ cup margarine with olive oil and sauté shallots. Break crab into chunks and add, with liquid, to sautéd shallots. Stir in parsley, pimiento, lemon juice and Italian seasoning; heat 8 to 10 minutes. Prepare vermicelli according to package directions; drain but do not rinse. While vermicelli is still hot, toss with ¼ cup margarine. To serve, ladle sauce over vermicelli and top with croutons and Parmesan cheese.

SHRIMP WITH SNOW PEAS

Simple, yet elegant!

12 large uncooked shrimp,
   in the shell
8 ounces snow peas
3 tablespoons virgin olive oil

1 tablespoon finely shredded
   fresh ginger
1 medium lime, juiced and
   peel grated
1 tablespoon soy sauce

Yield: 2 servings

Shell shrimp, leaving tail shells intact; remove veins and set shrimp aside. Remove ends and strings from snow peas and place in medium saucepan; cover with water and bring to a boil. Allow snow peas to boil 1 minute; drain and arrange on plates. In 12–inch skillet, heat olive oil. Add shrimp and ginger and cook gently, 5 minutes or until shrimp turn pink. Gently turn shrimp over halfway through cooking time. Add lime juice, grated lime peel and soy sauce. Cook 1 additional minute. Remove shrimp from pan and arrange atop snow peas; pour hot pan juices over shrimp and serve.

COCONUT–BEER SHRIMP WITH SPICY ORANGE DIP

1 pound medium size fresh
   shrimp
2¼ teaspoons red pepper
1⅛ teaspoons salt
1 teaspoon pepper
¾ teaspoon paprika
¼ teaspoon garlic powder
½ teaspoon onion powder
½ teaspoon ground thyme
½ teaspoon ground oregano

¾ cup, plus 2 tablespoons
   flour
¼ cup, plus 2 tablespoons
   beer
1 egg, beaten
½ teaspoon baking powder
1 7–ounce package flaked
   coconut
vegetable oil

Spicy Orange Dip:
1 10–ounce jar orange
   marmalade
3 tablespoons prepared
   horseradish

3 tablespoons spicy brown
   mustard
½ teaspoon grated lemon
   rind

Yield: 2–4 servings

Peel and devein shrimp, leaving tails on. Rinse and set aside. In small bowl, combine all seasonings. In separate bowl, combine flour, beer, egg and baking powder and mix well. Dip shrimp into seasoning and shake off excess. Dip seasoned shrimp into beer batter and dredge in coconut. Fry shrimp, 5 or 6 at a time in deep, hot oil (350°) about 15 seconds or until golden. Drain on paper towels and serve with spicy orange dip. To prepare dip, combine all ingredients in a small bowl and mix well.

VICTORIAN SHRIMP

1 medium onion, chopped
1 pound raw shrimp, shelled
   & deveined
2 tablespoons margarine
1 8–ounce can sliced
   mushrooms, drained

1 tablespoon flour
salt & pepper, to taste
1 cup sour cream
4 cups cooked rice

Yield: 4 servings

In skillet, sauté onion and shrimp in margarine for 10 minutes. Add mushrooms and sauté an additional 5 minutes. Stir in flour until smooth; add salt and pepper to taste. Add sour cream and simmer additional 10 minutes, stirring frequently. Serve hot over a bed of rice.

SNYDER SHRIMP

A bib & finger towel dish!

1 pound medium shrimp,
   shelled & deveined
juice of 1½ lemons
2½ sticks real butter, melted
3 cloves garlic, minced
2 teaspoons cracked pepper
½ teaspoon dry mustard

½ teaspoon Tabasco sauce
2 dashes Worcestershire
   sauce
½ teaspoon oregano
¼ teaspoon cayenne pepper
2 tablespoons dried parsley
   flakes

Yield: 2–3 servings

Arrange shrimp in single layer in 9 x 13–inch baking dish. Mix all remaining ingredients together and pour over shrimp. Broil approximately 14 minutes or until the shrimp turns pink.

SHRIMP FETTUCCINE

6–8 pounds medium to large shrimp, peeled
½ stick margarine
1 tablespoon vegetable oil
2 cloves garlic, chopped
1 teaspoon onion salt
1 teaspoon salt
1 teaspoon coarse ground pepper
1 teaspoon oregano
1 bunch green onions, sliced
1 14–ounce can artichokes, drained & quartered
1 14–ounce can roma tomatoes, drained & chopped
1 4½–ounce can sliced black olives
1 cup sliced fresh mushrooms, drained
1 cup white wine
½ cup chicken bouillon
2 ½ pint cartons whipping cream
1 12–ounce package fettuccine noodles

Yield: 6–8 servings

In large soup pot, boil shrimp until light pink; drain and set aside. Shrimp should not be allowed to overcook – (will cook additional time when added to sauce). In large skillet, heat margarine and oil. Over medium to high heat, sauté garlic and next 9 ingredients until thoroughly heated. Increase temperature to high, add white wine and chicken bouillon and heat additional 5 to 10 minutes. Blend in whipping cream and drained shrimp. Additional salt and pepper may be added to taste; heat 5 minutes. Prepare fettucine noodles according to package directions and drain. Serve hot shrimp and sauce over bed of fettuccine noodles.

SHRIMP CREOLE

½ cup chopped onion
1 4–ounce can chopped
  mushrooms, drain,
  reserve liquid
½ cup diagonally sliced
  celery
1 clove garlic, minced
3 tablespoons margarine
1 tablespoon flour

1 teaspoon sugar
1 teaspoon salt
1 tablespoon chili powder
water
2 cups canned tomatoes
1 tablespoon vinegar
1½ pounds cooked shrimp
steamed rice

Yield: 4 servings

In medium saucepan, sauté onions, mushrooms, celery and garlic in melted margarine until tender. Stir in flour, sugar, salt and chili powder, mixing well. Add water to mushroom liquid to equal one cup, pour into mixture, and allow to simmer 15 minutes. Add tomatoes, vinegar and shrimp and simmer additional 10 minutes. Serve over hot rice.

CHUCKWAGON BEAN BAKE

(See recipe in Oklahoma Specialties Section)

RED BEANS AND RICE

1 cup cooked rice
3 16–ounce cans red beans,
  drained
¼ teaspoon oregano
4 drops Tabasco sauce
1 tablespoon soy sauce
1 tablespoon garlic salt
1 small hot green chili
  pepper, diced

1 small hot red chili pepper,
  diced
1 tablespoon balsamic
  vinegar
¾ pound smoked sausage
2 tablespoons olive oil
1 pound colby cheese, finely
  grated

Yield: 6 servings

Over medium heat, combine all ingredients except sausage, oil and cheese in a large saucepan or Dutch oven. While simmering, cut smoked sausage in ½–inch slices and brown in olive oil. Add to bean mixture and continue to simmer for 20 to 30 minutes. When ready to serve, transfer beans to a serving bowl and top with grated cheese. Cover with lid or foil long enough to allow cheese to melt. Serve hot.

SOUTHERN JAMBALAYA

6 tablespoons vegetable oil, divided
1 pound smoked or Cajun sausage
(cut into ½–inch thick diagonal slices)
3½ pounds boneless chicken breasts
(cut into 2–3-inch pieces)
1 teaspoon cayenne pepper
3 large celery stalks, thinly sliced
1 large onion, coarsely chopped
2 large bell peppers, diced
3 cloves garlic, minced
1 tablespoon dried thyme, crumbled
3 cups long–grain rice
3 16–ounce cans Italian plum tomatoes
2–3½ cups chicken broth
2 cups bottled clam juice
1½ pounds medium shrimp, peeled & deveined
Tabasco sauce, salt, to taste

Yield: 12 servings

Preheat oven to 350° Heat 3 tablespoons oil in large, heavy skillet over medium heat. Add sausage and sauté until brown. Transfer sausage to medium bowl using slotted spoon; reserve drippings. Sprinkle both sides of chicken with cayenne pepper; sauté in sausage drippings, turning occasionally, until brown and thoroughly cooked, about 5 minutes. Transfer to bowl with sausage. Heat remaining 3 tablespoons of oil in skillet over medium heat; add celery, onions and bell peppers, cooking until onions are transparent. Add garlic and thyme and continue to cook an additional minute. Add rice to skillet and stir until coated with oil. Divide rice mixture between two 9 x 13-inch baking dishes. Drain juice from one can of tomatoes and discard juice. Add those tomatoes with 2 cups chicken broth, clam juice and remaining 2 cans of tomatoes and bring to boil, breaking up tomatoes with spoon. Divide mixture between baking dishes of rice, cover with foil and bake 35 minutes. Remove from oven and arrange shrimp, chicken and sausage over rice. If rice has absorbed most of liquid, add ¾ cup chicken broth to each baking dish. Cover and bake until rice is tender, shrimp are pink and chicken and sausage are hot, approximately 15–20 minutes. Stir gently before serving. Serve with Tabasco sauce and salt to taste.

"OKIE" GOOD LUCK PEAS

(See recipe in Oklahoma Specialties Section)

PANHANDLE BEANS

(See recipe in Oklahoma Specialties Section)

CAJUN BLACK BEANS AND RICE

A classic made easy!

2 15–ounce cans black
  beans, drained & rinsed
1 cup chopped onion
1 cup chopped green onion
½ cup chopped parsley
  (optional)
1 tablespoon garlic salt
¼ teaspoon dried oregano

1 tablespoon Worcestershire
  sauce
1 teaspoon pepper
1½ teaspoons hot sauce
1 8–ounce can tomato sauce
1 teaspoon red pepper
1 pound smoked sausage cut
  into ¼–inch slices
6 cups hot cooked rice

Yield: 4–6 servings

In large saucepan, combine all ingredients except sausage and rice. Allow to cook, over medium heat, approximately 30 minutes or until flavors begin to combine. In separate pan, brown sausage slices, drain and add to bean mixture. Cover and simmer 45 minutes, adding water if necessary. Serve over rice.

PIZZA CASSEROLE

1 medium onion, chopped
1 bunch green onions,
   chopped
1 green pepper, chopped
⅓ cup margarine
½ teaspoon salt
8 ounces fresh mushrooms,
   sliced
1 clove garlic, minced
1 teaspoon oregano
⅛ teaspoon tarragon,
   optional

1 28–ounce jar spaghetti
   sauce
1 12–ounce package egg
   noodles
1 6–ounce package sliced
   pepperoni
1 cup cooked sausage,
   drained
1 cup grated Muenster
   cheese
1 cup grated Monterey Jack
   cheese

Yield: 8–10 servings

Preheat oven to 350°. Sauté onions and green pepper in margarine for 6 minutes. Add salt, mushrooms, garlic, spices and spaghetti sauce to mixture and set aside. Cook noodles according to package directions and drain. In buttered 9 x 13-inch casserole dish, layer half of the cooked noodles, pepperoni slices, sausage, sauce mixture and cheeses. Repeat layers. Bake for 30 minutes or until bubbly. Serve warm.

GRILLED LAMB MARINADE

⅓ cup olive oil
¼ cup lemon juice

2 cloves garlic, minced
4 1–inch lamb chops

Yield: 4 servings

Mix olive oil, lemon juice and garlic. Pour over well–trimmed lamb chops and marinate in refrigerator at least 1 hour. Bring meat to room temperature and grill chops 5 minutes each side.

AMARETTO SAUCE FOR BAKED HAM

⅓ cup apricot juice
1 cup brown sugar
¼ cup amaretto

2 tablespoons lemon juice
1 tablespoon dry mustard

Yield: ½ cup

Mix all sauce ingredients together in small bowl until brown sugar is dissolved. Pour sauce over the top of scored ham and bake according to ham size.

BARBECUE SAUCE

½ cup vegetable oil
¾ cup chopped onion
¾ cup ketchup
¾ cup water
⅓ cup lemon juice
3 tablespoons sugar

3 tablespoons
   Worcestershire sauce
2 tablespoons prepared
   mustard
2 teaspoons salt
½ teaspoon pepper

Yield: 2½ cups

In medium saucepan sauté onion in oil until soft. Add remaining ingredients and allow to simmer 15 minutes.

Note: This sauce is best on chicken since it has a very light consistency.

TERIYAKI MARINADE

2 cups soy sauce
4 tablespoons whiskey
¾ cup sugar

4 teaspoons ginger
4 cloves garlic, minced

Yield: 2¼ cups

Mix all ingredients well and pour over meat. Cover and refrigerate, allowing to set at least 4 hours. This marinade works well with chicken, steak or burgers.

FLO'S BARBECUE SAUCE

1 cup apple cider vinegar
1 cup water
⅓ cup ketchup
1 onion, finely chopped
2 cloves garlic, chopped
1 teaspoon Worcestershire
   sauce

1 teaspoon celery seed
1 teaspoon black pepper
1 teaspoon paprika
1 teaspoon red pepper
1 pound brown sugar
1 stick margarine

Yield: 1 quart

In a medium saucepan, combine all ingredients, bring to boil, and allow to simmer approximately 20 minutes. When cool, pour into quart jar to store in refrigerator.

BAR–B–QUICK SAUCE

1 cup ketchup
1 tablespoon Worcestershire
   sauce

4 tablespoons brown sugar
4 tablespoons vinegar
2 tablespoons liquid smoke

Yield: 1¾ cups

In medium saucepan mix ingredients and simmer over low heat for 10 minutes, until thoroughly blended.

WOOD'S CAJUN BIRD MARINADE

1 cup vegetable oil
1 cup vinegar
2 tablespoons pepper
1 tablespoon cayenne
   pepper

1 cup prepared barbecue
   sauce
2 tablespoons salt
1 teaspoon Tabasco sauce
3 tablespoons dry mustard
2 teaspoons garlic salt

Yield: 3 cups

Mix all ingredients well and pour over bird that has been placed in a pan or dish appropriate to type of poultry. Marinate in refrigerator for a minimum of 3 hours (up to 12 hours), turning occasionally to spread marinade over bird. Take bird from marinade and bake or grill as desired.

BROWN SUGAR BEER GLAZE

Great combination of flavors for ham!

2 12–ounce cans beer
3 tablespoons Dijon mustard
1 cup firmly packed brown
   sugar

1 8–ounce can frozen orange
   juice, thawed

Bring all ingredients to a boil in medium saucepan. Allow to boil 2 minutes and remove from heat. Score ham, pour glaze on top and bake as needed for particular size ham. During cooking time, baste ham with glaze.

SALSA CRUDA

(See recipe in Oklahoma Specialties Section)

CAFE
OKLAHOMA

SWEETS

TERRITORIAL LADIES
AND TERRITORIAL "LADIES"

Settling the Oklahoma Territory took a special breed of man – and a special breed of woman.

Territorial women were enormously inventive, and enormously accomplished in the art of "making do". There was often no sugar, so they made do with sorghum. Cloth was precious, so after the kids' clothes were made, the scraps became beautiful quilts. Lumber was at a premium, so they helped their husbands build their first homes out of blocks of the tough sod cut from the prairie. And as the wagons passed each other on the plains, the women greeted each other by exchanging favorite recipes.

The customs of their time may have made them defer to the men, but still they thought for themselves, and they broke new ground in more ways than one.

There was the minister's wife from northwestern Oklahoma with the hatred of alcohol and the will to do something about it. As a leader of the Women's Christian Temperance Union, she roamed through Oklahoma Territory and Kansas for 15 years, denouncing strong drink and smashing with a hatchet the saloons that served it. She entered American legend as Carrie Nation, and her crusade had a resounding effect. On November 16, 1907 – Statehood Day – no fewer than 556 Oklahoma saloons had to close simultaneously, and for good. The new State was entering the Union as a dry State.

From Harrison, Arkansas, came Anne Ione Murphy, arriving a month after the Run. A beautiful 19-year-old, her father was establishing a law practice in the new city of Oklahoma City and, together with the rest of their family, they leased rooms from the very prominent – and very eligible – Henry Overholser. One thing led to another, and the following Spring the two were wed in a quiet ceremony in one of Henry's new red brick buildings downtown. Together, they helped set the tone for the city's cultural life, beginning with the Overholser Opera House and leading up to the rambling mansion they built just north of the burgeoning business district. Today it's a museum remembering their times, where you can almost hear the echoes of the dances and poetry readings they delighted in hosting.

Just as influential, although perhaps less reputable, was Anne Wynn. Intelligent, shrewd and possessed of a flair for fashion, "Big Anne" pitched a tent adjacent to the Santa Fe Railroad depot shack on the Day of the Run and proceeded to establish one of the West's poshest brothels. It grew over time into a discreet gathering place for much of the City's elite – they used to say that more business got transacted in Anne's parlor than in the mayor's office. For the better part of two decades "The Queen of the Red Light District" remained a power in the City's politics, until she was forced to leave the Territory.

Other Territorial women left us their achievements, but not their names. The women who waited at the starting line in the heavy wagons loaded with family and furniture, keeping the horses reined in while husbands raced ahead on horseback to stake claims. The woman who made the Run on foot – and kicked off her petticoat in midstride when the heavy garment got in her way. The "Button Woman" who wandered the streets of the new city, making a living by mending torn garments for "two bits." Their strength and determination is as much a part of Oklahoma history as any treaty or act of government.

And, comically (or tragically, depending on how things are going for you at the moment), there's the story of Bethsheba, the women-only town. Founded just after the Cherokee Strip Run of 1893, the residents had just had enough of men. So much so that a town ordinance forbade entry to all males – of any species whatever: no roosters, no stallions, no billygoats. To top it off, there was a shotgun-wielding sheriff in a long black dress to enforce it, too.

Whatever merit the idea may have had, it was short-lived: Bethsheba disappeared into legend.

Although the philosophy it stood for will probably never vanish entirely.

WHITE CHOCOLATE DREAMS

½ cup sugar
¼ cup firmly packed brown
    sugar
1 stick real butter, room
    temperature
1 teaspoon vanilla
1 egg

1 cup flour
½ teaspoon baking powder
½ teaspoon salt
1 cup white chocolate
    chunks
1 cup chopped macadamia
    nuts

Yield: 2 dozen

Preheat oven to 350°. Beat sugars with butter, vanilla and egg until smooth. Mix dry ingredients, then blend into sugar mixture. Add chocolate and nuts; mix well. Cover and refrigerate dough at least one hour. Drop by teaspoonful on cookie sheet that has been prepared with non-stick vegetable spray. Bake for 10–12 minutes on high rack below broiler, so chocolate on bottom of cookies will not scorch.

(A 10–ounce bag of vanilla milk chips may be substituted for white chocolate, if necessary.)

Note: This recipe, submitted by Margaret Kidd Robertson, won a baking contest at the State Fair of Oklahoma sponsored by a national cookie company.

MAMA'S BUTTER COOKIES

Gone in a minute!

Cookies:
1 pound real butter,
    softened
1¼ cups sugar

4 cups all–purpose flour
1½ teaspoons vanilla

Icing:
¼ cup real butter, softened
¼ cup milk

¼ teaspoon vanilla
2–3 cups powdered sugar

Yield: 4 dozen

Preheat oven to 350°. Cream together softened butter and sugar; gradually add flour and vanilla making sure to mix well. Drop by teaspoonful onto greased cookie sheet and make indentations on each with your thumb. Bake 10–12 minutes. For icing, combine softened butter with milk and vanilla; mix well. Add powdered sugar until thick. Fill each cookie indentation with icing and allow to set.

CHEESECAKE COOKIES

Absolutely fabulous!

1 cup real butter, softened	2 cups sugar
2 3–ounce packages cream cheese, softened	2 cups flour
	1 cup chopped pecans

Yield: 2 dozen

Preheat oven to 350°. Cream together butter and cream cheese; add sugar, beating until light and fluffy. Add flour and beat well. Stir in pecans. Drop by teaspoonful onto ungreased cookie sheet and bake for 12 minutes.

SANTA'S WHISKERS

Perfect for Christmas!

1 cup margarine, softened	¾ cup finely chopped red candied cherries
1 cup sugar	¾ cup finely chopped green candied cherries
2 tablespoons milk	½ cup chopped pecans
2 teaspoons vanilla	¾ cup flaked coconut
2½ cups flour	

Yield: 3 dozen

Preheat oven to 375°. In large bowl, cream together margarine and sugar. Blend in milk and vanilla. Stir in flour, candied cherries and nuts. Form into 2–3 rolls and roll each into coconut, coating the outside. Wrap in foil and chill overnight. Slice each roll into ¼-inch thick cookies and place on an ungreased cookie sheet. Bake for 12 minutes or until edges are golden.

COCOA KISS COOKIES

1 cup margarine, room
   temperature
$\frac{2}{3}$ cup sugar
1 teaspoon vanilla
1$\frac{2}{3}$ cups flour
$\frac{1}{4}$ cup cocoa powder

1 cup finely chopped pecans
1 9–ounce package milk
   chocolate kisses (about
   54)
powdered sugar

Yield: 4½ dozen

Preheat oven to 375°. Cream margarine, sugar and vanilla in large bowl. In separate bowl, combine flour and cocoa; blend into creamed mixture. Add pecans and beat on low speed until well-blended. Chill dough about 1 hour or until firm enough to handle. Meanwhile, unwrap kisses. Shape scant tablespoon of dough around each chocolate kiss covering completely. Shape into balls and place on ungreased cookie sheet. Bake 10–12 minutes. Cool slightly, remove to wire rack and allow all to cool completely; roll in powdered sugar.

KAHLÚA PECAN BALLS

2 cups chocolate sandwich
   cookie crumbs
   (approximately 22
   cookies)
½ cup powdered sugar
2 tablespoons cocoa powder

2 tablespoons light corn
   syrup
$\frac{1}{3}$ cup Kahlúa
1 cup chopped pecans
$\frac{1}{4}$ cup sugar

Yield: 3 dozen

In a large bowl, thoroughly mix all ingredients. Refrigerate and allow to chill for 1 hour. Roll dough into 1–inch balls and store in air tight container.

PEANUT BUTTER COOKIES

An old favorite stand–by.

1 cup margarine, softened
1 cup granulated sugar
1 cup firmly packed brown
  sugar
1 teaspoon salt

2 eggs
1 cup peanut butter
2½ cups flour
1 teaspoon baking soda

Yield: 3 dozen

Preheat oven to 375°. In large bowl, combine all ingredients, mixing well. Roll into 1-inch balls and place at least 1 inch apart on ungreased cookie sheet. Use fork dipped in sugar to make crisscross pattern on dough. Bake 15–18 minutes.

Note: The number of cookies can be increased by reducing size of balls to ¾ inch. If size is reduced, cooking time should be adjusted to 12–15 minutes.

PEANUT BUTTER SWIRLS

½ cup shortening
1 cup sugar
½ cup chunky style peanut
  butter
1 egg
2 tablespoons milk

1¼ cups flour
½ teaspoon salt
½ teaspoon baking soda
1 6–ounce package
  semisweet chocolate
  chips

Yield: 3–4 dozen

Preheat oven to 375°. Cream shortening and sugar until light. Beat in peanut butter, egg and milk. Sift together flour, salt and baking soda; stir into creamed mixture. Place dough on lightly floured wax paper; roll into 15 x 8 x ¼-inch thick rectangle. Melt chocolate pieces over hot water or in microwave. Cool slightly and spread over cookie dough. Roll jelly–roll fashion, lifting wax paper lightly with each roll. Chill dough ½ hour. Slice cookies ¼-inch thick. Place on ungreased baking sheet and bake 8–10 minutes.

TEA TIME GINGERSNAPS

¾ cup shortening
2 cups sugar, divided
¼ cup light molasses
1 egg
2 cups flour

¼ teaspoon salt
2 teaspoons baking soda
1 teaspoon cinnamon
1 teaspoon cloves
1 teaspoon ginger

Yield: 4–5 dozen

Preheat oven to 375°. Cream shortening and 1 cup sugar in a large bowl; add molasses and egg; beat well. In separate bowl, sift together flour, salt, soda, and spices; add to the sugar mixture and combine well. Roll in small balls and dip each in remaining cup of sugar. Place balls 2 inches apart on greased cookie sheet. Bake for 10–12 minutes.

PANCHETTA'S COOKIES

Great spice cookies!

⅓ cup shortening
⅔ cup firmly packed brown
 sugar
1 egg
⅔ cup flour
⅓ teaspoon cinnamon

⅓ teaspoon cloves
⅓ teaspoon nutmeg
⅓ teaspoon baking soda
½ cup chopped pecans
⅓ cup raisins, optional

Yield: 2 dozen

Preheat oven to 350°. Cream together shortening, brown sugar and egg. In separate bowl, sift together flour, spices and baking soda. Combine with creamed mixture. Add pecans and raisins. Drop by teaspoonful on greased cookie sheet. Allow space between each cookie, as they will double in size. Bake for 8–12 minutes.

Note: Panchetta was my grandmother's housekeeper in the early 1900's, and frequently made these cookies for us. Since that time, baking Panchetta's Cookies has become a treasured family tradition that I have passed on to my children and grandchildren. When I smell these wonderful spice cookies in the oven, I can picture Panchetta in Grandmother's kitchen. —Caroljean Reynolds

MOM'S FAMOUS DATE COOKIES

2 cups firmly packed brown
  sugar
1 cup shortening
2 eggs, well–beaten
2 tablespoons cream
3½ cups flour

½ teaspoon cream of tartar
1 teaspoon baking soda
1 teaspoon vanilla
1 cup chopped pecans
1 cup chopped dates
few drops maple flavoring

Yield: 100 cookies

Preheat oven to 410°. Cream together brown sugar and shortening. Add eggs and cream; mix well. Add sifted dry ingredients, pecans, dates and flavoring to creamed mixture and mix well. Form into 2 rolls and chill overnight. Thinly slice and bake on well–greased cookie sheet for 10 minutes or until delicately brown. Do not over bake.

OATMEAL SOUR CREAM COOKIES

(See recipe in Oklahoma Specialties Section)

SWEETHEART SUGAR COOKIES

1 cup powdered sugar
1 cup granulated sugar
2 sticks softened margarine
1 cup vegetable oil
2 eggs
1 teaspoon vanilla

1 teaspoon almond extract
4½ cups flour
1 teaspoon baking soda
1 teaspoon salt
1 teaspoon cream of tartar

Yield: 4 dozen

Preheat oven to 350°. In large bowl, on medium speed, combine powdered sugar, sugar, margarine, oil, eggs, vanilla and almond extract. Beat well. Add flour, baking soda, salt and cream of tartar. Refrigerate overnight. Form into small balls, approximately 1–inch in diameter. Place balls on cookie sheet sprayed with non–stick vegetable spray and press with fork dipped in sugar. Bake 12–13 minutes.

WAGON WHEEL COOKIES

(See recipe in Oklahoma Specialties Section)

POTATO CHIP COOKIES

An easy recipe that's a hit with the kids.

2 cups softened margarine
1 cup sugar
3 cups flour
2½ cups crushed potato
    chips

1 cup chopped pecans
2 teaspoons vanilla
powdered sugar

Yield: 6 dozen

Preheat oven to 350°. In a large bowl, mix all ingredients, except powdered sugar. Drop by teaspoonful onto ungreased cookie sheet. Bake for 15–20 minutes. Cool and sprinkle with powdered sugar.

ITALIAN MEATBALL COOKIES

5 cups flour
5 teaspoons baking powder
1 teaspoon cinnamon
1 teaspoon cloves
1 teaspoon nutmeg
¾ cup cocoa powder
1 cup shortening
1½ cups sugar

3 eggs
2 cups milk, divided
1 teaspoon vanilla
1 cup pecans
1 cup chocolate chips
1 cup raisins
¼ cup vegetable oil
powdered sugar

Yield: 6–8 dozen

Preheat oven to 375°. In large bowl stir together flour, baking powder, spices and cocoa powder; set aside. In large mixing bowl, cream together shortening and sugar; add eggs, 1 cup of the milk and vanilla. Gradually add flour mixture to batter making sure all are combined well. By hand, mix in nuts, chocolate chips and raisins. Batter will be very sticky. At this point, mixture can be refrigerated for 1 hour or more, if necessary. Dipping fingers in oil, roll dough into balls approximately 1–inch in diameter. Bake 10 to 15 minutes. When cookies are cooled, heat remaining 1 cup of milk to lukewarm. Dip balls in lukewarm milk and roll in powdered sugar. Return to cookie sheet or racks and allow to dry.

Note: This recipe is one of my favorites of my grandmother Congie Joy of Caledonia, NY. When my grandparents would visit Oklahoma, Gram would get off the plane carrying a box that I knew would be filled with Italian cookies. This year I've started making them for my family, trying to maintain the tradition. —Diane Joy–Sisemore

229

PECAN PRALINE COOKIES

Cookies:

1 cup real butter, softened
2 cups firmly packed brown
    sugar
2 tablespoons maple
    flavoring
2 teaspoons vanilla

2 eggs
4 cups flour
2 tablespoons baking
    powder
1 cup chopped pecans

Frosting:

1 cup firmly packed brown
    sugar
½ teaspoon vanilla
2 teaspoons maple flavoring

2 teaspoons light corn syrup
¼ cup milk
1½ cups powdered sugar

Yield: 4 dozen

Preheat oven to 350°. For cookies, cream margarine and brown sugar until fluffy. Add maple flavoring, vanilla and eggs; blend well. Add flour and baking powder to mixture until dough forms. Shape dough into 2 rolls and refrigerate 1 hour. When ready to prepare, slice ½–inch cookies from rolls and place on baking pan prepared with a non–stick vegetable spray. Top each cookie with chopped pecans and bake 8–10 minutes. Prepare frosting by bringing brown sugar, vanilla, maple flavoring, milk and corn syrup to a boil in small saucepan. Allow mixture to boil 1 minute and stir in powdered sugar. Drizzle frosting over cookies. (If frosting is too thick, additional milk may be added.)

GRANDMOTHER'S CHRISTMAS LIZZIES

1 cup real butter
1½ cups firmly packed light
    brown sugar
4 eggs
3 tablespoons milk
½ cup red wine
3 cups flour
1 teaspoon baking soda
1 teaspoon salt
1 teaspoon cinnamon

1 teaspoon ground cloves
1 teaspoon nutmeg
6 cups chopped pecans
1 pound white raisins
1 pound candied cherries,
    chopped
1 pound candied pineapple,
    chopped
1 pound dates, chopped

Yield: 12 dozen

Preheat oven to 350°. Cream together butter and sugar; add eggs, milk and wine. In separate bowl, combine dry ingredients. Gradually add flour mixture to the creamed mixture making sure all are thoroughly combined. By hand, stir in chopped pecans, raisins, candied fruit and dates. Drop by teaspoonful onto a lightly greased cookie sheet. Bake 15–20 minutes.

Note: Several recipes have come from love, through Rubye Atkinson, whose husband was founder of Midwest City, Oklahoma. She not only loved to cook, but loved to share her natural talents with family and friends. Her kitchen was always warm and smelled wonderful, with southern recipes being prepared. She was happiest planning and preparing for events to be held in her home. We all remember the special teas she had for Junior Service League. Grandmother was a gracious hostess who was able to show elegance, while expressing hospitality. — Cindy Mikeman

CANDY CANE COOKIES

A wonderful Christmas treat!

½ cup shortening
½ cup margarine, softened
1 cup sifted powdered sugar
1 egg, slightly beaten
1 teaspoon almond extract
1 teaspoon vanilla extract
2½ cups flour

1 teaspoon salt
½ teaspoon red food
 coloring
⅓ cup finely crushed
 peppermint candy
⅓ cup sugar

Yield: 4 dozen

Preheat oven to 375°. Cream shortening and margarine until fluffy; add powdered sugar and next 5 ingredients and mix well. Dough will be stiff. Divide dough in half; add food coloring to one portion, mixing well. On a lightly floured surface, roll a teaspoonful of each dough (plain and colored) into a 4½-inch rope. Place ropes side by side and carefully twist together; curve one end down to resemble a cane. Repeat procedure with remaining dough. Place cookies on ungreased cookie sheet and bake for 9 minutes. Combine crushed peppermint candy with sugar, mixing well. Remove cookies from cookie sheet while warm; immediately coat with candy mixture.

CHEESE BARS

Wonderful!

Crust:
1 18½–ounce box moist
 butter cake mix

1 cup chopped pecans
1 cup real butter, melted

Topping:
2 8–ounce packages cream
 cheese, softened

1 cup brown sugar, packed
1 cup chopped pecans

Yield: 24 bars

Preheat oven to 350°. For crust, combine all three ingredients until blended. Press into 13 x 9 x 2-inch pan. Blend cream cheese and brown sugar; spread over base and top with pecans. Bake 40–45 minutes until topping is set. Refrigerate before cutting.

CHERRY COCONUT BARS

Pastry:
1 cup flour
½ cup margarine, softened

3 tablespoons powdered
  sugar

Filling:
2 eggs, slightly beaten
1 cup sugar
¼ cup flour
½ teaspoon baking powder
¼ teaspoon salt

1 teaspoon vanilla extract
¾ cup chopped pecans
½ cup flaked coconut
½ cup chopped maraschino
  cherries

Yield: 12 bars

Preheat oven to 325°. For pastry crust, combine flour, margarine and sugar in small bowl; mix with hands until smooth. Spread thinly with fingers in 10 x 6 x 1½-inch pan. Bake for 25 minutes. Prepare filling by mixing all ingredients together in a large bowl. Spread over top of baked pastry (no need to cool pastry). Return to oven for 25 minutes. Cool and cut into bars.

DREAM BARS

Pastry:
1 cup flour
½ cup firmly packed brown
  sugar

½ cup margarine, softened

Filling:
1 cup firmly packed brown
  sugar
2 eggs
1 teaspoon vanilla

2 tablespoons flour
½ teaspoon baking powder
½ cup pecan pieces

Yield: 12 bars

Preheat oven to 350°. In a small bowl, mix flour, brown sugar and margarine. Press mixture firmly into an ungreased 9 x 9 x 2-inch pan and bake for 10 minutes. Prepare filling by beating brown sugar, eggs, vanilla, flour, baking powder and pecans. Pour over crust. Bake 15–20 minutes. Allow to cool before cutting into bars.

PECAN PIE TOFFEE BARS

1½ cups flour
⅓ cup powdered sugar
¾ cup margarine, well–
    chilled & cut into pieces
1 14–ounce can sweetened
    condensed milk

1 egg, beaten
1 teaspoon vanilla
1 cup chopped pecans
5 1⅛–ounce English toffee
    candy bars, diced

Yield: 36 bars

Preheat oven to 350°. Combine flour and powdered sugar in medium bowl. Cut in butter until mixture resembles coarse meal. Press firmly into bottom of ungreased 9 x 13-inch baking pan. Bake 15–20 minutes until lightly golden and edges begin to darken. Meanwhile, combine condensed milk, egg and vanilla in medium bowl. Stir in nuts and toffee pieces. Pour over prepared crust. Bake 20 minutes or until golden brown. Cool; refrigerate until well–chilled and cut into bars.

SUGARLESS DATE BARS

Crust:
1 cup margarine, softened
½ cup low calorie brown
    sugar replacement

1¾ cups flour
1¾ cups oatmeal
1 teaspoon baking soda

Filling:
1 pound dates, chopped
2 teaspoons low calorie
    sugar replacement

1 cup water

Topping:
½ cup margarine, melted
¼ cup low calorie brown
    sugar replacement

1 cup oatmeal

Yield: 12 bars

Preheat oven to 350°. To make crust, cream together margarine, brown sugar replacement, flour, oatmeal and baking soda. Pat into bottom of ungreased 9 x 13-inch pan and bake for 2 minutes. In a medium saucepan, prepare filling by cooking dates with sugar replacement in water until mixture is thick. Spread filling over baked crust. For topping, combine margarine, brown sugar replacement and oatmeal and spread over filling. Return to oven for 15 minutes. Allow to cool completely before cutting.

PUMPKIN BARS

*Great at Halloween and Thanksgiving when
pumpkins are abundant.*

Bars:

2 cups flour
2 teaspoons baking powder
2 teaspoons ground
   cinnamon
1 teaspoon baking soda

4 eggs
1 16–ounce can pumpkin
1⅔ cups sugar
1 cup vegetable oil
1-2 cups chopped pecans

Frosting:

2 3–ounce packages cream
   cheese, softened
½ cup melted margarine

2 teaspoons vanilla
4 cups powdered sugar
pecans, optional

Yield: 24 bars

Preheat oven to 350°. Combine flour, baking powder, cinnamon and baking soda; set aside. In a separate bowl, beat together eggs, pumpkin, sugar and oil. Add flour mixture and beat well. Stir in pecans. Spread in ungreased 15 x 10 x 1-inch baking pan. Bake 25–30 minutes or until toothpick inserted in center comes out clean. Cool on wire rack before frosting. For frosting, cream together cream cheese, margarine and vanilla. Gradually add powdered sugar, beating until smooth. Spread frosting on cooled cake and sprinkle with additional pecans.

LANDRUN BROWNIES

2 cups crushed graham
   crackers
½ cup chopped pecans
1 6–ounce package
   semisweet chocolate
   chips
1 cup butterscotch chips,
   optional

1 cup shredded coconut,
   optional
1 14-ounce can sweetened
   condensed milk
½ cup powdered sugar,
   optional

Yield: 10 brownies

Preheat oven to 350°. Mix together all ingredients except powdered sugar and pour into a well–greased 8 x 8-inch pan. Bake for 30 minutes. Remove from oven and cool 10 minutes. Cut into squares and remove from pan. Powdered sugar may be sprinkled on top if desired.

CHOCOLATE MINT BROWNIES
WITH FROSTING

Brownies:

4 squares unsweetened chocolate

1 cup margarine

4 eggs

2 cups sugar

¼ teaspoon peppermint extract

1 teaspoon vanilla

1 cup flour

1 12–ounce package chocolate chips

Frosting:

6 tablespoons margarine, softened & divided

2 cups powdered sugar

2 tablespoons milk

1 teaspoon peppermint extract

2 squares unsweetened chocolate

Yield: 15 bars

Preheat oven to 350°. Prepare brownies by melting chocolate and margarine in small saucepan. In a large bowl, beat eggs; add sugar gradually. Stir in melted chocolate, peppermint and vanilla. Mix well. Stir in flour and chocolate chips until well combined. Pour into a 9 x 13-inch baking dish and bake 25 to 30 minutes. Allow to cool before frosting. Prepare frosting by creaming together 4 tablespoons of the softened margarine with the powdered sugar. Add milk and peppermint extract and spread over cooled brownies. In small saucepan, melt together remaining 2 tablespoons of margarine with chocolate squares. Drizzle over frosting. Refrigerate brownies before cutting to serve.

OKLAHOMA CRUDE CAKE

(See recipe in Oklahoma Specialties Section)

SOUR CREAM CHOCOLATE CAKE

2 cups sugar
1¾ cups all–purpose flour
1 cup cocoa powder
2 teaspoons cinnamon
1½ teaspoons baking
   powder

1 teaspoon salt
2 eggs, lightly beaten
1 cup milk
½ cup melted sweet butter
1 cup boiling water
2 teaspoons vanilla extract

Frosting:
1 16-ounce package
   semisweet chocolate
   pieces

2 cups sour cream, at room
   temperature, divided
1 teaspoon vanilla extract
½ teaspoon salt

Yield: 10–12 servings

Preheat oven to 350°. Grease and flour two 9–inch cake pans; set aside. In a large bowl combine all dry ingredients. Stir in eggs, milk and melted butter until fully combined. Add boiling water and vanilla; stir to combine. Pour batter into prepared pans. Bake for 35–40 minutes or until a knife inserted in the center of cakes comes out clean. Allow to cool and turn out of pans. For frosting, melt chocolate in double boiler. Remove from heat and stir in ½ cup of sour cream. Stir chocolate mixture into remaining sour cream and add vanilla and salt. Allow to cool. Spread ⅓ of frosting over one cake. Place second cake on top. Spread top and sides of cake with remaining frosting. Refrigerate cake for at least one hour before serving.

THE ULTIMATE CHOCOLATE CAKE

1 cup margarine, softened
1⅓ cups sugar
4 eggs
½ teaspoon baking soda
1 cup buttermilk
2½ cups flour
1⅓ cups chocolate mini–morsels, divided

2 4–ounce bars sweet baking chocolate, melted and cooled
⅓ cup chocolate syrup
2 teaspoons vanilla extract
4 ounces white chocolate, chopped
2 tablespoons plus 2 teaspoons shortening, divided

Yield: 16 servings

Preheat oven to 300°. In a large mixing bowl, cream softened margarine and sugar. Add eggs, one at a time, beating well after each addition. Dissolve baking soda in buttermilk, stirring well. Add to creamed mixture alternating with flour, beginning and ending with flour. Add 1 cup mini–morsels, melted sweet baking chocolate, chocolate syrup and vanilla, stirring just until ingredients are blended. Do not overbeat. Spoon batter into a heavily greased and floured 12 cup (10–inch) Bundt pan. Bake for 1 hour and 25–35 minutes or until cake springs back when touched. Invert cake on serving platter and allow to cool completely. For topping, combine 4 ounces chopped white chocolate and 2 tablespoons shortening in top of double boiler. Allow water to boil, reduce heat to low and allow to cook until mixture is melted and smooth. Remove from heat. Drizzle melted white chocolate mixture over cooled cake, allowing to drip from the sides. Melt remaining ½ cup mini–morsels and 2 teaspoons shortening in small saucepan over low heat, stirring until smooth. Remove from heat, and let cool; drizzle over white chocolate. Allow chocolate to set, cut and serve.

CINNAMON CHOCOLATE SHEET CAKE

(See recipe in Oklahoma Specialties Section)

WHITE CHOCOLATE CAKE

Cake:

¼ pound white chocolate, melted

1 cup margarine, softened

2 cups sugar

4 eggs, separated

1 teaspoon vanilla

2½ cups flour

1 teaspoon baking powder

1 cup buttermilk

1 cup chopped pecans

1 cup flaked coconut

Icing:

2 cups sugar

1 5.33–ounce can evaporated milk

1 cup melted margarine

1 teaspoon vanilla

Yield: 12 servings

Preheat oven to 350°. For cake, melt chocolate in double boiler and set aside. Cream margarine and sugar, beat in egg yolks; add vanilla and melted chocolate and mix well. Sift together flour and baking powder, and add alternately with buttermilk to chocolate mixture. Beat egg whites until stiff and fold into cake batter. Gently stir in nuts and coconut. Pour into a greased 13 x 9 x 2-inch pan and bake 45 minutes. For icing, mix all ingredients in saucepan and let stand one hour before heating, stirring occasionally. Cook over medium heat until soft ball is formed in cold water or temperature reaches 235° on candy thermometer. Beat mixture until consistency for spreading. Spread mixture over top of cake with spatula.

ITALIAN CREAM CAKE

Cake:

1 stick margarine, softened
½ cup shortening
2 cups sugar
1 teaspoon baking soda
1 cup buttermilk

2 cups sifted all–purpose
   flour
5 eggs, separated
1 cup chopped pecans
2 cups flaked coconut

Icing:

1 8–ounce package cream
   cheese, softened
1 stick margarine, softened

1 1–pound box powdered
   sugar
1 teaspoon vanilla

Yield: 16–18 servings

Preheat oven to 325°. To prepare cake, in a large bowl, cream margarine and shortening together; blend in sugar. Dissolve baking soda in buttermilk and alternate with flour to creamed mixture. Add egg yolks, one at a time, beating well after each addition. Add in pecans and coconut. Stiffly beat egg whites and fold into batter. Spoon into 3 greased and floured 8–inch cake pans. Bake for 25 minutes; allow to cool before icing. To prepare icing, blend cream cheese and margarine, mixing well. Add powdered sugar and vanilla, mixing to spreading consistency. Spread icing between cake layers as well as on the sides and top of cake.

CHOCOLATE DELIGHT CAKE

1 18½-ounce box chocolate
  cake mix
1½ cups sugar, divided
1½ cups evaporated milk,
  divided

24 large marshmallows
1 14-ounce package
  shredded coconut
1½ cups chocolate chips
1½ cups chopped pecans

Yield: 24 servings

Preheat oven to temperature indicated on cake mix. In large bowl, pre-pare cake mix according to package directions, and pour into greased and floured 15 x 10 x 1-inch baking pan. Bake 15–20 minutes. While cake is baking, in a medium saucepan, heat 1 cup sugar and 1 cup canned milk. Boil 1 minute. Add marshmallows and coconut to mixture, stirring until marshmallows are melted. When cake is done, pour this mixture, while still warm, over hot cake, spreading to edges. Allow to cool completely. Heat ½ cup sugar and ½ cup canned milk in small saucepan. Boil 1 minute. Add chocolate chips and pecans to mixture stirring until chips are melted. Spread warm mixture over coconut layer, covering completely. Allow to cool slightly prior to cutting cake.

PINEAPPLE NUT CAKE

2 eggs
2 cups sugar
1 teaspoon vanilla
2 cups flour

2 teaspoons baking soda
1 20-ounce can crushed
  pineapple, drained
1 cup chopped walnuts

Cream Cheese Icing:
1 8-ounce package cream
  cheese, softened
1 stick margarine, softened

1½ cups powdered sugar
1 teaspoon vanilla

Yield: 8-10 servings

Preheat oven to 350°. Beat eggs, sugar and vanilla until sugar is dis-solved. Beat in flour, baking soda and pineapple. Fold in walnuts. Pour into a greased and floured 13 x 9 x 2-inch pan. Bake 40-45 minutes or until firm. Cool on cake rack in pan. For icing, mix cream cheese and margarine together until well blended. Add powdered sugar and vanilla and beat until creamy. Spread on cooled cake.

APPLE CAKE WITH HOT BUTTER SAUCE

¼ cup shortening
1 cup sugar
1 egg
1 cup flour
1 teaspoon salt

1 teaspoon baking soda
1 teaspoon cinnamon
2 cups finely chopped,
   peeled apples
¾ cup chopped pecans

Hot Butter Sauce:
2 cups sugar
⅔ cup evaporated milk
1 egg yolk

⅔ stick margarine
1 teaspoon vanilla

Yield: 8 servings

Preheat oven to 350°. Cream together shortening and sugar in large bowl; add egg and beat. Sift together flour, salt, baking soda and cinnamon. Add to first mixture and combine well. Add apples and pecans to batter and mix well. Pour batter into a greased and floured 9 x 5 x 3-inch loaf pan. Bake 30–35 minutes. Before serving cake, prepare Hot Butter Sauce by heating sugar, evaporated milk, egg yolk and margarine over medium heat. Bring mixture to a boil and allow to boil 3 minutes, stirring occasionally. Add vanilla to mixture and beat to spreading consistency. Serve warm over individual pieces of apple cake.

APPLE PUDDING CAKE

1 cup sugar
¼ cup melted margarine
1 egg
1 cup flour
½ teaspoon cinnamon
½ teaspoon allspice
½ teaspoon nutmeg

½ teaspoon baking soda
¼ teaspoon salt
1 teaspoon vanilla
2 cups peeled and sliced
   apples
½ cup chopped pecans
whipped topping

Yield: 9 servings

Preheat oven to 350°. In large bowl, combine first 10 ingredients; mix well. Add apples and pecans and mix until blended. Pour into well-greased 8-inch glass baking dish. Bake for 30 minutes. Cool slightly and serve with whipped topping.

BANANA CAKE

Cake:

2 cups sugar
1 cup shortening
4 ripe bananas, mashed
4 tablespoons buttermilk
4 eggs

2 cups flour
1 teaspoon baking soda
1 teaspoon vanilla
½ cup chopped pecans

Frosting:

1 8–ounce package cream
   cheese, softened
¼ cup softened margarine

1 1–pound box powdered
   sugar
1 cup chopped pecans (if
   desired)

Yield: 16–18 servings

Preheat oven to 350°. For cake, cream together sugar and shortening. Add remaining cake ingredients and mix well. Pour batter into a greased 11 x 16-inch sheet pan. Bake for 30 minutes. To prepare frosting, mix together all frosting ingredients until thoroughly blended. Spread on cooled cake.

EASY POPPY SEED CAKE

This is a wonderful cake to take to bake sales and school carnivals!

1 18.5–ounce box butter
   recipe yellow cake mix
1 8–ounce container of sour
   cream

¾ cup vegetable oil
¼ cup poppy seeds
½ cup sugar
4 large eggs

Yield: 12–14 servings

Preheat oven to 350°. In a large bowl, combine all ingredients well. Pour into a greased and sugared Bundt pan. Bake for 1 hour.

Note: Instead of using flour to dredge your Bundt pan, you can use sugar and you will not need any icing for this cake.

CARROT CAKE AND CREAM CHEESE FROSTING

Cake:

2 cups flour	2 cups sugar
2 teaspoons baking soda	1 teaspoon vanilla
1 teaspoon baking powder	4 eggs
½ teaspoon salt	3 cups grated carrots
2 teaspoons cinnamon	½ cup chopped pecans
1½ cups vegetable oil	

Frosting:

1 1–pound box of powdered sugar	½ cup butter, softened
	1 teaspoon vanilla
1 8–ounce package cream cheese, softened	

Yield: 16–18 servings

Preheat oven to 350°. For cake, sift first five dry ingredients together and set aside. In a large bowl, combine oil and sugar; mix thoroughly. Add vanilla and eggs one at a time, beating well after each addition. Gradually add dry ingredients and mix well. Stir in carrots and pecans. Pour batter into greased 9 x 13-inch baking pan. Bake for 50–60 minutes. Mix all frosting ingredients together in small bowl. Spread frosting onto cooled cake. If desired, sprinkle with pecans.

CHOCOLATE POUND CAKE

3 sticks margarine, softened	½ cup cocoa
3 cups sugar	2 tablespoons vanilla
5 eggs	1 cup milk
3 cups flour	powdered sugar
1 teaspoon baking powder	

Yield: 12-14 servings

Preheat oven to 350°. Cream together margarine, sugar and eggs. In separate bowl mix together flour, baking powder, cocoa and vanilla. Add dry ingredients to creamed mixture, alternately with milk; mix well. Pour into well-greased Bundt pan. Bake for 1½ hours. Let cool, and remove from pan. Before serving sprinkle top with powdered sugar.

POUND CAKE

3 cups sifted cake flour
¼ teaspoon baking soda
2 sticks margarine, softened
3 cups sugar
6 egg yolks

1 teaspoon butter extract
1 teaspoon vanilla extract
1 teaspoon almond extract
1 cup sour cream
6 egg whites, stiffly beaten

Yield: 12 servings

Preheat oven to 325°. Sift together cake flour and baking soda and set aside. On medium speed of electric mixer, cream together margarine, sugar and egg yolks; add in butter, vanilla and almond extracts. Alternate flour mixture and sour cream, beginning and ending with flour, making sure to blend well after each addition. By hand, gently fold in stiffly beaten egg whites. Pour batter into greased and floured Bundt pan and bake 1 hour. Allow to cool prior to cutting.

CHOCOLATE CHIP PECAN PIE

Pie:
1 cup light corn syrup
½ cup sugar
¼ cup margarine, melted
1 teaspoon vanilla
3 eggs, slightly beaten

1 cup semisweet chocolate
    chips
1½ cups chopped pecans
1 9–inch pastry shell,
    unbaked

Topping:
2 tablespoons semisweet
    chocolate chips

10 pecan halves
whipped topping

Yield: 6–8 servings

Preheat oven to 325°. Combine corn syrup, sugar, margarine, vanilla and eggs; mix all well. Stir in chocolate chips and chopped pecans. Spread entire mixture evenly in unbaked pastry shell. Bake 60 to 65 minutes. For topping, melt 2 tablespoons chocolate chips in small saucepan. Line small cooking sheet with wax paper. Dip pecan halves in melted chocolate and place on cookie sheet. Place in refrigerator for 15 to 20 minutes. Garnish pie with whipped topping and chocolate covered pecans.

DEEP DISH APPLE PIE

(See recipe in Oklahoma Specialties Section)

APPLE TODD BEST

Pie:
7-8 apples, peeled and
   sliced
1 cup water
1 teaspoon cinnamon

½ teaspoon allspice
1 lightly baked 9–inch pie
   shell

Topping:
¾ cup sugar
¾ cup flour

½ cup softened margarine

Yield: 8 servings

Preheat oven to 350°. In large saucepan cover sliced apples with water and add cinnamon and allspice. Over medium heat allow apples to cook 10 minutes and drain. Arrange apples in lightly baked pie shell. Make crumb topping by blending sugar, flour and softened margarine with fork until it resembles coarse meal. Sprinkle on top of apple mixture and bake for one hour. If desired, sprinkle on additional cinnamon and allspice.

SOUR CREAM APPLE PIE

Pie Filling:
2 tablespoons flour
⅛ teaspoon salt
¾ cup sugar
1 egg
1 cup sour cream

1 teaspoon vanilla
¼ teaspoon nutmeg
2 cups diced, peeled apples
½ cup raisins (optional)
1 unbaked 9–inch pie shell

Topping:
⅓ cup sugar
⅓ cup flour

1 teaspoon cinnamon
¼ cup margarine, softened

Yield: 8 servings

Preheat oven to 400°. Sift together flour, salt and sugar. Add egg, sour cream, vanilla and nutmeg; beat until batter is thin and smooth. Stir in apples and raisins, if desired. Pour into pie shell. Bake for 15 minutes at 400°; reduce heat to 350° and bake an additional 30 minutes. While pie is in oven, prepare topping by mixing sugar, flour and cinnamon; cut in margarine. Sprinkle topping over pie; return oven to 400° and bake another 10 minutes to brown.

PARADISE PUMPKIN PIE

Pie:

1 8–ounce package cream
  cheese, softened
¼ cup sugar
½ teaspoon vanilla
1 egg, beaten
1 unbaked 9–inch pastry
  shell
1¼ cups canned pumpkin
1 cup evaporated milk

½ cup sugar
2 eggs, slightly beaten
1 teaspoon cinnamon
¼ teaspoon ginger
¼ teaspoon nutmeg
dash of salt
¼ cup maple syrup
pecan halves to garnish

Spiced Whipped Topping:

½ cup firmly packed brown
  sugar
⅓ teaspoon cinnamon

⅛ teaspoon nutmeg
¾ cup whipping cream
½ teaspoon vanilla

Yield: 8 servings

Preheat oven to 350°. Combine softened cream cheese, sugar and vanilla, mixing until well–blended. Blend in egg. Spread onto bottom of
pastry shell. Combine remaining pie ingredients except maple syrup and
pecan halves and mix well. Carefully pour over cream cheese mixture.
Bake 1 hour and 5 minutes. Allow to cool and brush with maple syrup
and garnish with pecan halves if desired. For topping, mix brown sugar,
cinnamon and nutmeg in medium–sized bowl. Stir in whipping cream
and vanilla and allow to chill for 1 hour. Take from refrigerator and whip
until stiff. Makes 1½ cups. Spread on top.

PRALINE PUMPKIN PIE

Praline layer:
3 tablespoons softened
   margarine
⅓ cup firmly packed brown
   sugar

½ rounded cup chopped
   pecans
1 unbaked 8–inch pie shell

Custard layer:
1 cup evaporated milk
½ cup water
3 eggs, beaten
1½ cups pumpkin
1½ teaspoons pumpkin
   spice

½ teaspoon salt
½ cup white sugar
½ cup firmly packed brown
   sugar
whipped cream

Yield: 8 servings

Preheat oven to 400°. For praline layer, cream margarine with brown sugar and stir in pecans. Press over bottom of pie crust in even layer and bake at 400° for 10 minutes. Remove and cool on rack. For custard layer, scald evaporated milk with water in small saucepan. In separate bowl, combine beaten eggs, with remaining ingredients. Beat in scalded milk mixture and pour into cooled pastry shell. Cover crust edges with aluminum foil to keep from burning. Reduce heat to 350° and bake for 50 minutes or until center is set but still soft. Serve with whipped cream.

STRATFORD PEACH FRIED PIES

(See recipe in Oklahoma Specialties Section)

DOUBLE LAYER PEACH COBBLER

(See recipe in Oklahoma Specialties Section)

JOE'S FAVORITE SWEET POTATO PIE

Sweet Potato Filling:

1 cup baked sweet potato
   pulp
¼ cup packed light brown
   sugar
2 tablespoons granulated
   sugar
½ egg, beaten until frothy
   (after beating egg, just
   divide in half)

1 tablespoon heavy cream
1 tablespoon unsalted butter
1 tablespoon vanilla
¼ teaspoon salt
¼ teaspoon cinnamon
⅛ teaspoon allspice
⅛ teaspoon nutmeg
1 9–inch unbaked pie shell

Pecan Pie Syrup:

¾ cup granulated sugar
¾ cup dark corn syrup
2 small eggs
1½ tablespoons unsalted
   butter, melted

2 teaspoons vanilla
pinch of salt
¼ teaspoon cinnamon
¾ cup pecan pieces

Yield: 1 pie

Preheat oven to 325°. To prepare pie filling, combine all ingredients in mixing bowl. Beat 2–3 minutes until smooth. Pour into unbaked 9–inch pie shell. Prepare syrup by combining all ingredients except pecans. Mix on slow speed for 1 minute. Stir in pecans and pour syrup on top of filling. Bake for 1¾ hours.

EGGNOG PIE

1 teaspoon unflavored gelatin	3 egg yolks, beaten
1 tablespoon cold water	1 tablespoon margarine
1 cup milk	1 teaspoon vanilla
½ cup sugar	1 cup heavy cream, whipped
2 tablespoons cornstarch	1 9-inch baked pie shell
¼ teaspoon salt	nutmeg

Yield: 8 servings

In small bowl, soak gelatin in cold water and set aside. Heat milk in double boiler until scalded. In separate bowl, combine sugar, cornstarch and salt; mix well. Add sugar mixture to the scalded milk; stir and cook until mixture thickens and continue cooking 15 additional minutes. Stir a small amount of milk mixture into the beaten egg yolks, then add yolks to double boiler mixture. Stir well and heat 3–4 minutes. Remove from heat; add gelatin and margarine. Cool. Add vanilla and mix well. Fold in whipped cream and pour into baked pie shell, sprinkle top with nutmeg.

"I CAN DO THIS" PIE CRUST

1 cup flour	2-3 tablespoons cold water
½ teaspoon salt	

⅓ cup plus 1 tablespoon
    butter flavored vegetable
    shortening	

Yield: 1 crust

In medium bowl, combine flour and salt. Cut in shortening until mixture resembles coarse meal. Sprinkle with water as needed and shape into a ball. Roll out dough to ½-inch thickness on lightly floured surface, or in between waxed paper. Place rolled dough into 9-inch pie pan. Flute edges and use according to your favorite pie recipe.

APPLE DESSERT

Pie Crust:

1½ cups graham cracker
   crumbs
2 tablespoons sugar

3 tablespoons melted
   margarine

Filling:

1 14–ounce can sweetened
   condensed milk
1 8–ounce carton sour cream

¼ cup lemon juice
1 21–ounce can apple pie
   filling

Topping:

1 cup chopped pecans

½ teaspoon cinnamon

Yield: 8 servings

Preheat oven to 350°. In a small bowl, mix graham cracker crumbs and sugar; stir in melted margarine. Press mixture into bottom and sides of a 9–inch deep dish pie pan. Bake for 10 minutes; remove from oven and allow to cool. Combine condensed milk, sour cream and lemon juice and mix well. Pour into pie crust. Carefully spread apple pie filling over sour cream mixture making sure sour cream mixture is totally covered. In small bowl, mix together cinnamon and pecans and spread evenly over pie filling. Bake for 20 minutes.

Note: May serve warm or make ahead and refrigerate until needed.

NEVER FAIL PIE CRUST

3 cups flour
1 teaspoon salt
1½ cups shortening

1 egg, beaten
3 tablespoons water
2 tablespoons vinegar

Yield: 3 pie crusts

In a large bowl, blend together flour, salt and shortening. In a small bowl, combine egg, water and vinegar. Pour liquid mixture into flour mixture and blend until all flour is moistened and a ball forms. Divide into 2 or 3 portions, depending upon size of pans. Roll out on lightly floured surface. Use according to pie directions.

WHITE CHOCOLATE CHEESECAKE WITH RASPBERRY SAUCE

Crust:
¾ cup almonds, ground
¾ cup quick cooking oats
¾ cup graham cracker crumbs
¼ cup sugar
6 tablespoons margarine, melted

Filling:
1 10-ounce package white chocolate chips
3 8-ounce packages cream cheese, softened
¾ cup sugar
3 eggs
½ cup amaretto
1 8-ounce carton sour cream
2 tablespoons whipping cream
2 teaspoons vanilla

Sauce:
1 10-ounce package frozen red raspberries, thawed
¼ cup currant jelly (or other mild flavored jelly)
1 tablespoon cornstarch

Yield: 10 servings

Preheat oven to 350°. Prepare crust by combining ingredients and press into bottom and 2 inches up the sides of a 10-inch springform pan. Bake for 5 minutes; remove from oven and allow to cool on rack. For filling, melt chocolate in top of double boiler. Beat cream cheese until fluffy, gradually adding sugar, mixing well. Add eggs, one at a time, beating well after each addition. Add remainder of ingredients except chocolate, scraping sides of bowl often to avoid lumps. Gently stir in melted chocolate, combining well. Pour into prepared pan and bake for 45 minutes. Remove from oven and let cool slightly. Loosen the cake from the rim of the pan; refrigerate and allow to cool completely before removing sides of pan. Prepare Raspberry Sauce by draining thawed raspberries, reserving ⅔ cup of juice. In small saucepan combine reserved juice, jelly and cornstarch. Cook and stir until slightly thickened and glossy. Allow to cool and gently stir in raspberries. Serve sauce over cheesecake slices.

EASY SOUR CREAM CHEESE CAKE

Cake:

4 3–ounce packages
   softened cream cheese
2 eggs
¾ cup sugar

2 teaspoons vanilla
½ teaspoon lemon juice
1 9–inch graham cracker
   crust

Topping:

1 cup sour cream
3½ tablespoons sugar

1 teaspoon vanilla

Yield: 6 servings

Preheat oven to 350°. Combine cream cheese and next 4 ingredients beating until light and frothy. Pour into prepared graham cracker crust and bake 25 minutes. Allow to cool 15 minutes. Mix all topping ingredients together, blending well. Pour over cooled cheesecake and bake an additional 15 minutes.

Note: May also add your favorite fruit topping in addition to sour cream topping.

STRAWBERRY CHEESECAKE

Crust:

1½ cups graham cracker
   crumbs
2 tablespoons sugar

3 tablespoons melted
   margarine

Filling:

3 9–ounce containers
   strawberry cream cheese
1 cup sugar

½ teaspoon vanilla
3 eggs

Topping:

1 12–ounce container frozen
   whipped topping

fresh strawberries to garnish

Yield: 10–12 servings

Preheat oven to 350°. In a small bowl, mix graham cracker crumbs and sugar; stir in melted margarine. Press mixture into bottom and sides of a 9–inch deep dish pie pan. Bake for 10 minutes; remove from oven and allow to cool. Reduce oven to 300°. Beat cream cheese and sugar in large bowl; add vanilla. Beat in eggs, one at a time. Pour over crumbs and bake at 300° for 60 minutes or until center is firm. After cheesecake has cooled, top with whipped topping and garnish with strawberries.

ROCA CHEESECAKE

Crust:
¾ cup graham cracker crumbs
¼ cup firmly packed brown sugar
½ cup chopped Almond Roca candy
¼ cup margarine, melted

Filling:
3 8-ounce packages cream cheese, softened
1 14-ounce can sweetened condensed milk
3 eggs
1¼ teaspoons vanilla

Topping:
⅔ cup firmly packed brown sugar
⅔ cup whipping cream
1 cup chopped Almond Roca candy

Yield: 12 servings

Preheat oven to 300°. Mix all crust ingredients together and press into a 9 x 13 x 2-inch baking dish; set aside. Prepare cheesecake filling by beating cream cheese until fluffy; slowly add milk. Gradually beat in eggs and vanilla; pour over crumb mixture. Bake 45 minutes or until center is set. Cool. For topping, combine brown sugar and whipping cream in small saucepan; cook 10 to 12 minutes until thickened. Stir in candy; pour over cooled cake. Chill before cutting.

IRISH CREAM CHEESECAKE

Crust:
1⅓ cups graham cracker
   crumbs
3 tablespoons sugar

3 tablespoons unsweetened
   cocoa
⅓ cup melted margarine

Cheesecake:
3 8-ounce packages
   softened cream cheese
1¼ cups sugar

5 jumbo eggs
½ cup Irish Cream liqueur

Topping:
1 cup sour cream
3 tablespoons sugar

¼ cup Irish Cream liqueur

Yield: 8 servings

Preheat oven to 350°. For crust, in medium bowl, mix together cracker crumbs, sugar and cocoa. Add melted margarine and work with fork to dampen all crumbs. In a 9 or 10-inch springform pan, spread mixture on bottom and up sides 1 inch. Refrigerate. Make cheesecake by blending cream cheese and sugar until light and fluffy. Add eggs one at a time, blending well after each. Continue beating mixture until smooth; add Irish Cream and continue to beat on medium speed for 2 minutes. Pour entire mixture into chilled crust and bake 25 minutes. Allow to cool while preparing topping. Thoroughly blend together sour cream, sugar, and Irish Cream. Spread mixture on top of cheesecake, allow to set until firm.

ALMOND LEMON TART

An easy, but elegant dessert!

Crust:
2⅔ cups flour
1⅓ cups sugar
1⅓ cups real butter,
    softened

½ teaspoon salt
1 egg

Filling:
1 cup finely chopped
    almonds
½ cup sugar

1 egg, slightly beaten
1 teaspoon grated lemon
    peel

Yield: 8–10 servings

Preheat oven to 325°. Blend together all crust ingredients at low mixer speed until dough forms. Spread half of dough in bottom of greased 9 or 10-inch springform pan. Prepare filling by blending remaining ingredients and spreading over bottom crust to within ½ inch of sides of pan. Roll or press remaining dough to 9 – 10 inch circle and place over filling. Gently press dough into place. Bake for 45–55 minutes or until a light golden brown. This recipe often takes over an hour to bake. Cool 15 minutes, remove from pan and allow to cool completely.

Note: While cooking, place pan on cookie sheet to catch any dripping butter.

BLUEBERRY STREUSEL

Streusel:
1 pint blueberries, washed
   and drained
1 14–ounce can sweetened
   condensed milk
2 teaspoons grated lemon
   rind

¾ cup, plus 2 tablespoons
   cold margarine, divided
2 cups biscuit baking mix,
   divided
½ cup firmly packed brown
   sugar
½ cup chopped pecans

Blueberry Sauce:
½ cup sugar
1 tablespoon cornstarch
½ teaspoon cinnamon
¼ teaspoon nutmeg

½ cup water
1 pint blueberries, washed &
   drained

Yield: 6 servings

Preheat oven to 325°. In medium bowl, combine blueberries, condensed milk and lemon rind and set aside. In separate large bowl, cut ¾ cup margarine into 1½ cups biscuit mix until crumbly; fold in berry mixture. Spread in greased 9 x 13-inch baking pan. In small bowl, combine ½ cup biscuit mix and brown sugar; cut in 2 tablespoons margarine until crumbs form and mix in pecans. Sprinkle mixture evenly over top of blueberry mixture. Bake for 1 hour or until golden. Prepare sauce by combining sugar, cornstarch, cinnamon, nutmeg and water in medium saucepan. Cook over medium heat until thickened. Add blueberries; cook and stir until hot. Serve over blueberry streusel.

Note: This recipe is great served hot with your favorite ice cream.

CHILLED CHOCOLATE TORTONI

**1 6–ounce package
  semisweet chocolate
  chips**
⅔ cup light corn syrup
2 cups heavy cream, divided

**1½ cups broken, chocolate
  wafers**
**1½ cups coarsely chopped
  pecans, divided**
**whipped topping
  shaved chocolate**

Yield: 15–18 servings

Line 2½-inch muffin cups with foil liners. In 3–quart saucepan, stir chocolate and corn syrup over low heat just until chocolate melts; remove from heat. Stir in ½ cup heavy cream until blended. Refrigerate 15 minutes or until cool. Beat remaining cream until soft peaks form; gently stir into chocolate mixture. Stir in cookies and 1 cup chopped pecans. Spoon mixture into muffin cups. Freeze 4–6 hours or until firm. Garnish as desired with whipped topping, shaved chocolate, drizzled chocolate or remaining chopped nuts. Let stand a few minutes before serving. Store covered in freezer up to 1 month.

GLAZED APPLE RINGS

¼ cup margarine
**4 apples, cored and cut into
  ½-inch rings**
**½ cup dry white wine or
  apple juice**

1 tablespoon lemon juice
¼ teaspoon ginger
¼ teaspoon cinnamon
½ cup sugar

Yield: 6 servings

Heat margarine in 10–inch skillet over medium heat until melted. In margarine, fry several apple rings at a time, turning until golden brown. (Add more margarine if necessary) Return all apple rings to skillet. In a small bowl, mix wine or apple juice, lemon juice, ginger and cinnamon. Pour over apples. Sprinkle all with sugar. Cover skillet and cook over medium heat until apples are tender and glazed, approximately 5 minutes.

CURRIED FRUIT

A warm winter treat!

⅓ cup margarine
¾ cup plus 3 tablespoons firmly packed brown sugar, divided
½ to 1 tablespoon curry powder
1 16–ounce can sliced peaches, drained

1 16–ounce can sliced pears, drained
1 15¼–ounce can pineapple chunks, drained
1 16–ounce can apricots, drained

Yield: 8 servings

Preheat oven to 350°. Melt margarine in a small saucepan and mix in ¾ cup brown sugar and curry powder. Arrange drained fruit in a 2–quart ovenproof baking dish. Pour curry mixture over fruit and sprinkle with remaining 3 tablespoons brown sugar. Bake 30–45 minutes. Serve warm.

Note: Can add cherries or plums to recipe for different taste.

Adjust curry powder to your individual taste.

TROPICAL DELIGHT

2 cups finely crushed graham crackers or vanilla wafers
1½ cups margarine, divided
2 cups powdered sugar
1 8–ounce package softened cream cheese
6–8 firm bananas, sliced

2 20–ounce cans crushed pineapple, very well drained
1 8–ounce carton frozen whipped topping, thawed
1 10–ounce jar maraschino cherries, drained
1 cup chopped pecans

Yield: 12 servings

Mix together cracker or cookie crumbs with ½ cup margarine, melted, and pat into a 9 x 13-inch baking dish to form crust. Cream together remaining softened margarine, powdered sugar and cream cheese. Spread over crust. In the following order, evenly layer sliced bananas, drained pineapple, whipped topping, cherries and pecans. Refrigerate until ready to serve.

CHOCOLATE LOVER'S DREAM COME TRUE

1 quart heavy cream
1 cup brown sugar, divided
2 tablespoons sugar

8 ounces milk chocolate,
   chopped
7 egg yolks
1 teaspoon vanilla

Yield: 8–10 servings

Preheat oven to 350°. In saucepan, over medium heat, bring cream, ½ cup brown sugar, and sugar to a boil. Add chocolate and remove from heat; stir until chocolate is melted. Allow to cool slightly. In mixing bowl, whisk egg yolks and vanilla until blended. Whisk ¼ cup of chocolate mixture into eggs. Pour in remaining chocolate mixture and whisk until blended. Pour mixture through a strainer into a 13 x 9 x 2–inch glass baking pan. Place pan in a larger baking pan. Add water to larger pan to come halfway up side of inner pan. Bake 1 to 1½ hours or until knife inserted in center comes out clean. Cool to room temperature. Cover with plastic wrap and refrigerate 6 to 8 hours. When ready to serve, set oven on broil. Pat top of dessert with paper towel to remove excess moisture. Cover top evenly with ½ cup brown sugar. Place dessert under broiler just until sugar begins to melt (watch carefully). Serve warm or chilled with whipped cream. Refrigerate leftovers.

Note: This seems to get better and better the longer it sets.

CHOCOLATE VELVET

⅔ cup chocolate syrup
⅔ cup sweetened condensed
   milk

2 cups heavy cream
½ teaspoon vanilla
1 cup chopped pecans

Yield: 12 servings

Combine chocolate syrup, condensed milk, cream and vanilla in large bowl; chill. Whip chilled mixture until soft peaks form. Fold in ¾ cup pecans. Spread into 8 x 8-inch pan and top with remaining pecans. Serve chilled.

STRAWBERRY BANANA SHERBET

1 14–ounce can sweetened
   condensed milk
2 10–ounce cartons frozen
   strawberries, thawed

2 medium bananas, chopped
6 12–ounce cans strawberry
   soda

Yield: 1 gallon

Combine all ingredients in the drum of a 1 gallon ice cream freezer; stir gently to mix. Process mixture in ice cream freezer according to individual machine directions until firm, about 30 minutes. Sherbet should not be frozen solid.

APRICOT ICE CREAM

1 quart half–and–half
2 8–ounce cans apricot
   nectar
¾ cup fresh lemon juice
   (approximately 4 medium
   lemons)

1 cup fresh orange juice
   (approximately 2 medium
   oranges)
2¾ cups sugar
1 quart milk

Yield: 1 gallon

Combine all ingredients, except milk, in container of ice cream freezer. Add milk to the fill line. Process in ice cream freezer according to individual machine directions until firm, about 30 minutes.

BANANA NUT ICE CREAM

3 eggs, well beaten
2½ cups sugar
½ teaspoon salt
2 teaspoons vanilla

1 13–ounce can evaporated
   milk
3 bananas, mashed
1 cup chopped pecans
½ gallon milk

Yield: 12 servings

In container of ice cream freezer, mix together all ingredients except milk, making sure all are thoroughly blended. Fill remainder of container with milk. Process in ice cream freezer according to individual machine directions until firm, about 30 minutes.

Note: See special note on page 6 regarding uncooked eggs.

VANILLA ICE CREAM

6 eggs
2½ cups sugar
1½ tablespoons vanilla

dash of salt
1½ pints whipping cream
milk

Yield: 12 servings

In a large bowl, beat eggs until creamy. Add sugar, vanilla and salt to eggs and continue to beat until sugar is dissolved. Add whipping cream and mix well. Pour into gallon canister of ice cream freezer. Add milk to fill line on container; stir well. Process mixture in ice cream freezer according to individual machine directions until firm, about 30 minutes.

Note: If making fruit ice cream, use only 1 teaspoon vanilla.

See special note on page 6 regarding uncooked eggs.

MISS JUNE'S PEANUT PATTIES

2½ cups sugar
⅔ cup white corn syrup
1 cup evaporated milk
3 cups raw peanuts

1 teaspoon vanilla
1 teaspoon butter
red food coloring

Yield: 3 dozen

Mix sugar, corn syrup, milk and peanuts together and cook over low heat, stirring frequently for 1 hour. Peanut skins will dissolve during cooking. Remove from heat and add butter and vanilla and beat until creamy. Add a few drops of red food coloring, to tint mixture, while beating. Spoon out on wax paper to form patties, let cool.

PEANUT BRITTLE

2 cups sugar
1 cup light corn syrup
1 cup cold water
2 cups raw peanuts

2 tablespoons margarine
1 teaspoon vanilla
2 teaspoons baking soda

Yield: 36 pieces

Combine sugar, corn syrup and water in a large and very heavy pot. Bring mixture to a boil and add peanuts and margarine, stirring constantly. The mix will turn to a light brown color. Continue cooking and stirring mixture until candy thermometer reaches 300°. Remove from heat and add vanilla and baking soda; stir well. Pour mixture on to buttered non–stick 9 x 13-inch pans. Allow to cool well and break into pieces. Store in a tightly covered container.

MICROWAVE PEANUT BRITTLE

1 cup sugar
½ cup light corn syrup
1 cup raw peanuts
½ teaspoon salt

1 teaspoon butter
1 teaspoon vanilla
1 teaspoon baking soda

Yield: 20 pieces

Combine sugar, corn syrup, peanuts and salt in glass bowl; stir well. Microwave on high for 8 minutes. Gently stir in butter and vanilla until well–mixed. Microwave on high for 2 minutes. Slowly add baking soda; mix well. Pour onto a buttered cookie sheet to cool. Break apart.

AUNT ANNIE'S CARAMELS

7 cups white corn syrup
8 cups sugar
2 pounds real butter

8 cups evaporated milk,
   divided
4 teaspoons vanilla
4 cups chopped pecans

Yield: 36-45 pieces

In a large soup pot, combine corn syrup, sugar, butter and 4 cups of evaporated milk. Stir with a wooden spoon over low heat until mixture reaches a rolling boil. Slowly add 4 more cups evaporated milk. Cook slowly and stir constantly for 1½ hours until it reaches a firm, soft–ball stage. Add vanilla, and pecans. Pour into 2, 9 x 13-inch buttered pans. Cool. Cut into strips and remove 1 strip at a time to slice into individual caramels. Wrap in waxed paper.

My father's Aunt Annie always made these wonderful caramels. Her daughter later started Land of the Midnight Sun Candy Company from her home in Alaska. The company is now based in Seattle, run by her children. These are the best caramels I've ever eaten. It really takes 2 people to make them because you have to stir them so long.
— Pat Owens

OKLAHOMA DEPRESSION CANDY

(See recipe in Oklahoma Specialties Section)

PRALINES

1 cup white sugar
½ cup brown sugar
¼ cup milk

1 tablespoon butter or
   margarine
1 cup pecan pieces
1 teaspoon vanilla

Yield: 2 dozen

In a medium saucepan mix sugars, milk, butter and pecans and bring to a boil. Boil 1½ minutes. Remove from the heat, add vanilla and beat until creamy. Drop by spoonfuls onto wax paper. Let cool.

AUNT BILL'S BROWN CANDY

(See recipe in Oklahoma Specialties Section)

AUNT BILL'S MICROWAVE CANDY

2 cups sugar
1 teaspoon baking soda
1 cup buttermilk

¾ cup butter or margarine
1 teaspoon vanilla
2 cups chopped pecans

Yield: 2 dozen

Combine sugar, soda, buttermilk and margarine in large bowl. Cover with plastic wrap; punch holes with fork in wrap. Microwave at 70% power for 15 minutes. Stir and continue cooking at 70% for 13 to 15 minutes until soft ball forms in cold water (236° on the candy thermometer – do not put thermometer in microwave.) Add vanilla and beat with electric mixer until soft peaks form. Watch closely. Stir in pecans and pour into buttered 12 x 7-inch dish. Cool completely and cut into pieces.

Note: Cook this in a microwave–safe cooking container which holds three times the amount of ingredients or it will boil over.

CINNAMON CANDY

2 cups sugar
1 cup light corn syrup
6–8 drops red or green food
    coloring

⅛ ounce cinnamon oil
powdered sugar

Yield: 24 pieces (depending on size)

Place sugar and corn syrup in 4–quart saucepan and add food coloring. Bring to a boil while stirring frequently. Add cinnamon oil and continue to stir. When candy thermometer reaches crack stage, 290°, pour onto greased cookie sheet and allow to cool. Turn cooled candy onto waxed paper and break into small pieces. Sprinkle with powdered sugar. Store in air tight container.

QUICK APPLE DIP

1 8–ounce package cream
  cheese, softened
¾ cup firmly packed brown
  sugar

⅓ cup white sugar
1 teaspoon vanilla

Yield: 2 cups

Cream together all ingredients until smooth. Serve with apple sticks or any fruit as dippers.

PRALINE SAUCE

1 cup light corn syrup
½ cup sugar
⅓ cup margarine

1 egg, beaten
1 tablespoon vanilla
1 cup chopped pecans

Yield: 2 cups

Combine first four ingredients in a heavy saucepan and mix well. Bring to a boil over medium heat, stirring constantly; allow to cook 2 minutes longer without stirring. Remove pan from heat; stir in vanilla and pecans. Serve warm or at room temperature over ice cream.

EASY CHOCOLATE DIP

1 16–ounce can chocolate
  syrup
1 14–ounce can sweetened
  condensed milk

dash salt
1½ teaspoons vanilla

Yield: 3¾ cups

Combine in 1–quart glass casserole dish the chocolate syrup, condensed milk and salt; mix well. Microwave mixture on high for 2 minutes. Stir in vanilla and microwave an additional 2 minutes. Serve warm with dippers: angel food cake cubes, marshmallows, bananas, strawberries, etc.

THE VANISHED NATIONS: CHOCTAWS, CHEROKEES AND CONFEDERATES

The very first history of Oklahoma is Indian history. And in a very real sense, the phrase "Gone With The Wind" applies to the Choctaws and Cherokees as much as to the Old South.

Forced to leave their homes in the South, the Five Civilized Tribes – Choctaw, Cherokee, Chickasaw, Creek, Seminole – were brought to what would become Oklahoma in the 1820's and '30's, 60,000 of them in all. They called it the "Trail of Tears" – many of them died along the way.

Once here, each Tribe established itself as an independent Nation, with its own constitution, elected representatives, laws and schools. It was hard, starting again in an unfamiliar country, and each person did it in his own way.

The full-bloods tended to live as their ancestors had lived for generations – as hunters, far back in the heavily forested hills. The mixed bloods, though, had acquired many of the white man's ways, and established themselves as the southern white man would, as farmers and plantation owners. Being originally from the South, many of them had brought slaves with them to Indian Territory. They became prosperous – one observer described the average Choctaw as "immensely wealthy," and some had cattle herds numbering in thousands. Then in 1861, the Civil War broke out.

As people originally from the South, many of the Indians naturally sympathized with the South, and the Confederate government in Richmond was eager to secure the Territory's abundant food production. So, between July and October, 1861, alliances were signed between the Confederate States and all five Indian Nations. It would forever change their fate.

The War divided each of the Indian Nations in the same way it divided the Nation as a whole: both armies had Indian soldiers from all five tribes. Confederate Stand Watie of the Cherokees led a brigade of cavalry into battle in neighboring Arkansas. Meanwhile, Unionist Opothleyahola of the Creeks led 5,000 of his people out of Indian Territory to refuge in Kansas and the Union lines. Many pro-Union Indians of other tribes followed suit, and their lands were ravaged by Confederate soldiery in their absence. By the end of the war, much of the Indian Nations had been laid waste, just like the rest of the South.

Because they had rebelled against the Union, the Indian Nations now faced a hostile government in Washington. Even more ominously, they faced an explosive westward expansion that would finally surround and overrun them. In time, the Five Indian Nations would vanish as geographic expressions, although they survive today as entities devoted to furthering the interests of their peoples.

Robert E. Lee surrendered to U.S.Grant on April 9, 1865, but the war really went on a little longer. The last Confederate to surrender was Brigadier General Stand Watie of the Cherokees, three months later.

To this day, the southeastern part of Oklahoma – the old Choctaw Nation – is called Little Dixie.

Thank you for your financial support of the Junior Service League of Midwest City. Your purchase of Cafe Oklahoma will help to support projects such as:

Breakfast With The Easter Bunny

A project allowing children from all economic backgrounds the opportunity to have a morning of springtime fun with arts, crafts and educational programs presented by members and other local organizations.

FOOD YIELDS & EQUIVALENTS

	THIS MUCH	EQUALS THIS MUCH
Apples	1 pound (3 medium)	3 cups sliced
	1 medium	1 cup chopped
Bacon	1 pound, thin sliced	24 slices
	8 slices, cooked	½ cup crumbled
Beans		
Dried	1 pound (2½ cups)	6 - 7 cups, cooked
Green	1 pound	2 cups cut
Bread	1 slice from sandwich loaf	1 ounce
Bread Crumbs		
Dry	1 slice bread	¼ cup
Soft	1 slice bread	¾ cup
Butter or Margarine	1 stick	½ cup
	1 pound	2 cups
Cauliflower	1 pound	3 cups flowerets
Cabbage	1 head (about 1 pound)	4½ cups shredded
Carrots	1 pound	3 cups shredded
	2 medium	1 cup sliced
Celery	1 medium rib	½ cup sliced
Cheese		
American or	1 pound	4 cups grated
Cheddar	4 ounces	1 cup grated
Cottage	1 pound	2 cups
Cream	3 ounces	6 tablespoons
Chicken	3½ pound fryer, cooked	4 cups chopped
Chocolate	1 ounce	1 square or 4 tablespoons grated
Morsels	6 ounces	1 cup
Cocoa	1 pound	4 cups
Coconut	1 pound	5 cups shredded
	3½ ounce can, flaked	1⅓ cups
Coffee	1 pound	5 cups (40-45 cups perked)
Corn	2 medium ears	1 cup kernels
Cornmeal	1 pound	3 cups
Cornstarch	1 pound	3 cups
Crumbs		
Chocolate wafer	19 wafers	1 cup fine crumbs
Graham	14 crackers	1 cup fine crumbs
Saltine	28 crackers	1 cup fine crumbs
Vanilla wafer	22 wafers	1 cup fine crumbs

THIS MUCH	EQUALS THIS MUCH

	THIS MUCH	EQUALS THIS MUCH
Eggs	5 large, 6 medium or 7 small whole eggs	1 cup yolks and whites
Whites	8 - 10 large egg whites	1 cup
Yolks	12 - 14 large egg yolks	1 cup
Flour		
All-Purpose	1 pound	4 cups sifted
Cake	1 pound	4¾ cups sifted
Whole wheat	1 pound	3½ cups unsifted
Green Pepper	1 large	1 cup diced
Honey	1 pound	1⅓ cups
Lemon	1 medium	2 - 3 tablespoons juice 1 - 3 teaspoons grated rind
Lettuce	1 pound head	6¼ cups torn
Lime	1 medium	1½ - 2 tablespoons juice
Marshmallows	¼ pound	16 large
	1 large	10 miniature
	11 large	1 cup
Milk Products		
Evaporated	5.33 ounce can	⅔ cup
	14.5 ounce can	1⅔ cups
Sweetened condensed	14 ounce can	1⅓ cups
Cream,		
heavy or whipping	1 cup	2 cups whipped
Mushrooms	1 pound	5 cups sliced
	3 cups raw (8 ounces)	1 cup sliced, cooked
Nuts, shelled		
Almonds	1 pound	3¼ cups
Peanuts	1 pound	3¼ cups
Pecans or Walnuts	1 pound	4½ cups or 3¾ cups chopped
Onion	1 medium	½ cup chopped
	1 pound	3 - 3½ cups diced
Orange	1 medium	⅓ - ½ cup juice or 1½ - 2 tablespoons grated
Pasta		
Macaroni	8 ounces	4 cups cooked (2 cups, uncooked)
Noodles	8 ounces	6 cups cooked (3 cups, uncooked)
Spaghetti	8 ounces	4 cups cooked (2 cups, uncooked)
Potatoes	1 medium	½ cup diced
	1 pound	4 medium potatoes
	1 pound	3½ - 4 cups diced or 2 cups mashed

	THIS MUCH	EQUALS THIS MUCH
Raisins	1 pound	3 cups
Rice	1 pound	2½ cups uncooked
Uncooked	1 cup	3½ cups cooked
Precooked	1 cup	2 cups cooked
Strawberries	1 pint	2 cups sliced
Sugar		
Brown	1 pound	2¼ cups packed
Granulated	1 pound	2 cups
Powdered	1 pound	3½ cups sifted
Tomatoes	1 pound	3 - 4 medium
	1 pound	2½ cups cooked

Equivalents are only estimates to help determine the amount of food to purchase.

INGREDIENT SUBSTITUTIONS

	IF A RECIPE CALLS FOR:	YOU MAY USE:
Butter	1 cup butter	⅞ cup corn oil plus a pinch of salt ⅞ cup solid vegetable shortening plus ½ teaspoon salt 1 cup margarine
Chocolate	1 square unsweetened (1 ounce)	1 envelope soft baking chocolate (1 ounce) 3 ounces (½ cup) semi-sweet morsels, decrease shortening by 1 tablespoon and sugar by ¼ cup 3 tablespoons cocoa plus 1 tablespoon oil
	3 squares semi-sweet baking chocolate (3 ounces)	3 ounces semi-sweet morsels (½ cup)
	¼ cup cocoa powder	1 envelope soft baking chocolate (1 ounce) 3 ounces (½) cup semi-sweet morsels, decrease shortening by 1 tablespoon and sugar by ¼ cup

IF A RECIPE CALLS FOR: YOU MAY USE:

Flour	1 cup sifted cake flour	1 cup sifted all-purpose less 2 tablespoons
	1 cup sifted self-rising	1 cup sifted all-purpose plus 1 teaspoon baking powder and ½ teaspoon salt
	1 cup all-purpose	1 cup plus 2 tablespoons cake flour
	1 cup biscuit mix	1 cup flour plus 1½ teaspoons baking powder and 2 tablespoons shortening
Leavening Agents	1 teaspoon baking powder	¼ teaspoon baking soda plus ½ teaspoon cream of tartar 2 egg whites ¼ teaspoon baking soda plus ½ cup buttermilk and reduce liquid in recipe by ½ cup
	1 package active dry yeast (2 tablespoons)	1 cake compressed yeast
Liquids	1 cup barbecue sauce	1 cup ketchup plus 2 tablespoons Worcestershire sauce
	juice of 1 lemon	3 tablespoons bottled lemon juice
	1 teaspoon lemon juice	½ teaspoon vinegar (for cooking only)
	juice of 1 orange	⅓ - ½ cup orange juice
Milk/Cream	1 cup whole milk	¼ cup dry whole milk plus 1 cup water ¾ cup dry non-fat milk plus 1 cup water and 3 tablespoons butter ½ cup evaporated milk plus ½ cup water 1 cup buttermilk plus ½ teaspoon baking soda
	1 cup light cream	⅞ cup milk plus 3 tablespoons butter
	1 cup heavy cream	¾ cup milk plus ⅓ cup butter

Help On The Range

IF A RECIPE CALLS FOR:	YOU MAY USE:
1 cup buttermilk or sour milk	1 cup sweet milk plus 1 tablespoon vinegar or lemon juice, let stand 5 minutes 1 cup sweet milk plus 1¾ teaspoons cream of tartar
1 cup sour cream	⅓ cup butter and ⅔ cup sour milk 1 tablespoon lemon juice plus evaporated milk to equal 1 cup
1 cup yogurt	1 cup sour milk or buttermilk

Seasonings and Spices

1 teaspoon dried herbs	1 tablespoon fresh herbs
1 teaspoon allspice	1 teaspoon equal parts cinnamon, clove, and nutmeg
1 teaspoon basil	1 teaspoon oregano
1 teaspoon caraway	1 teaspoon anise
1 teaspoon cayenne	1 teaspoon chile peppers
⅛ teaspoon garlic powder	1 small clove garlic or ½ teaspoon garlic salt
1 tablespoon prepared mustard	1 teaspoon dry mustard
1 tablespoon dried minced onion	1 small fresh onion
1 tablespoon onion powder	1 medium fresh onion
1 teaspoon oregano	1 teaspoon marjoram
1 teaspoon sage	1 teaspoon thyme

Sugar
In the following, reduce liquid in recipe by ¼ cup

1 cup sugar	1 cup molasses plus ½ teaspoon baking soda 1 cup honey plus ½ teaspoon baking soda 1 cup maple syrup plus ¼ teaspoon baking soda 1 cup maple syrup plus ¼ cup corn syrup
Sweeteners 1 cup corn syrup	1 cup sugar plus additional ¼ cup of any liquid in recipe
1 cup honey	1¼ cups sugar plus additional ¼ cup any liquid in recipe 1 cup molasses

273

Help On The Range

IF A RECIPE CALLS FOR: YOU MAY USE:

Thickening Agents	1 ounce flour (2 tablespoons)	3½ whole eggs 7 egg yolks ¾ ounce bread crumbs 1 tablespoon cornstarch 1 tablespoon tapioca
Vegetables	1 pound fresh mushrooms	6 ounces canned mush-rooms
	1 cup fresh chopped tomato	½ cup tomato puree
	15 ounce can tomato sauce	6-ounce can tomato paste plus 1 cup water
	1 cup canned tomatoes	1⅓ cups fresh tomatoes, cut and simmered 10 minutes
	1 cup tomato juice	½ cup tomato sauce plus ½ cup water
	1 cup tomato sauce	3 ounces tomato paste plus ½ cup water

MEASUREMENTS TO REMEMBER

3 teaspoons	= 1 tablespoon
2 tablespoons	= ⅛ cup
4 tablespoons	= ¼ cup
5 tablespoons plus 1 teaspoon	= ⅓ cup
8 tablespoons	= ½ cup
10 tablespoons	= ⅝ cup (or ½ cup plus 2 tablespoons)
12 tablespoons	= ¾ cup
16 tablespoons	= 1 cup
⅛ cup	= 2 tablespoons
¼ cup	= 4 tablespoons

⅓ cup	= 5 tablespoons plus 1 teaspoon
½ cup	= 8 tablespoons
¾ cup	= 12 tablespoons
1 cup	= 16 tablespoons
1 ounce	= 2 tablespoons liquid
4 ounces	= ½ cup
8 ounces	= 1 cup
16 ounces	= 1 pound
2 cups	= 1 pint
4 cups	= 1 quart
2 pints	= 1 quart
4 quarts	= 1 gallon

Acknowledgments

Every effort has been made to include the names of all individuals contributing to the publication of Cafe Oklahoma, by donating time, talent, energy and recipes. If any names have been omitted, it was purely accidental.

Debi Alleman
Debbie Anderson
Cindy Andrulonis
Michelle Ashley
Rubye Atkinson
Sandra Austin
Ann Bain
Scotty Barnett
Norma Bartlett
Toady Beaver
Wanda Bennett
Julie Bishop
Karen Boehm
Brenda
   Bodenheimer
DeAnn Bower
Sharon Breeden
Shannon Brewer
Jolene Browning
Beverly Broyles
Caralee Buchanan
Cheryl Buchanan
Suzi Byrne
Missy Cain
Denise Caram
Virginia Carlile
Darlene Case
Charles Cedena
Nacia Cedeno
June Cermak
Linda Chard
Debbie Clark
Janice Clark
Jeanette Clemons
Charlene Cole
Clara Colvin
Aaron Corwin
Naomi Coston
Mary Ann Cox
Bill Croak
Linda Croak
Sherri Croak
Linda Cunningham
Wanda Dalrymple
Eugenia Davis
Joe Davis
Mitsy Davis
Martha Dearing
Kathy Dickey

Pam Dimski
Ann Dixon
Katherine Dockery
Pauline Dow–
   Gibson
Jean Leckness
   Dunlap
Cindy Enix
Rita Finney
Gayle Fisher
Don Flynn
Connie Fogarty
Wyvonna Folks
Bobbie Freeman
Martha Gillaspy
Elveree Golff
Carolyn Green
Sandy Gregory
Susan Gust
Pamela Hall
Mary Hardy
Leigh Ann Harrison
Susan Harroz
Lola Hartley
Sue Hawk
Jerry Hearn
Terry Henson
Kristy Holinsworth
Karen Holland
Joyce Honey
Diann Howell
Joy Howell
Lezlie Hudiburg
Kay Hughes
Sue Hugus
Jane Huffaker
Karen Hurst
Becky Issac
Cheryl Johnson
JoAnn Johnson
Marie Jordan
Joe Joy
Carolyn Joy
Diane Joy–Sisemore
Allison Kaiser
Bill Kaiser
Diane Keen
Lola Kelly
Lucille Kerr

Mary Kuettel
Linda Lane
Susie Larsen
Glenda Lee
Annette Lopp
Charlotte Mann
Wanda Markham
Dale Matherly
Pam Matherly
Susan Matlock
Betty Lewis
   Matthews
Dara McGlamery
Kathy McLaughlin
Cindy Mikeman
Kathryn Mikeman
Betty Miller
Connie Milloer
Joye Miller
Necia Miller
Reda Miller
George Mohr
Jerre Moore
Tiny Moore
Lerae Morrison
Kay Mott
Robin Murphy
Dorothy Mussatto
Sylvia Nash
Karel Nichols
Carmon Noland
Andrea Ohmann
Ellen Olsen
Bertha Owen
Elaine Owen
Pat Owens
Sandra Pittman
Jean Powers
Gara Prather
Peggy Premo
Gloria Prewett
Lynn Pulliam
Faye Pyles
Carolejean Reynolds
Cheryl Ritterskamp
Darlene Roach
Cheryl Robicheaux
Linda Roberts
Margaret Robertson

Greena Rogers
Teresa Sanders
Burnie Sanderson
Laurine Schulz
Darlene Sellars
Nancy Simmons
Lillie Simon
Susan Simon
C. A. Smith
Lee Smith
Nadine Smith
Nona Smith
Susan Stanley
Jamie Stark
John L. Stark
David Steen
Kelly Stephens
Pam Stephenson
Donna Strahorn
Naomi Strawn
Lois Strickland
Mary Strunk
Dixie Swain
Nadine Swindell
Susanne Tapp
Shirley Thomas
Theresa Todd
Wileeta Treadway
Laura Tribble
Joan Valanejad
Teri Wagnon
Beverly Watson
Cheri Weintraub
Rita White
Margenia Wicker
Debbie Wiersig
Lee Williams
Tammy Williams
Jan Williamson
Barbara Wilson
Ginger Wilson
Eileen Wilson
Ann Womak
Betty Woodruff
Donna Woodward
Karen Young
Diana Zeckser

Contributors

Our sincere thanks go to the following financial sponsors of Cafe Oklahoma. Without their support, this endeavor would not have been possible.

Oil Tycoons

First National Bank of Midwest City

David & Lezlie Hudiburg

Hudiburg Enterprises

Liberty Bank

Midwest City Regional Hospital

Cattle Barons

ABC Tobacco Stores

City Bank & Trust

Dr. John P. and Jeanette W. Clemons

Community Bank

Dr. Bob Dimski

First Dealer Resources, Inc.

Four Seasons Nursing Home

Jim Glover Dodge

Jim Glover Nissan

Matherly Mechanical Contractors, Inc.

Midwest Radiology Associates, Inc.

Oklahoma Consulting Service

Oklahoma Gas & Electric

Oklahoma Natural Gas

Dr. Richard Wilson

Wildcatters

Century Management Company

Dr. Stanley R. Chard

Buckaroos

Dr. Zaheer U. Baber

Index

278

Index

Index

Index

284

Index